D0912665

BLACKWELL'S POLITICAL TEXTS

General Editor: WILFRID HARRISON

KARL MARX

EARLY TEXTS

KARL MARX
EARLY TEXTS

Translated and edited by
DAVID McLELLAN
University of Kent at Canterbury

OXFORD
BASIL BLACKWELL
1971

ISBN 0 631 11630 3 Cloth bound edition
ISBN 0 631 12920 0 Paper bound edition

Library of Congress Catalog Card Number: 73-129588

Printed in Great Britain by
Alden & Mowbray Ltd at the Alden Press, Oxford
and bound at Kemp Hall Bindery

Preface

Considering the amount of discussion that they have aroused, it is surprising that no comprehensive English translation of Marx's early writings appeared during the thirty years after their original publication. More recently, T. B. Bottomore's edition (*Karl Marx, Early Writings*, London, 1963) contains three important pieces, but gives no idea of the range and development of Marx's thought during this period. The edition by Lloyd D. Easton and Kurt H. Guddat entitled *Writings of the Young Marx on Philosophy and Society* was published when I had already completed the first draft of this book. My aim has been to include in one volume all the texts that are relevant to the discussion of Marx's early thought and to accompany them with enough commentary for the student of Marx to be able to see when and why they were written and to situate them in Marx's intellectual development.

I am grateful to Sir Isaiah Berlin for reading through the Introduction and to my colleagues Derek Crabtree and Martin Minogue for help with the translation; also to Charles Lucken. Any remaining deficiencies are entirely my responsibility.

Littlecroft, Chilham, Kent   DAVID MCLELLAN

To My Parents

Contents

Introduction

Intellectual Background

THE HEGELIAN SCHOOL

When Hegel, the greatest of the German idealist philosophers, died in
1831, he left behind him a system which had increasingly dominated
German philosophical thought since his appointment to the chair of
philosophy at Berlin in 1821 and which was to remain the predominant
German philosophy for a further ten years. The centre of the school that
Hegel had created was, naturally, in Berlin, but it had adherents all
over Germany. Hegel had conceived of his philosophy as in some way
a definitive summing-up of all previous philosophies and it was widely
felt among his disciples that their task was merely to apply the principles of the Master to various fields in which time had prevented him
from elaborating them. One of Hegel's closest disciples likened the
philosophical climate to the break-up of Alexander's empire: no one
person could succeed to the throne and the *diadochi* would divide the
provinces between themselves.

Plainly it would be difficult to remain for long limited to such a
quietist programme. Prussia, it is true, had long been in the grip of
Frederick William III's unimaginative autocracy; but a year before
Hegel's death the July Revolution in France had installed Louis
Philippe as king 'by the will of the people', and a year after Hegel's
death the Great Reform Bill was passed in Britain. In Germany itself,
liberal ideas were on the increase in the Rhineland and the south-west
and even the socialist ideas of Saint-Simon and Fourier were beginning
to be heard of. The repercussion of all this on the Hegelian School was
aided by the essential ambivalence of much of Hegel's thought. For
Hegel was capable of many interpretations: the accent could either be
put on dialectical progress and negation as the chief agent of change, or
else on the static 'system' in which philosophy was 'the owl of Minerva'
whose only business was interpretation *post factum*. Engels wrote later of
this period: 'Hegel's doctrine was vast enough to give shelter to conceptions of the most varied groups. In the Germany of that time, whose

ix

character was essentially theoretical, two things above all presented a practical interest: religion and politics. One who put the accent on Hegel's system could be quite conservative in these two fields, whereas one who considered the dialectical method as essential could belong, in both religion and politics, to the opposite extreme.'

Politics, however, under Frederick William III was a thorny subject, and the first signs of opposition to the prevailing way of thinking came in the less dangerous field of religion. The disagreements here were focused by the book by D. F. Strauss, *Das Leben Jesu*, published in 1835. Strauss concentrated upon the Gospels as historical documents (Hegel had only been concerned with their philosophical content) and interpreted them as myths embodying the aspirations of the first Christian communities. These aspirations were outmoded, for Strauss considered the fundamental truth of Christianity—the unity of divine and human natures—could not be realized merely in the person of Christ, but only in humanity as a whole. These views naturally aroused the opposition not only of orthodox Lutherans but also of the more conservative Hegelians, and Strauss, writing two years later and using the current description of the French Parliament, divided the parties into Right, Centre and Left. It was the last group which came to be called the Young Hegelians and inside which Karl Marx began to elaborate his ideas.

THE YOUNG HEGELIAN MOVEMENT

The Young Hegelians were a very tight-knit group and were, in effect, the first political party in Germany. The most prominent were Bauer, Feuerbach, Hess, Engels, Stirner and Köppen.[1] They all had similar backgrounds: they came from well-to-do middle class homes, were university-educated and almost all had either held university posts or intended to do so. One result of the radicalism of their views was that they were debarred from university life and found themselves jobless intellectuals. This lack of attachment to contemporary society may explain the extravagant theories that they entertained. Another result of their being debarred from the lecture theatre was that their only means of publicizing their views was by the printed word. The activities of

1 See: S. Hook, *From Hegel to Marx*, 2nd ed., Michigan, 1962; D. McLellan, *The Young Hegelians and Karl Marx*, London, 1969.

the Young Hegelians were centred on their reviews and journals, usually very short-lived, which, it has been calculated, ran to as many as 40,000 pages in the space of four years. Their thought showed a rapid process of secularization. Many of them had started off studying theology and had switched to philosophy and the book that was the immediate cause of a split in the Hegelian school was a theological one. But the church in Prussia was established and criticism of religion involved political criticism which became more and more radical until their journals were suppressed. Disillusioned at the failure of the German bourgeoisie to support them in their struggle some, like Marx, found a way forward in socialist ideas, while others faded out of the picture with an idealism that became increasingly detached from any political reality. A surprising number had acquired conservative attitudes by the time of the 1848 revolution and the Bismarck era.

Marx the Student

Trier, where Marx was born in 1808, was a town in which considerable attention was paid to new ideas. The Rhineland in general was the most progressive of the German provinces for, as well as being the most industrialized, it had also been under French occupation since the Napoleonic wars. Thus the influence of the principles of the French Revolution was strong, the archbishop of Trier was impelled to issue a condemnation of Saint-Simon and an enthusiastic disciple of Fourier, Ludwig Gall, used Trier as a centre for his activity.

Marx's father, Heinrich Marx, fitted well into the atmosphere of the town. He was a well-to-do lawyer who, although descended from a line of rabbis, had become a convert to protestantism about 1816 probably to escape the anti-Jewish laws. Heinrich Marx was a cultivated man, a disciple of the Enlightenment, a 'true eighteenth-century Frenchman' who 'knew Voltaire and Rousseau by heart',[1] according to Marx's daughter, Eleanor. Marx's mother, who also came from a rabbinic family, was of Dutch–Hungarian origin, rather narrow minded and without influence on her son. The Jesuit school that Marx attended in Trier had a headmaster who was a disciple of Kant and it was suspected by the government of being a hotbed of liberal ideas. A

[1] *Reminiscenses of Marx and Engels*, Moscow, n.d., p. 130.

further influence on Marx in Trier was Baron v. Westphalen who lived next door and whose daughter, Jenny, Marx later married. The Baron taught Marx the love of Shakespeare and Homer that he always kept and was also interested in social questions and encouraged in Marx an interest in the personality and work of Saint-Simon.

In 1835 Marx left home to study law at the small university of Bonn. Here romanticism predominated, and W. Fr. Schlegel was one of the leading lecturers. Marx began to write poetry, joined a poets' club, and went to as many lectures on literature and aesthetics as he did on law. Soon his attendance at lectures dropped considerably and he received a slight duelling wound. The year at Bonn seemed to have been wasted and his father decided to send him to Berlin.

The city of Berlin had an unusually large population of shopkeepers and civil servants and all intellectual life was concentrated in the university, the intellectual centre of Germany and focal point of Hegelianism. Marx's *Letter to his Father*[1] written after a year at Berlin gives a vivid account of how he spent his first year in writing poems and composing philosophical systems. He felt an initial repugnance for the 'grotesque and rocky melodies' of Hegel's philosophy, but he found himself forced to accept Hegel's conclusions. He had read Hegel from end to end while recovering from the strain of overwork and resolved thereafter to 'seek the idea in the real itself'.

This allegiance to Hegel led to his joining a Graduates' Club composed mostly of university lecturers, all adepts in Hegelian philosophy. This club was the nucleus of the Young Hegelian movement in Berlin and flourished in the early 1840s under the name of 'The Free Men'. Adolf Rutenberg, editor of the *Rheinische Zeitung* before Marx, was a member, as was also Karl Köppen whose book on the Greeks Marx mentions in the preface to his *Dissertation*.[2] Max Stirner, the anarchist, and Friedrich Engels belonged to the club a little later. Its most prominent member was Bruno Bauer who was a lecturer at the university and at first an opponent of Strauss. However, in 1838 Bauer went even further than Strauss and began a criticism of the Gospels even more radical than that of Strauss. All his writings revolved round the notion of religion as the self-alienation of man and were inspired by an anti-theological obsession. Bauer was moved to Bonn by the Minister of

[1] See pp. 1 ff. below.   [2] See pp. 11 ff. below.

Culture but he was eventually dismissed in 1842, and it was this dismissal that caused the break-up of the Young Hegelian movement. There are not many documents concerning Marx's development at this time. Marx had given up law for philosophy and discussed with Bauer the project of writing a polemic against the Old Hegelians and actually wrote a book on G. Hermes, professor of theology at Bonn, who had attempted to reconcile catholicism with Kant's philosophy. The book, however, was never published, and Marx turned his attention, in close co-operation with Bauer to post-Aristotelian Greek philosophy. There were two reasons for Marx's choosing this period: first, as he explained in the preliminary notes to his *Dissertation*,[1] he felt that the situation of Greek thinkers after the 'total philosophy' of Aristotle was similar to that of Hegel's disciples after the 'total philo-sophy' of their Master; secondly, Marx was here following Bauer, who had put the concept of self-consciousness, the human mind developing dialectically and freeing itself from enslavement to its own creations, at the centre of his own philosophy. Bauer had drawn heavily here on Hegel, who had connected 'self-consciousness' with the period of the post-Aristotelian philosophies and the rise of Christianity. No doubt also Marx wrote the *Dissertation* as a help to his academic career, as he hoped, through the influence of Bauer, to get a post teaching philo-sophy at the university of Bonn, and even went as far as to discuss with him the content of the lectures he would give. The bulk of the *Disserta-tion*, comparing the natural philosophies of Democritus and Epicurus, is devoid of interest. According to the preface, the object of the work was, as commonly among Hegel's disciples, to elaborate on a field only very sketchily dealt with by the Master. In the preliminary notes Marx defends Hegel against his critics by appealing, as did the rest of the Young Hegelians, to an 'esoteric' Hegel that often contradicted the 'exoteric' one. The other notes are mainly concerned with the general Young Hegelian problem of how philosophy was possible after Hegel. The solution to this question was largely inspired by August v. Cieszkowski, a Polish count, who studied philosophy in Berlin. In 1838 Cieszkowski published a small book entitled *Prolegomena to Historiosophy*, the object of which was to advocate, in the place of purely speculative philosophy, one that brought action within its

[1] See pp. 11 ff. below.

reach. Hegel had only considered the past and the present: his followers must now use these principles to change the world in the future. For this synthesis of thought and action he coined the term, so influential later, 'praxis'. The more personal parts of Marx's *Dissertation* convey very vividly a similar desire for a secularization of Hegel's philosophy. Eventually, after much badgering from Bauer, Marx submitted his *Dissertation* to the university of Jena in April 1841 and was awarded his degree *in absentia*.

Marx made a great impression on his contemporaries even at this stage. Georg Jung, a Cologne lawyer and one of the backers of the Young Hegelians, wrote to Arnold Ruge in 1841: 'Although he is the devil of a revolutionary, Dr. Marx is one of the most penetrating minds I know.'[1] And Moses Hess, the first German communist, wrote at the same time: 'Dr. Marx, that is the name of my idol, is a very young man, aged 24 at the most, who will give the finishing stroke to mediaeval religion and politics.'[2] But Marx, in spite of all his potential, still had no job. In June 1841 he moved to Bonn and planned to edit with Bauer a journal to be called *Atheistic Archives*. This, however, came to nothing, and Bauer and Marx began to write a book with the intriguing title *The Last Trump over Hegel the Antichrist*. It was a very clever piece of double bluffing, appearing to be written by a pietist putting his co-religionists on guard against the atheistic implications of Hegel's philosophy. Marx's contribution, however, never appeared, and Bauer published his own work separately. Marx, both now and later, had great difficulty in getting material into a state in which it could be published, as he always wanted to pursue in depth anything of interest that he came across, whether it was of relevance to the subject he was studying or not.

Marx the Journalist

In January of 1842 Marx moved to Trier and began his career as a journalist by sending to Arnold Ruge, editor of the *Hallischer Jahrbücher* an article entitled 'Remarks on the latest Prussian instruction on

[1] *Karl Marx, Friedrich Engels: Historische-Kritische Gesamtausgabe*, Frankfurt–Berlin–Moscow, from 1927 (edition referred to hereafter as MEGA) I i (2) p. 262.

[2] Moses Hess, *Briefwechsel*, ed. E. Silberner, The Hague, 1959, p. 80.

censorship'.[1] However, the article was itself censored and only appeared a year later in a collection of censored articles that Ruge published in Switzerland under the title *Anekdota zur neuesten deutschen Philosophie und Publicistik*. The *Hallischer Jahrbücher* for which this article was destined well reflected the progress of the Young Hegelian movement. Founded in 1838, it gradually became more and more radical as it concentrated on politics. Some of its original contributors left it and in June 1841 it was banned in Prussia and moved to Dresden where it appeared under the title of *Deutsche Jahrbücher*. The Young Hegelians had great hopes for the new king, Frederich William IV, but these were crushed as the king, a weak-witted romantic of whose character Marx gives an excellent sketch in his letter to Ruge of May 1843,[2] gradually suppressed all the Young Hegelian publications. And since these were their only public means of expression, the movement was effectively suppressed at the same time. The new king could not, however, immediately make up his mind what course of action to take and he at first ordered his censors to relax the censorship. Marx's article was designed to show the internal contradictions involved in this apparent liberalism.

Marx also wrote at this time a second article, which he did not send to Ruge until some time later, and which was also published in *Anekdota*. Its title was 'Luther as Judge between Strauss and Feuerbach',[3] and it consisted of a long quotation from Luther to support Feuerbach's interpretation of miracles as simply a projection of human desires, as opposed to that of Strauss which retained, however vaguely, a supernatural interpretation. This is the first occasion on which Marx mentions Feuerbach whose influence on him was profound, though often misinterpreted. Feuerbach had attended Hegel's lectures at Berlin, held several academic posts, but eventually had to give up his academic career because of his unorthodox view and retired to his farm at Bruckberg where he devoted himself to study. From 1838 onwards his writings had a considerable influence on the Young Hegelians and this became more pronounced with the publication in April 1841 of his book *The Essence of Christianity*. The theme of the book was, to use Feuerbach's own words, as follows: 'The objective essence of religion,

---

[1] See pp. 26 ff. below.   [2] See pp. 74 ff. below.
[3] See pp. 23 ff. below.

particularly the Christian religion, is nothing but the essence of human, and particularly Christian feeling, the secret of theology therefore is anthropology. . . . The foundation of a new science is laid here in that the philosophy of religion is conceived of and presented as esoteric or secret anthropology or psychology'.[1] According to Engels, in his over-schematic account of the Young Hegelian movement written fifty years later, the effect of the book was extraordinary: 'The spell was broken; the "system" was exploded and cast aside. . . . Enthusiasm was general; we all became at once Feuerbachians.'[2]

This account is greatly exaggerated, at least so far as Marx was concerned. Engels was never as deeply influenced by Hegel as was Marx. Bruno Bauer had already taught Marx atheism. Moreover, if one looks at the actual passages in which Marx refers to Feuerbach's achievements and his debt to him it is plain that it was not *The Essence of Christianity* that influenced Marx, but Feuerbach's writings of a year or two later in which he specifically attacks Hegel's philosophy. The first edition of *The Essence of Christianity* was still fairly Hegelian in passages that Feuerbach later amended.

On 1st January 1842, thanks to the relaxation of censorship that Marx had criticized in his *Anekdota* article, a new paper, the *Rheinische Zeitung* was founded in Cologne. Its financial backers were mainly business men from the Rhineland who wanted a paper to replace the dominant *Kölnische Zeitung* which was extremely reactionary. The government, too, was pleased to see the advent of the *Rheinische Zeitung*, because they hoped that it would be an antidote to the ultra-montane tone of the *Kölnische Zeitung*. Moses Hess had played a leading part in the founding of the paper, but his communist ideas deprived him of the editorship which he had expected and he was given the job of editing correspondence from France. The editor-in-chief, Höffken, was a man of moderately liberal tendencies. Two of the directors, who had been converted by Hess to a radical Young Hegelian position, put pressure on Höffken to include articles written from that standpoint and he resigned in protest, declaring himself 'no adept of neo-Hegelian-ism'. Adolf Rutenberg, whom Marx had described in his letter to his father as 'the most intimate of my Berlin friends' and who was Bruno

[1] L. Feuerbach, *Briefwechsel*, Leipzig, 1963, pp. 140 f.
[2] K. Marx, F. Engels, *Selected Works*, Moscow, 1962, vol. 2, p. 368.

Bauer's brother-in-law, was then chosen as editor and the columns of the paper immediately became open to the Young Hegelians.

In March 1842, Marx, who had participated in the founding of the *Rheinische Zeitung*, decided on a more active collaboration with it. He had previously been thinking of publishing his thesis with a view to an academic career, but he finally had to give up this idea because Bauer's position at the university of Bonn was becoming more and more precarious. Marx's first contribution to the *Rheinische Zeitung* was an article commenting on the debate in the Rhenish Parliament on the freedom of the press and the publication of its proceedings.[1] Marx's article was written in a larger context than the previous one and set out to show how, in relationship to the whole political situation, the government's attitude on censorship was typical of the reactionary Prussian state. Marx was still writing in very idealist terms. He treated the state, following Hegel, as the expression of Reason and the highest incarnation of morality. The law, for him, was the form in which objective liberty was realized, was something beyond the scope of individual devising and it could not have an arbitrary character. The press, too, he considered to be an area for the manifestation of Reason, and History itself was the product of Spirit.

The next article Marx wrote was prompted by an attack on the *Rheinische Zeitung* by Hermes, editor of the rival *Kölnische Zeitung*, who accused the paper of attacking Christianity and asked the government to forbid all discussion of philosophical and political questions. Marx, in his reply,[2] vindicated the right of the press to discuss all questions and argued that the Christian state was the antithesis of the rational state, whose progress was shaped by critical philosophy which had now to become a philosophy of action. Shortly afterwards Marx published a criticism of the historical school of law that he had originally intended to send to Ruge.[3] The principal theoretician of this school was Hugo who, taking up Kant's principle that an object was not knowable in itself, concluded that laws had to be accepted as one found them since there was no possible standard of criticism. Marx's article argued that this position involved internal contradictions.

Meanwhile the Young Hegelians' collaboration with the *Rheinische*

[1] See pp. 35 ff. below.   [2] See pp. 37 ff. below.
[3] See pp. 31 ff. below.

Zeitung was becoming more radical. Their articles were militantly atheistic and politically they rejected any policy that they called *juste milieu*. Hess, by reporting on the French scene, managed to give excellent accounts of communist ideas. Bakunin, too, was represented pseudonymously under the name of Elysard by a very revolutionary-sounding article which emphasized the change that the Young Hegelians had operated in Hegel's dialectic. For Hegel's three-term dialectic had become with them a two-term dialectic of which one term was destined for complete and utter victory. All 'mediation' was rejected. Bakunin's article ended with the sentence 'the joy of destruction, too, is a creative joy'.

Marx had been growing more and more involved in the affairs of the paper, and eventually in October 1842, he became its editor. His first task was to reply to an accusation by the *Augsburger Allgemeine Zeitung* that the *Rheinische Zeitung* was becoming a platform for communist ideas. Marx, in his reply[1] said that his paper was opposed to communism and considered it unrealizable, but he promised to publish later a profound critique of communist ideas.

Marx's next article was a commentary on the debate in the Rhenish Parliament on the law to suppress the stealing of wood.[2] Wood-stealing, poaching and similar offences accounted for two-thirds of all the crimes committed in Prussia at this time and it was proposed to increase the penalities involved. Marx was full of indignation, but his criticism of the debates was based on moral and juridical grounds rather than on anything that approached socialism. He had nothing to say against private property and he still looked for social and political development from a reform of the state, though, as he later said,[3] this incident was the first to draw his attention to the importance of economic influences.

Under the editorship of Marx the *Rheinische Zeitung* prospered and its circulation went up by leaps and bounds. However, the paper was under increasing threat of closure from the authorities, and Marx was forced to temporize on a number of points. This led to difficulties with the 'Free Men' in Berlin, whose articles Marx had to censor himself. Things came to a head when Ruge and the radical poet George

---

[1] See pp. 44 ff. below.   [2] See pp. 49 ff. below.
[3] K. Marx, F. Engels, *Selected Works*, Moscow, 1962, vol. i, pp. 361 f.

Herwegh visited the 'Free Men' in Berlin with a plan to found a free university. They found the 'Free Men' both frivolous and extravagant in their ideas, and a quarrel ensued. Both sides appealed to Marx who eventually published his correspondence with Herwegh and finally broke with the Berlin Young Hegelians.[1]

However, a wave of suppression followed shortly afterwards, depriving the Young Hegelians of their means of expression. In December 1842 the great liberal paper the *Leipziger Allgemeine Zeitung* was suppressed, in January 1843 the Saxon Government decreed the end of Ruge's *Deutsche Jahrbücher*, and at the same time it was decided that the *Rheinische Zeitung* should cease publication on 31st March 1843 which it did, with its last number printed in red. Marx welcomed the decision, for the censorship had made his job virtually impossible. 'The government has given me back my liberty', he wrote to Ruge, 'I can undertake nothing further in Germany, where one is forced to corrupt oneself.'[2]

Marx in Paris

THE CRITIQUE OF HEGEL'S PHILOSOPHY OF THE STATE

The suppression of their journals split the Young Hegelian movement into two groups. The two wings are seen united for the last time in the *Anekdota* that Ruge published in Switzerland in March 1843. The first wing led by Bruno Bauer retreated more and more from active political life. Bauer wrote later: 'When the new law on censorship was published by the newspapers, the friends of progress, having lost their rallying point through the suppression of the three big dailies, used this as an excuse for declaring that they could do nothing more . . . each retired from the struggle'.[3] In effect, the 'Free Men' kept meeting as a club until at least 1845 and Bruno Bauer, together with his brother Edgar, kept up his journalistic activity. Indeed, Marx and Engels took Bauer and his school seriously enough to devote the first book they published together to a criticism of them. Bauer's writings, they said, were increasingly removed from political reality, as he despised 'the

---

[1] See Marx's letter to Ruge, pp. 52 f. below.   [2] MEGA, I i (2) p. 294.
[3] B. Bauer, *Vollständige Geschichte der Parteikämpfe in Deutschland*, Charlottenburg, 1847, vol. I, pp. 245 f.

Masses' and took refuge in an idealism understood and propagated by a small elite.

The other wing of the Young Hegelians, led by Ruge, Marx and Hess, was eager to continue the struggle and immediately began to look for new facilities for publication. They approached Julius Froebel, professor of mineralogy at Zurich University, who controlled a publishing house in Zurich, was another of Hess's converts to communism and readily agreed to help. It was at first proposed to produce a continuation of the banned *Deutsche Jahrbücher*, and Marx accepted Ruge's offer of a co-editorship with him. Among other reasons he wanted a secure situation in order to get married, which he did soon after the contract was signed. He suggested to Ruge at the same time that the title of the review should be *Deutsch-französische Jahrbücher*, that it should involve a close collaboration with the French and that it should be published in Strasbourg. The idea of this kind of Franco-German alliance was very popular among German radicals. Heine and Ruge had suggested it, and Hess in particular had praised France as the land *par excellence* of political action and thus a necessary complement to German theory. And Feuerbach had recently lent his authority to the idea by declaring that 'the true philosopher who identifies himself with life and man must be of Franco-Germanic blood'.[1] By May 1843 preparations were well advanced, and Marx and Froebel went to see Ruge at Dresden to make the final arrangements. However, Froebel was prosecuted because of his other radical publications, and sentenced to two months' imprisonment, so the publication of his review was delayed until the end of the year.

Marx occupied himself in the summer of 1843, during this delay, by undertaking a detailed study of Hegel's view of the State. His articles in the *Rheinische Zeitung* had still looked to some form of rational (i.e Hegelian) State as the answer to social and political problems. But the suppression of the radical press had compelled the Young Hegelians to abandon any hope of political reform. Marx's reaction to this state of affairs took the form of a paragraph by paragraph analysis of Hegel's *Philosophy of Right*.[2] According to Marx, Hegel had not drawn his

[1] L. Feuerbach, *Anthropologische Materialismus, Ausgewählte Schriften*, Frankfurt, 1967, vol. I, p. 92.
[2] See pp. 61 ff.

philosophy of law from an analysis of social and political organization and the existing relationships between individuals, society and the State. He had made law the expression of objective morality, a transcendent entity that determined political organization *a priori*. Hegel 'mystifies' politics by making objective reality a product or mode of being of the idea. He had made the predicate into the subject and the subject into the predicate. Marx's actual proposals were the same as those of Ruge and Froebel: the inauguration of a 'true' democracy by means of a Republic and universal suffrage.

This is the first of Marx's writings which shows important influences of Feuerbach, from whom Marx borrowed in particular the ideas of mystification and of the reversal of subject and predicate. Feuerbach had in 1843 taken over the intellectual leadership of the radicals by the publication of his *Theses for the Reform of Philosophy* and *Principles of the Philosophy of the Future*. Even though he did not participate actively in the radical movement, these two writings gave him a dominant position. Previously, and in particular in *The Essence of Christianity*, Feuerbach had dealt with religion: in these articles he for the first time attacked Hegel's system as such. The opening words of the *Theses* make clear the connection with, and difference from, his previous book: 'The secret of theology is anthropology, but the secret of speculative philosophy is theology.'[1] The outstanding instance of speculative philosophy was the Hegelian system, and Feuerbach proposed to apply to it the same analysis that he had already applied to Christianity: here, too, the reversal of subject and object would uncover the truth. Feuerbach summed up his general point of view thus: 'The true relationship of thought to being is this: being is the subject, thought the predicate. Thought arises from being, being does not arise from thought.'[2]

THE 'DEUTSCH-FRANZÖSISCHE JAHRBÜCHER' AND THE
ORIGINS OF GERMAN SOCIALISM

Feuerbach's simple style, reiterating the same point in a thousand different ways, gained him a wide audience and his method of reducing

[1] L. Feuerbach, *Anthropologische Materialismus, Ausgewählter Schriften*, Frankfurt, 1967, vol. I, p. 82.
[2] L. Feuerbach, op. cit., p. 95.

all ideas to their basis in 'Man' was the only position held in common by the radical group that launched the *Deutsch-französische Jahrbücher*. Apart from this, as Marx wrote in September 1843, 'none of the reformers has any exact idea of what ought to happen'. Froebel had declared himself in favour of a 'true democracy' and Ruge, in his last article for the *Deutsche Jahrbücher* entitled 'A self-critique of Liberalism' had rejected liberalism in favour of a democracy based on Feuerbach's humanism and to be realized by a union of Germany's rational thought and France's combative energy. In order to clarify their ideas before approaching the French, Ruge, Marx, Bakunin and Feuerbach exchanged letters that were subsequently printed in the *Deutsch-französische Jahrbücher*.[1] This correspondence well reflected the differences of opinion: Ruge and Feuerbach were pessimistic about the chances of a revolution in Germany. Bakunin thought that revolution was the only answer, while Marx was quite hopeful for the future, placing his confidence in a true democracy. Marx had written to Feuerbach,[2] pressing him to write for the new review a critique of Schelling, who had been appointed to the chair of philosophy in Berlin in order, in the words of the king, to 'root out the dragon seed of Hegelianism'.[3] But Feuerbach thought that political activism was premature and had already replied to Ruge that 'we are not yet at the point of transition from theory to practice, because our theory is still faulty'.[4]

In his three letters published in the *Deutsch-französische Jahrbücher* Marx was still very idealistic in his approach to the questions of the day, considering that the most important of these was spiritual emancipation. He also referred to 'suffering humanity' as an element in any future revolution. For the second time Marx criticized socialism, and more particularly communism, as one-sided and abstract. Unlike Engels, who as Hess wrote later, after a discussion on current problems 'left me the keenest of communists',[5] Marx was a slow convert to socialism.

In Germany it was only in the 1830s that socialism began to have any appreciable effect on intellectuals. The ideas of Saint-Simon entered via

---

[1] See pp. 73 ff. below.   [2] See pp. 83 ff. below.
[3] C. v. Bunsen, *Aus seinen Briefen*, Leipzig, 1896, vol. 2, p. 133.
[4] L. Feuerbach, *Briefwechsel und Nachlass*, Leipzig, 1876, vol. 1, p. 358.
[5] M. Hess, *Briefwechsel*, The Hague, 1959, p. 103.

the Rhineland and south-west Germany and were propagated by men like Heine and Edward Gans whose lectures Marx had followed at Berlin; but their influence was very small. Abroad, the first German workers' associations date from 1832 in Paris and a little later in Switzerland, and here the most influential figure was Wilhelm Weitling, the rhetorical communist tailor whose first book, *Humanity as it is and as it ought to be* was published in 1838. Social questions did not come to the fore inside Germany until after 1840. Ruge wrote that his colleague Echtermeyer's work on romantic politicians had become dated from the practical point of view by the 'critique of society and state that Anglo-French socialism offered and whose principles had already in 1842 aroused the attention of Germany'.[1] Among the Young Hegelians Feuerbach, and, in particular, Hess, had prepared the ground, but the book that did most to present socialism to the intellectual public was Lorenz v. Stein's *The Socialism and Communism of Contemporary France*. Stein was a young conservatively-inclined Hegelian academic who, on finishing his studies in Berlin, had been given a scholarship by the Prussian Government to go to Paris and report on socialist and communist doctrines and the activities of the German workers there. This book was the result of his researches, and it presented socialism and communism (terms that in German were virtually interchangeable at this time) as the logical result of the French Revolution. Stein pointed to the increasingly uneven distribution of wealth in society and warned that, if the state did not intervene, it would give rise to a proletarian revolution. Stein condemned the doctrines he was describing and his book was conceived by him as an appeal to the ruling classes, but it helped greatly to spread knowledge of socialism inside Germany.

Among those founding the new review future differences of opinion, particularly on the subject of communism, were not yet apparent and the atmosphere was full of hope. Ruge arrived in Paris in August 1843, accompanied by Hess, who was to act as intermediary and introduce him to the socialist leaders whom he knew well from his stay in Paris as correspondent of the *Rheinische Zeitung*. Ruge later described his attitude to Paris as follows: 'At the end of our journey we shall find the vast valley of Paris, the cradle of the new Europe, the great laboratory where world history is being developed. . . . It is in Paris that we shall

[1] A. Ruge, *Zwei Jahre in Paris*, Leipzig, 1846, vol. 2, p. 152.

live our victories and our defeats. Even our philosophy, the field in which we are in advance of our time, will only triumph after being manifested at Paris and impregnated with the French spirit.'[1] However, the results of this endeavour were a great disappointment, and their tour of the Paris salons only led to an almost total incomprehension between them and the French. For in general the French considered that they were making quite satisfactory progress without German missionaries, and they did not see the need for a new ideology, particularly an atheistic one couched in Hegelian terminology. The first person Ruge and Hess visited was Lammenais, whom Ruge described as shocked by the idea of a science independent of religion. From Louis Blanc they only got the practical advice that anti-religious propaganda was useless and merely served the purposes of the liberal bourgeoisie: they would do best to join a political party and not go round the detour of humanism. Lamartine was at first willing to collaborate, but withdrew when he learnt that the review might have a revolutionary tone. Considérant shared Lamartine's attitudes, Proudhon was in Lyons and Leroux was too busy with other things. Finally Cabet, author of the Utopian communist book, *Journey to Icaria* was astonished that Ruge declared himself an atheist yet would not definitely say he was a communist.

This reduced the number of possible collaborators, and those who remained were not very numerous: Feuerbach persisted in his refusal, Herwegh was on his honeymoon and Bakunin, expelled from Zurich, was out of contact wandering from city to city. This left Ruge, Hess, Heine, Marx, Engels and Bernays, a journalist who had written for the *Rheinische Zeitung* and had recently been expelled from Baden. By October 1843 the preparations for launching the review were completed and the collaborators, such as they were, assembled. Froebel and Herwegh had arrived in September, Marx arrived with his wife in October and Ruge in December, after fruitless attempts in Germany to obtain more collaborators. The first and last number of the *Deutsch-französische Jahrbücher* appeared in February 1844 and contained articles by Ruge, Heine, Marx, Engels, Hess, Bernays and Herwegh. Ruge wrote an editorial setting out the aims of the review: it was to help in the struggle for political freedom by informing the Germans of what

[1] A. Ruge, *Zwei Jahre in Paris*, Leipzig, 1846, vol. I, pp. 4 ff.

the French had already achieved in this field, and it was also to tell
the French of the anti-religious campaign of the Germans and thus help
to liberate them from religious oppression and the Germans from
political oppression: this, it seemed to Ruge, the most effective way of
achieving humanism. However, Ruge fell ill soon after his arrival in
Paris, and most of the editing was left to Marx.

Marx's stay in Paris had the same effect on him as Engels's stay in
England had on Engels. Paris had two things lacking in Germany: a
numerous and class-conscious proletariat, and a revolutionary tradi-
tion. Marx frequented some of the workers' secret societies, but did
not actually join any of them. His first article in the *Deutsch-französische
Jahrbücher*, entitled 'On the Jewish Question,'[1] had been for the most
part written previously at Kreuznach, and so was not so much influenced by Paris but was rather a specific application of themes already
treated in the *Critique of Hegel's Philosophy of Right*. A Prussian edict of
1816 had excluded Jews from public office, and social and political
equality for the Jews had been one of the most insistent demands of the
liberals and of the Young Hegelians in particular. Bauer had dealt with
the question in a series of articles published in the *Deutsche Jahrbücher*
in November 1842 and re-issued as a brochure in 1843. He had also
written another article entitled 'The Capacity for Liberation of
Contemporary Jews and Christians' which he published in the collection of articles, *Twenty-one pages from Switzerland*, edited by Herwegh.
Bauer's position was roughly as follows: Judaism, being confined to
one race, was inferior to Christianity with its promise of universal
salvation. The Jews had separated themselves from other men, so why
should they object if other men did the same to them? In his second
article Bauer maintained that Christianity, being universal in scope,
was nearer to total emancipation than Judaism. This did not mean that
Jews had to become Christians, but only that they would find total
emancipation more difficult since it involved two steps for them as
opposed to one for Christians, i.e. the abolition of the 'Christian' State.

Marx's main point against Bauer was that a desire from a political
point of view for the abolition of religion was not sufficient; for political emancipation was not human emancipation, as was proved
particularly in North America, where religion flourished without any

[1] See pp. 85 ff. below.

political enforcement. This was just one example of the separation between civil society, where man led his real life, and the political state where his life was an imaginary one. Marx goes on to analyse the Rights of Man and the Citizen as defined by the French Revolution, the highest point of political emancipation. Bauer had regarded these rights as general and had denied their applicability to separatist Jews. Marx, on the other hand, regarded them as privileges belonging to bourgeois society, and different from the rights of the citizen that belonged to man as a member of the state. All these Rights of Man, beginning with the right to freedom, were the rights of men conceived of as private individuals, isolated nomads withdrawn into themselves. In order to achieve true emancipation the distinction between society and the state would have to be abolished and political man re-incorporated into social man. In the second part of his article Marx again viewed the problem from the social angle of the relationship of Judaism to general human emancipation. According to Marx, the main difficulty was the Jews' commercial instinct, their thirst for profit that was reflected in their religion. Jewish emancipation would involve the emancipation of the whole of society from the domination of money, for the whole of contemporary Christian society had been impregnated with the Jewish spirit.

Some of the main themes of Marx's article, and in particular the second part of it, were borrowed from Hess, who had been the first to apply Feuerbach's ideas of religious alienation to the field of economics. Hess had elaborated these ideas in an article 'On the Essence of Money' which he had sent to Marx to be included in the *Deutsch-französische Jahrbücher* (it was not published until eighteen months later). Hess's article had included the idea that the principles of the French Revolution were in some ways a regression from the principles of mediaeval times when corporations at least conserved the link between creative and individual life; it also included the idea that the Rights of Man were selfish and egoistic, and the idea that money in the economic sphere had become parallel to God in the religious, embodying the alienated essence of man.

The second of Marx's articles entitled 'Introduction to a Critique of Hegel's Philosophy of Right'[1] was much more influenced by his stay in

---

[1] See pp. 115 ff.

Paris. This article began with a series of brilliant similes on religion as the flowers on mankind's chains, the halo above the valley of tears and the opium of the people. Criticism of religion was now perfected and was giving way to criticism of politics in which field Germany's social situation, turned towards the past, did not afford much hope. However, Germany was in advance of other nations philosophically. In these circumstances, two parties had grown up: the first, consisting of some disciples of Feuerbach, thought that philosophy could be abolished without being realized in practical terms, that is, that only practical action was important. The second, Bruno Bauer's group, thought that philosophy could have its full effect without ceasing to exist, that is, only theory was important. It was difficult to see how Germany could have a radical revolution that would raise practice to the level of theory and thus enable Germany to take the lead in European emancipation. Just because Germany was so backward, no partial, that is political, emancipation was possible. Only a total, that is social, emancipation could free Germany. A political revolution occurred when a particular class, the bourgeoisie, undertook to reform society from its particular standpoint. Total emancipation was only possible for a class that was totally deprived of any of the goods of society. This class was the proletariat which would find in philosophy its theoretical weapons.

This article, so clearly inspired by the studies of the French Revolution that Marx was beginning to undertake, contained no ideas that were peculiarly communist; it was rather the article of an extreme democrat.

Shortly after the publication of the *Deutsch-französische Jahrbücher* the Prussian Government issued warrants for the arrest of Ruge, Marx, Heine and Bernays. Many copies of the review were seized on entering Germany, and financial difficulties, particularly as the French press paid scant attention to the publication, added to the disarray among the contributors. Froebel changed his mind about giving the review financial backing and withdrew his support.

Doctrinal divergences increased the difficulties: Ruge had become disillusioned with the German communists, who, he said, attached too great importance to private property and money (presumably his). In May 1844 he wrote to Feuerbach: 'Neither the complicated plans of Fourier's followers nor the communists' suppression of private property can be clearly formulated. Both end in a police state and slavery. In order to free the proletariat intellectually and physically from the weight of their misery, people dream of organizing society so as to generalize this misery and make all men carry its weight.'[1] Ruge had not entirely approved of Marx's essays in the *Deutsch-französische Jahrbücher* thinking them too stylized and epigrammatic. The direct cause of their quarrel was the poet Herwegh, whom Ruge attacked as being dissolute and lazy. Marx was offended and seized the opportunity to break off relations with Ruge.

THE 1844 MANUSCRIPTS AND BREAK WITH RUGE

Marx's time in Paris was particularly taken up with studies of the French Revolution. Already in 'On The Jewish Question' he had defined the character and limitations of this revolution, and in his introduction he had explained how the bourgeoisie had been able to seize power as the representative of the whole of society. Marx continued these studies and intended to write a history of the Convention. He even sketched out a table of contents for a book entitled 'Bourgeois Society and Communist Revolution', of which the first chapter was 'History of the Origin of the Modern State, or the French Revolution'. None of these plans resulted in anything definite. Ruge described Marx at this time as follows: 'He (Marx) reads a lot. He works in an extraordinarily intensive manner. He has a critical talent that sometimes degenerates into a purely dialectical game, but he never finishes anything, he interrupts each piece of research to plunge into a fresh ocean of books. . . . . He is more excited and violent than ever, above all when he has been made ill by working and has not gone to bed three or four nights in a row.'[2]

However, Marx did, during this period, manage to write some extended notes which, like the *Critique of Hegel's Philosophy of Right*, were preliminary drafts of a work on Hegel's philosophy of right to which Marx's second essay in the *Deutsch-französische Jahrbücher* was to serve as an introduction. These notes,[3] which form the largest single item in the following texts, are usually known as the *Paris Manuscripts*,

---

[1] A. Ruge, *Briefwechsel*, Berlin, 1886, vol. I, p. 346.
[2] A. Ruge, op. cit., p. 343.   [3] See pp. 130 ff. below.

1844 Manuscripts or *Economic and Philosophical Manuscripts*: Marx himself gave them no collective title. They begin with sections on the wages of labour and the rent of land that are largely excerpts from the writings of Adam Smith and other economists. There follow sections on alienated labour, private property and communism, and the manuscripts conclude with a long section devoted to a critique of Hegel's dialectic. Their two main themes are the alienation of man and the suppression of this alienation in communism. Although the *Manuscripts* are the first work in which Marx declares himself for communism, they do not represent the decisive turning point between the 'young' and the 'mature' Marx, supposing that such a turning point exists. If it does, it will be found more plausibly in *The Holy Family* published early in 1845. For it is there that Marx's characteristic doctrine, historical materialism, first appears. In the *Manuscripts* there is very little history, and materialism is explicitly rejected: 'We see here how consistent naturalism or humanism is distinguished from both idealism and materialism, and constitutes at the same time their unifying truth.'[1]

It is easy to point to the influences that nourished Marx's thought here: Engels' essay 'Zur Kritik der politischen Oekonomie' in the *Deutsch-französische Jahrbücher* had given him the idea of the internal contradictions of capitalism and its necessary failure; Hess had emphasized that work was central to any discussion of contemporary man, and had also demonstrated that the concept of alienation could be transferred to the social and economic spheres; Wilhelm Schulz in his book *Die Bewegung der Produktion*, published in 1843, had traced the link between production, division of labour and different forms of society; Feuerbach's humanist criticism of Hegel is present everywhere in the *Manuscripts;* finally there is Hegel's all-pervasive idea of the self-creation of man as a process in which the principal factor is man's own labour.

It is not quite clear exactly when the *Manuscripts* were written, but they were probably largely complete before Marx wrote his last piece of work before *The Holy Family* and his expulsion from Paris. This was an attempt to clarify his differences with Ruge.[2] The opportunity was provided by an article by Ruge on the Silesian weavers' revolt and

[1] See p. 167 below.   [2] See pp. 204 ff. below.

the nature and role of revolution. This article was published in the Prussian German-language newspaper *Vorwärts*, a paper that had originally been reactionary but whose owner had recently been converted to revolutionary ideas. He had invited Ferdinand Bernays, who had previously been in charge of the *Mannheimer Abend-Zeitung*, to become its editor, whereupon the group centred on the *Deutsch-französische Jahrbücher* began to contribute. The owner of *Vorwärts* had asked Ruge in an open letter to clarify his differences with Marx, who seemed to criticize the Rights of Man while Ruge defended them. Ruge replied by trying to make out that there were no real differences between Marx and himself, because Marx was only applying Ruge's principles. In July 1844 Ruge wrote an article entitled 'The King of Prussia and Social Reform', and signed it 'A Prussian', which could have given the impression, since Ruge was a Saxon, that Marx was the author. In this article Ruge took Louis Blanc to task for saying that the King of Prussia's ordinances to combat pauperism were the result of fear. According to Ruge, Germany was so backward that no political sense at all existed there and so pauperism was viewed as a natural calamity and there was no hope of a revolution. Marx in his reply pointed out that pauperism was not solved by a political sense, as was shown by the example of Britain where pauperism was so far developed as to be a state institution. Pauperism was of such a nature that no administrative measures would deal with it. In the second part of his article Marx disagreed with Ruge's view of the revolt as merely a local event. It was the first revolutionary act of the German proletariat, who were destined, as Weitling's writings showed, to be the theoreticians of the European proletariat. Moreover, any manifestation of social revolution, however small, was important since, as distinct from a political revolution, it posed the problem from a universal point of view.

In effect, this article took up the attack on political solutions that Marx had already elaborated in his articles for the *Deutsch-französische Jahrbücher*. Marx's next piece of writing was his first book, *The Holy Family*, which he wrote with Engels in the autumn of 1844. This book, and, of course, *The German Ideology*, written a year later, contain the outlines of historical materialism and both are thus outside the scope of the texts which follow, because these have been chosen in order to show

the development of Marx's thought before it achieved full systematization.

The 'Young Marx' and Marxism

In the century or so during which Marx has been recognized as a great
thinker, there have been many different views of what it was that was
central to his thought. Among the European Social Democrats at the
turn of the century Marx was above all an economist who, in the
Critique of Political Economy and *Capital* had analysed the bases of
bourgeois society and had demonstrated that its collapse was imminent.
Rudolph Hilferding, writing in 1905, said: 'Logically, taken simply as a
scientific system . . . Marxism is only a theory of the laws of social
movement, laws which are formulated in general by the Marxist conception of history, whereas Marxist economics applies them to the age
of commodity production.'[1]

When the centre of gravity of Marxism then shifted eastwards, Lenin
concentrated more on those of Marx's writings—the *Critique of the
Gotha Programme*, for example—that discussed political theory and
revolution. During the whole of this period those of Marx's early
writings that were known were considered as immature works that
were only of interest as stages towards the formulation of historial
materialism. Mehring wrote in 1918 of the *Deutsch-Französische
Jahrbücher*: 'Marx is still ploughing the philosophic field, but in the
furrows turned over by his critical ploughshare the first shoots of the
materialistic conception of history began to sprout, and under the warm
sun of French civilization, they soon began to flower.'[2]

But by the 1930s two factors, particularly in Western Europe, made
for a reappraisal of Marx's thought. The first was the political situation: the rise of Fascism on the one hand and of Stalinism on the other,
created a climate in which the critical and yet undogmatic humanism of
Marx's early writings was welcomed as a basis for the reformulation of
socialist ideals. Secondly, there was the publication in 1932 of Marx's

---

[1] Quoted in: E. Thier, 'Etappen der Marxinterpretation', in: *Marxismusstudien*,
Tübingen, 1957, vol. I, p. 15.
[2] F. Mehring, *Karl Marx*, London, 1936, p. 73.

early writings, and particularly the *Paris Manuscripts*, which had hitherto been unknown. The publication of these writings, together with the
advent of Existentialism and the revival of an enthusiasm for Hegel,
led to an immense interest in the 'young Marx'. This aspect of Marx's
thought inspired many new courses at universities where Marxism
had never figured before: one has only to consider the intensity of, for
example, the debate on 'alienation' in order to realize the extent of the
influence of these early texts. Instead of the economic forecasts of
Capital, or even the truth of dialectical materialism, the debate is
increasingly about Marx's understanding of history and human nature
—Marx's 'humanism'. Inevitably there arose the idea that there had
been 'two Marxes' and the question became: were the early writings
implicitly rejected by the mature system of Marx's later years? Or did
they reveal Marx's true philosophical inspiration? Was Marx an
economist or a philosopher? The recent tendency has been to divide
Marx into two and to elevate the 'young' at the expense of the 'mature'
Marx. Eric Fromm, for example, had said, 'it is impossible to understand Marx's concept of socialism, and his critique of capitalism as
developed in later years except on the basis of the concept of man
that he developed in his earlier years'.[1] Robert Tucker, in his portrayal
of Marxism as a religious myth again misunderstands the true location
of alienation when he says '. . . human self alienation and the overcoming of it remained always the supreme concern of Marx and the
central theme of his thought'.[2] On the other hand, the editors of the
latest, practically complete, edition of the works of Marx and Engels
justify their exclusion of the *Paris Manuscripts* by saying that their
edition is 'intended for a wide readership and is not a complete academic
edition'.[3]

To answer the question, what importance to attach to the early
writings of Marx both in themselves and in an understanding of Marx's
thought as a whole, it is relevant to ask how Marx himself regarded his
pre-1845 works. Certainly he did not care much about the fate of his
early manuscripts. In the preface to his *Critique of Political Economy*, he
said that he and Engels had abandoned the manuscript of *The German*

[1] E. Fromm, *Marx's Concept of Man*, New York, 1961, p. 79.

[2] R. Tucker, *Philosophy and Myth in Karl Marx*, Cambridge, 1961, p. 238.

[3] K. Marx, F. Engels, *Werke*, Berlin, 1961, vol. 1, p. xii.

Ideology (1846) 'to the gnawing criticisms of the mice all the more willingly as we had achieved our main purpose—self-clarification'.[1] When in 1867 a German friend, Dr. Kugelmann, an enthusiastic admirer of Marx, presented Marx with a copy of *The Holy Family* (1844) he wrote to Engels: 'he [Kugelmann] possesses a much better collection of our works than both of us put together. Here I also found *The Holy Family* again; he has presented it to me and will send you a copy. I was pleasantly surprised to find that we do not need to be ashamed of this work, although the cult of Feuerbach produces a very humorous effect upon one now.'[2] Engels, writing in 1888 dismissed *The German Ideology* very curtly: 'before sending these lines to press, I have once again ferreted out and looked out the old manuscript of 1845–1846. The section dealing with Feuerbach is not completed. The finished portion consists of an exposition of the materialistic interpretation of history which proves only how incomplete our knowledge of economic history still was at that time.'[3] Engels's attitude is very clearly shown in a conversation that a Russian visitor, Alexis Voden, had with him in 1893. Voden, recalling in 1927 a conversation concerning the early works of Marx and Engels reported:

'Our next conversation was on early works by Marx and Engels. At first Engels was embarrassed when I expressed interest in those works. He mentioned, too, that Marx had written poetry in his student years, but that it would hardly interest anybody. Then he asked which of Marx's and his works interested Plekhanov and his fellow thinkers, and what was the exact reason for that interest. Was not the fragment on Feuerbach, which Engels considered the most meaty of those 'old works', sufficient?

I gave all Plekhanov's arguments in favour of publishing as soon as possible the whole of Marx's philosophical legacy and his and Engels's joint works. Engels said he had heard that more than once from certain Germans, the seriousness of whose interest in those 'old works' he had no reason to doubt; but he asked me for an honest answer to the question: which was more important—for him, Engels—to spend the rest of his life publishing old manuscripts from publicistic work of the forties, or to set to work, when Book Three of *Capital* came out, on the publication of Marx's manuscripts on the history of the theories on surplus value?

[1] K. Marx, F. Engels, *Selected Works*, Moscow, 1962, vol. 1, p. 364.

[2] K. Marx, F. Engels, *Selected Correspondence*, London, 1936, p. 217.

[3] K. Marx, F. Engels, *Selected Works*, Moscow, 1962, vol. 2, p. 359.

I availed myself of what seemed to me the most favourable moment to urge Engels to redeem from undeserved oblivion at least the most essential of Marx's earlier works, Feuerbach alone being insufficient. Engels said that in order to penetrate into that 'old story' one needed, in fact, to have an interest in Hegel himself, which was not the case with anybody then, or, to be exact, 'neither with Kautsky nor with Bernstein'.[1]

Nevertheless, though Marx and Engels later avoided the 'philosophical' language of their early years, and in the *Communist Manifesto* mocked at the German *literati* who 'beneath the French criticism of the economic function of money, wrote "Alienation of Humanity" ',[2] they always recognized that 'the German working class movement is the inheritor of classical German philosophy'.[3] Marx's contemporaries may have been incapable of understanding Hegel, but Marx himself never lost his interest in him. In 1858, he wrote to Engels: 'I am getting some nice developments. For instance, I have thrown over the whole doctrine of profit as it has existed up to now. In the *method* of treatment, the fact that by mere accident I have again glanced through Hegel's *Logic* has been of great service to me—Freiligrath found some volumes of Hegel's which originally belonged to Bakunin and had sent them to me as presents. If there should ever be time for such work again, I should greatly like to make accessible to the ordinary human intelligence, in two or three printers' sheets, what is *rational* in the method which Hegel discovered but at the same time enveloped in mysticism.' In 1873, in the Afterword to the second German edition of *Capital* Marx made clear his position with regard to Hegel and specifically alluded to his early writings on the subject:

the mystifying side of Hegelian dialectic I criticized nearly thirty years ago, at a time when it was still the fashion. But just as I was working on the first volume of *Das Kapital*, it was the good pleasure of the peevish, arrogant, mediocre epigoni who now talk large [*sic*] in cultured Germany, to treat Hegel in the same way as the brave Moses Mendelssohn in Lessing's time treated Spinoza i.e. as a 'dead-dog'. I therefore openly avowed myself the pupil of that mighty thinker,

[1] *Reminiscences of Marx and Engels*, Moscow, n.d., pp. 330 f.
[2] K. Marx, F. Engels, *Selected Works*, Moscow, 1962, vol. 1, p. 54.
[3] K. Marx, F. Engels, *Selected Works*, Moscow, 1962, vol. 2, p. 402. The following few pages are a slightly different version of the final section of my book *Marx before Marxism*, London–New York. 1970.

and even here and there, in the chapter on the theory of value, coquetted with the modes of expression peculiar to him. The mystification which dialectic suffers in Hegel's hands, by no means prevents him from being first to present its general form of working in a comprehensive and conscious manner. With him it is standing on its head. It must be turned right side up again if you would discover the rational kernel within the mystical shell.[1]

This was also the view of Engels in his essay on Feuerbach. He wrote:

with Hegel philosophy comes to an end: on the one hand, because his system is its whole development in the most splendid fashion; and on the other hand, because even though unconsciously, he showed us the way out of the labyrinth of systems to real positive knowledge of the worlds.[2]

If, then, as these quotations suggest, there is some unity in Marx's thought, what does this unity consist in, and what are the themes which are common both to the early and to the later writings? One possible answer is that attempts to read Marxism as a 'scientific' account of social development are mistaken, and that the central inspiration of Marx is always ethical, and that the evidence for this is clearest in Marx's earliest writings.[3] The most usual answer, however, is that the problem of the unity of Marx's thought is closely bound up with the question of the relationship of Marx to Hegel; that Marx always remained in some sense a Hegelian; and that the early writings are important since they document the formation of Marx's attitude to Hegel's philosophy. Lenin himself lent support to this view by writing in 1914: 'it is impossible to fully grasp Marx's *Capital* and especially the first chapter, if you have not studied or understood the whole of Hegel's *Logic*. Consequently, none of the Marxists for the past half century has understood Marx!'[4] The most usual document quoted here is the *Paris Manuscripts*. Lately, however, it has been said that Marx's decisive encounter with Hegel was a year earlier in his *Critique of Hegel's Philosophy of Right*, and that Marx's basic ideas on materialism, the disappearance of the State, and communism, are to be found here.[5]

[1] K. Marx, *Capital*, Moscow, 1954, vol. I, pp. 19 f.

[2] K. Marx, F. Engels, *Selected Works*, Moscow, 1962, vol. 2, p. 365.

[3] For this view, see particularly: M. Rubel, *Karl Marx: Essai de Biographie Industrielle*, Paris, 1957.

[4] V. Lenin, *Aus dem philosophischen Nachlass*, Berlin, 1949, p. 99.

[5] See: S. Avineri, *The Social and Political Philosophy of Karl Marx*, Cambridge, 1968.

If there is a theme running through the whole of Marx's writings, the most obvious candidate would be 'alienation', a concept that Marx adopted directly from Hegel, although its origins are, of course, much earlier. Those who claim to find a break between the 'young' and the 'old' Marx usually maintain that alienation is a concept that was central to Marx's early thought but which he abandoned later. Sidney Hook, for example, wrote recently: 'it is easy to show that the notion of human alienation—except for the sociological meaning it has in *Capital*—is actually foreign to Marx's conception of man'.[1] And Daniel Bell has said that 'whereas in the young Marx there was a double vision of the nature of alienation . . . Marx's thoughts developed along one narrow road of economic conceptions, of poverty and exploitation, while the other road, which might have led to new, humanistic concepts of work and labour, was left unexplored'.[2] These statements are, however, inaccurate. Not only the concept but also the term itself occurs on several occasions in *Capital*.[3] Marx writes, for example; 'the character of independence and estrangement which the capitalist modes of production as a whole gives to the instruments of labour and to the product, as against the workman, is developed by means of machinery into a thorough antagonism'.[4] Yet it is not only a question of terminology; the content, too, of *Capital* is a continuation of Marx's early thoughts. The main theme of Volume I of *Capital*, surplus-value, rests on the equation of work and value that goes back to the conception of man as a being who creates himself and the conditions of his life —a conception outlined in the *Paris Manuscripts*. It is man's nature, according to the Marx of the *Paris Manuscripts*, to be constantly developing, in co-operation with other men, himself and the world about him. What Marx in *Capital* is describing is how this fundamental role of man, to be the initiator and controller of the historical process, has been transferred, or alienated, and how it belongs to the inhuman power of capital. The counterpart to alienated man, the unalienated or

[1] S. Hook, *From Hegel to Marx*, 2nd. ed., Michigan, 1962, p. 6.
[2] D. Bell, 'The Debate on Alienation', in: *Revisionism*, ed. L. Labedz, London, 1962, p. 210.
[3] See, for example: K. Marx, F. Engels, *Werke*, Berlin, 1962, vol. 23, pp. 455, 596, 635, 674; vol. 25, pp. 95 f., 274.
[4] K. Marx, *Capital*, Moscow, 1954, vol. I , p. 432.

'total' man of the *Manuscripts*, also appears in *Capital*. In the chapter of Volume I on 'Machinery and Modern Industry' Marx makes the same contrast between the effects of alienated and unalienated modes of production on the development of human potentiality. He writes:

Modern industry, indeed, compels society, under penalty of death, to replace the detail-worker of today, crippled by life-long repetition of one and the same trivial operation, and thus reduced to the mere fragment of a man, by the fully developed individual, fit for a variety of labours, ready to face any change of production, and to whom the different social functions he performs, are but so many modes of giving free scope to his own natural and acquired powers.[1]

The fact that, in *Capital*, the conclusion is supported by a detailed analysis of the effects of advanced technology, should not obscure the continuity.

The section of *Capital* that most recalls the early writings, is a final section of Chapter I, entitled 'Fetishism of commodities'. The whole section is reminiscent of the section on alienated labour in the *Paris Manuscripts* and of the notes on James Mill which Marx composed in 1844. Marx writes:

A commodity is therefore a mysterious thing, simply because in it the social character of man's labour appears to them as objective character stamped upon that labour; because the relation of the producers to the sum total of their own labour, is presented to them as a social relation, existing not between themselves, but between the products of their labour.[2]

He goes on, as so often in his earlier writings, to draw a parallel with religion:

In order, therefore, to find an analogy, we must have recourse to the mist-enveloped regions of the religious world. In that world the productions of the human brain appear as independent beings endowed with life, and entering into relation both with one another and the human race. So it is in the world of human commodities with the products of men's hands.[3]

It should be remembered, of course, that *Capital* is only an unfinished fragment of the task that Marx set himself. He complained frequently to Engels of the time he was forced to spend studying economics. In the

[1] K. Marx, *Capital*, Moscow, 1954, vol. I, p. 488.
[2] K. Marx, op. cit., p. 72.
[3] Ibid.

Preface to the *Paris Manuscripts* he had outlined the programme of his life's work:

I will therefore present one after another a critique of law, of morality, politics, etc. in different independent brochures and then finally in a separate work try to show the connection of the whole and the relationship of the parts to each other and end with a criticism of the elaboration of the material by speculative philosophy. Therefore, in the present work the connection of the political economy with the State, law, morality, civil life, etc. is only dealt with in so far as political economy itself professes to deal with these subjects.[1]

In fact, Marx never got beyond his first 'brochure' on political economy.

The continuity in Marx's thought has been demonstrated beyond all doubt by the publication, under the title *Grundrisse der Kritik der Politischen Oekonomie* (*Elements of a Critique of Political Economy*), of the 1,000 page draft that served Marx as a basis both for his *Critique of Political Economy* (1859) and of *Capital* (1867). The *Grundrisse*, written in 1857/8 was published for the first time in Moscow in 1939. The time and place of their publication prevented their attracting attention and it was not until 1953 that there was even an accessible German edition; it has still not been translated into English.[2] The *Grundrisse*, of which the *Critique of Political Economy* and *Capital* are only partial elaborations, is the centrepiece of Marx's work. It is the basic work which permitted the generalizations in the famous *Preface* of the *Critique of Political Economy*. The *Preface* is not matched by the work that follows it. Marx himself describes it in a letter to Lassalle as: 'the result of 15 years research, that is to say the best years of my life'.

The *Grundrisse* consists of an introduction in two parts, the first dealing with money and the second, much larger, dealing with capital, in the form of production, circulation and profit. Since it was written for personal clarification, some parts of the *Grundrisse* are very difficult to follow, since they are in note form and extremely elliptical. But in spite of the draft's somewhat fragmentary character, the Hegelian categories in which Marx forms his thought are obvious. Questions that were prominent in Marx's writing in 1844—such as the true nature of

[1] See pp. 131 below.
[2] See further: M. Nicolaus, 'The Unknown Marx', *New Left Review*, 1967.

labour and the resolution of the conflict between individual and community—are taken up again and filled out with a wealth of detail. Something of the tone of the *Grundrisse* is given by the following passage:

The ancient conception, in which man always appears (in however narrowly national, religious or political a definition) as the aim of production, seems very much more exalted than the modern world, in which production is the aim of man and wealth the aim of production. In fact, however, when the narrow bourgeois form has been peeled away, what is wealth, if not the universality of needs, capacities, enjoyments, productive powers, etc. of individuals, produced in universal exchange? What, if not the full development of human control over the forces of nature—those of his own nature as well as those of so called 'nature'? What, if not the absolute elaboration of his creative dispositions, without any preconditions other than antecedent historial evolution which makes the totality of this evolution—i.e. the evolution of all human powers as such, unmeasured by any previous established yardstick—an end in itself? What is this, if not a situation where man does not produce himself in any determined form, but produces his totality? Where he does not seek to remain something formed by the past, but is in the absolute movement of becoming? In bourgeois political economy—and in the epoch of production to which it corresponds—this complete elaboration of what lies within man, appears as the total alienation, and the destruction of all fixed, onesided purposes as the sacrifice of the end in itself to a wholly external compulsion.[1]

The *Grundrisse*, then, are as Hegelian as the *Paris Manuscripts* and their publication make it impossible to maintain that only Marx's early writings are of philosophical interest, and that in the later Marx specialist economic interests have obscured the early humanist vision. The concept of alienation is thus seen to be central to Marx's whole thought, including *Capital*.[2] However, the concept of alienation, so central to Marx's writings, needs examination, for its meaning and implications are far from self-evident.[3]

---

[1] K. Marx, *Pre-capitalist Economic Formations*, ed. E. Hobsbawm, London, 1964, pp. 84 f.

[2] See further, Maximilien Rubel's Preface to his superb edition of Marx's economic writings: K. Marx, *Oeuvres*, Paris, 1968, vol. 2, pp. vxii ff.

[3] It is necessary to add something on the translation of this term. Marx uses two words to express the concept of alienation: *Entfremdung* and *Entaüsserung*. His distinction between these two words is by no means as precise as that of

Particularly in his early writings Marx discusses several types of alienation, moving, in the rapid process of secularization common to the thinking of all the Young Hegelians, from religious alienation to philosophical, political and finally to economic alienation. This last Marx considered to be fundamental in as much as work was man's fundamental activity. In all fields the common idea was that man had forfeited to someone or something what was essential to his nature— principally, to be in control of his own activities, to be the initiator of the historical process. In the different forms of alienation some other entity had obtained what was proper to man: in religion it was God, in politics the State, in economics the market process.

Marx's notion of alienation came most directly from Hegel, though its roots are much earlier. For Hegel, reality was Spirit realising itself. Later Spirit perceived this world to be its own creation. Spirit, which existed only in and through its productive activity, gradually became conscious that it was externalizing or alienating itself. Alienation, for Hegel, consisted in this failure to realize that the world was not external to Spirit. Alienation would therefore cease when men saw that their environment and culture were creations of Spirit. When men saw this, they would be free, and this was the aim of history.[1] Marx's central

---

Hegel. Often they appear to be synonyms and are used together for rhetorical effect. If anything, *Entfremdung* conveys the sense of alienation in which two people are said to be alienated from each other; while *Entaüsserung* has more the sense of 'making external to oneself' with legal and commercial overtones. To mark this distinction (realizing at the same time that Marx does not rigidly adhere to it) I translate *Entfremdung* by 'alienation' and *Entaüsserung* by 'externalization'. Neither of these words should be confused with *Vergegenständlichung* (= 'objectification') which, in Marx, is a process that can either be good or bad according to the circumstances. For further views on the difficulties of translation, see: Karl Marx, *Economic and Philosophical Manuscripts*, trans. M. Milligan, Moscow, 1961, pp. 10 ff.; Karl Marx, *Early Writings*, trans. T. Bottomore, London, 1963, p. xix; D. Bell, 'The Debate on Alienation' in *Revisionism*, ed. L. Labedz, London, 1962, pp. 195 f.; D. Braybrooke, 'Diagnosis and Remedy in Marx's Doctrine of Alienation', in *Social Research*, 1964, pp. 326 f.

[1] Such a compressed summary of Hegel must necessarily be extremely deficient. See further: J. Plamenatz, *Man and Society*, London, 1963, vol. 2.

criticism of Hegel was that alienation would not cease with the supposed abolition of the external world. The external world, according to Marx, was part of man's nature and what was vital was to establish the right relationship between man and his environment.[1] Marx therefore rejected the notion of Spirit and replaced its supposed antithesis to the external world by the antithesis between man and his social being.

It is, however, only recently that alienation has emerged as the central concept in many discussions of Marxism. The reasons for this emphasis are not hard to find. Much of what Marx wrote was only relevant to the nineteenth century, and much of the thought of his would-be followers has remained imprisoned inside conceptions that have become swiftly outmoded. For both the evolution of capitalist societies and the gap between ideology and reality in the socialist ones have shown the orthodox analysis to be insufficient. In the post-Stalinist atmosphere of Eastern Europe, and particularly in Czechoslovakia, Poland and Yugoslavia, the early writings of Marx have had an increasing influence on intellectuals. As far as the West is concerned, of Marx's two major analyses of capitalist society, the first, that of the progressive pauperization of the proletariat and its necessary evolution to the realization of its revolutionary role, has been rendered obsolete. The creation of labour unions and the growth of reformism demonstrates that, far from aiding a proletarian revolution, the economic infrastructure of society has made for the progressive integration of the working classes into the existing social order. Nevertheless, the second of Marx's major analyses, which aimed at showing that in a commodity society the products of men's labour acquired an independent, anti-human power, has become far more relevant than he could have imagined. For the very wealth and complexity of highly developed societies has, in this respect, reinforced Marx's views.

Its topicality, however, is in danger of rendering the concept of alienation vacuous. Often it seems to be used to designate any state of affairs that is considered unsatisfactory. It has recently been said, without any exaggeration, that 'its evident resonance for "neo-marxist" thinkers, in both the West and the East, for existentialist philosophers and theologians, for psychiatrists and industrial sociologists, for

[1] The central passage for Marx's critique of Hegel is pp. 157 below.

déraciné artists and intellectuals and student rebels, has meant that it has been widely extended and altered in the interests of a number of contemporary preoccupations; as a result the core of Marx's concept has been lost'.[1]

However, Marx's account of alienation, particularly as contained in the *Paris Manuscripts*, is by no means as vacuous as many contemporary accounts.[2] For it contains both a hypothesis of the relationship between social conditions and psychological states and also a far from vague view of human nature. Because it contains both of these, it is also a concept in which facts and values are inextricably bound together, and so one which runs counter to the prevailing demand for a sharp distinction between normative and descriptive statements. Thus, although Marx is always writing with certain initial value judgements presupposed, empirical criteria are, to some extent, applicable to his hypotheses. One example of such a test would be to ask whether (as Marx implies) alienation increases in proportion to the division of labour under capitalism.[3] Marx's concept can be further clarified by asking in what, for him, would non-alienation consist. The positive side of Marx's critique is less well-known. But the passage on 'alienated labour' in the *Paris Manuscripts* should always be read in close conjunction with his description of 'production in a human manner' contained in his notes on James Mill.[4]

Of course, it is still possible either to dispute that the future communist society, even as painted by Marx, is superior to different forms

[1] S. Lukes, 'Alienation and Anomie', in *Politics, Philosophy and Society*, ed. Peter Laslett and W. G. Runciman, *Third Series*, Oxford, 1967, pp. 134 f. This article contains a very illuminating analysis of Marx's concept of alienation and a comparison with Durkheim's concept of 'anomie'.

[2] Nor, it may be added, is it quite as bizarre as some contemporary exegeses would indicate. For the view that Marx's thinking 'is closely allied to the thinking of Zen-Buddhism' see: E. Fromm, *Marx's Concept of Man*, New York, 1961. And for the view that ' "alienation" as first used by Marx . . . was a romantic concept with a preponderantly sexual connotation', see: L. Feuer, 'What is Alienation? The Career of a Concept', in *Sociology on Trial*, ed. M. Stein and A. Vidich, Englewood Cliffs, 1963.

[3] For a recent attempt to modernize and test Marx's ideas, see R. Blauner, *Alienation and Freedom*, Chicago, 1964.

[4] See pp. 188 ff. below.

of society, or to reject the blueprint as irrelevant because unrealizable. To this second position Marx would have replied, in the words of his *Theses* on Feuerbach, 'it is in practice that man must prove that his thought is true'.[1]

[1] K. Marx, F. Engels, *Werke*, Berlin, 1959, vol. 3, p. 533.

Letter to his Father[1]

Written: 10th November 1837
First published: By Eleanor Marx-Aveling in *Die Neue Zeit,* year 16, vol. I, (1897–98) no. 1, pp. 4–12
Reprinted: MEGA, I (2), pp. 213–221. *Frühe Schriften,* pp. 7–17
Translated: Molitor, Volume IV, pp. 1–16. By William Glen-Doepel, in B. Delfgaauw, *The Young Marx,* London, 1967, pp. 135–147. Easton and Guddat, *Writings of the Young Marx,* pp. 40–50

Seventeen letters of his father to Marx have been preserved, but only this one of Marx in reply: it was written towards the end of Marx's first term at the University of Berlin when Marx was 19 years old. Usually Marx's letters were short, and the length of this one indicates its importance. It is dominated by Marx's search for unity and a synthesis of the various currents of thought which influenced him at the time. He mentions here many of the themes that run right through his work: that, for example, of historical consciousness, an attempt to situate himself within an evolving process, and the desire, following Hegel, to find the identity of the real and the rational.

Berlin, 10th November

Dear Father,

There are moments in one's life that represent the limit of a period and at the same time point clearly in a new direction.

In such a period of transition we feel ourselves compelled to consider the past and present with the eagle eye of thought in order to come to a realization of our actual position. Yes, History itself likes this sort of stock-taking and introspection which often makes it look as though it were going backwards or standing still, whereas it is merely throwing itself into an armchair to understand itself and comprehend intellectually its own mental processes.

An individual, however, becomes lyrical at such moments, for every change is partly a swansong, partly an overture to a new epic that is trying to find a form in brilliant colours that are not yet distinct.

[1] See Introduction, p. xiii f., above.

Yet we want to erect a memorial to our past experiences so that they may find again in our emotions the place that they have lost in our actions; and there could be no more sacred home for this memorial than the heart of parents, the mildest of judges, the most intimate sympathizers, a sun of love whose fire warms the inmost centre of our endeavours. How better could much that is disgraceful and blame-worthy find forgiveness and excuse than when it appears as the result of an essentially necessary state of affairs, how else could the often untoward fall of chance and the mind's errors escape being thought the products of a deformed spirit?

So now that I am casting an eye back over the events of the year that I have lived here and thus answering, my dear father, your most precious letter from Ems, allow me to consider my situation (as I do life in general) as the result of an intellectual activity that finds expression on all sides—in science, art and personal matters.

When I left you, a new world had just begun to exist for me, the world of love that was at first drunk with its own desire and hopeless. Even the journey to Berlin which would otherwise have charmed me completely, excited me to an admiration of nature and inflamed me with a zest for life, left me cold and even, surprisingly, depressed me; for the rocks that I saw were not rougher, not harsher than the emo-tions of my soul, the broad cities not more full of life than my blood, the tables of the inns not more overladen and indigestible than the stocks of fantasies that I carried with me, nor, finally, was any work of art as beautiful as Jenny.

When I arrived in Berlin I broke off all the connections that I had hitherto contracted, made rare and reluctant visits and tried to steep myself in science and art.

Considering my state of mind then it was inevitable that lyric poetry should be my first project and certainly the pleasantest and readiest to hand. But my attitude and all my previous development made it purely idealistic. My heaven and art became a Beyond as distant as my love. Everything real began to dissolve and thus lose its finiteness, I attacked the present, feeling was expressed without moderation or form, nothing was natural, everything built of moonshine; I believed in a complete opposition between what is and what ought to be and rhetorical reflections occupied the place of poetic thoughts, though there was perhaps also a certain warmth of emotion and desire for exuberance. These are the characteristics of all the poems of the first three volumes that Jenny received from me. The whole scope of a longing that sees no limits is expressed in many forms and broadens poetry out.

But poetry was to be, and had to be, only a sideline; I had to study jurisprudence and felt above all impelled to struggle with philosophy. Both were so interconnected that I examined Heineccius, Thibaut and the sources completely uncritically like a schoolboy and thus translated the first two books of Pandects into German and at the same time tried to elaborate a philosophy that would cover the whole field of law. As introduction I prefixed a few metaphysical propositions and continued this unhappy opus as far as public law, a work of almost three hundred pages.

Here the same opposition of 'is' and 'ought' which is the hallmark of idealism was the dominating and very destructive feature and engendered the following hopelessly mistaken division of the subject-matter: firstly came what I had so graciously christened the metaphysics of law, i.e. first principles, reflections, definitions distinct from all actual law and every actual form of law—just as you get in Fichte only here more modern and with less substance. This meant that from the outset the unscientific form of mathematical dogmatism where one circles round a subject, reasoning back and forth, without letting it unfold its own rich and living content, prevented any grasp of the truth. The mathematician constructs and proves the triangle, but it remains a pure abstraction in space and does not develop any further; you have to put it beside something else and then it takes up other positions and it is the juxtaposition of these different things that gives it different relationships and truths. Whereas in the practical expression of the living world of ideas in which law, the state, nature and the whole of philosophy consist, the object itself must be studied in its own development, arbitrary divisions must not be introduced and it is the ratio of the object itself which must develop out of its inner contradictions and find unity within itself.

The second part consisted of the philosophy of law, i.e. in accordance with the opinion I held at that time, a discussion of the development of ideas in positive Roman law, as though the development of the ideas of positive law (I don't mean in its purely finite terms) could ever be anything different from the formation of the concept of law which the first part should already have dealt with!

Moreover, I had further divided this section into formal and material legal doctrine, the first of which was to describe the pure form of the system in its consistent development, its divisions and range, while the second was to describe the self-incarnation of the form in its content. This was an error that I held in common with Herr v. Savigny, as I found out later in his learned work on property, only with the difference that he calls the formal definition of the idea 'the finding of the place that such and such a doctrine occupies in the (fictional) Roman system', and material 'the doctrine of the positive content that the Romans included in a concept thus defined' whereas I meant by form the necessary structure of the expressions of an idea and by matter the necessary quality of these expressions. The fault here was that I believed that the one could and must develop itself independently of the other and thus I did not obtain a true form but merely a desk into whose drawers I proceeded to pour sand.

A concept is the mediator between form and content. So in a philosophical treatment of law the one must emerge into the other; indeed the form should merely be the development of the content. So I arrived at a division that the mind could only form for an easy and superficial classification, while the true spirit of the law went by the board. The whole field of law was divided into contractual and non-contractual. In order to make this clearer let me set out the plan up to the division of *ius publicum* which is also treated in the formal part.

I   II

IUS PRIVATUM   IUS PUBLICUM

I. IUS PRIVATUM

A. Codified contractual private law
B. Uncodified non-contractual private law

A. Codified contractual private law

(a) Law of persons
(b) Law of things
(c) Law of persons relating to things

(a) Law of persons

I. Comercial contracts
II. Warranties
III. Contracts of bailment

I. Commercial contracts

2. Contracts of legal entities (*societas*)
3. Contracts of easements (*locatio conductio*)

3. *Locatio conductio*

(i) In as much as it refers to *operae*
    a. Actual *locatio conductio* (excluding letting or leasing in the Roman sense)
    b. *mandatum*
(ii) In as much as it refers to *usus rei*
    a. On land: *usus fructus* (again not just in the Roman sense)
    b. On houses: *habitatio*

II. Warranties

1. Arbitration agreement or contract of indemnity
2. Insurance contracts

III. Contracts of bailment

2. Promissory contract
    (i) *fide iussio*
    (ii) *negotiorum gestio*
3. Contract of gift
    (i) *donatio*
    (ii) *gratiae promissum*

(b) Law of things

I. Commercial contract

2. *Permutatio stricte sic dicta*
    (i) *Eigentliche permutatio*
    (ii) *mutuum (usurae)*
    (iii) *emptio, venditio*

D

II. Warranties *pignus*

III. Contracts of bailment

2. *commodatum*

3. *depositum*

But why should I go on filling up pages with what I have rejected? The whole is full of hair-splitting, it is written with boring prolixity and Roman conceptions are barbarously misused in order to force them into my system. On the other hand, this did give me, at least to some extent, a love and knowledge of the material.

At the end of material private law I saw the falsity of the whole conception (whose outline borders on the Kantian but when elaborated veers completely away), and it again became plain to me that I could not get by without philosophy. So I was forced again with a quiet conscience to throw myself into her arms and composed a new basic system of metaphysics at the end of which I was forced to realize the perversity of this and that of all my previous efforts.

This had put me in the habit of making excerpts from all the books that I read and so I scribbled down thoughts from Lessing's *Laokoon*, Solger's *Erwin*, Winckelmann's *History of Art*, Luden's *German History*; and others.

At the same time I translated Tacitus's *Germania* and Ovid's *Tristia* and began to learn English and Italian on my own, i.e. out of grammars, though I have not yet got anywhere with them. I also read Kelin's *Criminal Law* and his *Annals* and all the latest literature, though this latter only as a sideline. At the end of the term I again sought the dances of the Muses and the music of the Satyrs and in the last volume that I sent you the forced humour of *Scorpion and Felix* and the misconceived fantastic drama of *Oulanem* are shot through with idealism which finally changes completely, dissolving into purely formal art which has no objects to inspire it and no exciting progress of ideas.

And yet these last poems were the only ones in which suddenly, as though at the touch of a magic wand—oh! the touch was at first shattering—the kingdom of true poetry glittered opposite me like a distant fairy palace and all my creations dissolved into nothingness.

With these various occupations I had been forced during the first term to sit up through many nights, to fight through many a struggle and endure much excitement from within and without and yet was not much richer at the end in spite of having deserted nature, art and the world, and spurned friends. These thoughts were registered by my body and a doctor advised me to go to the country and so for the first time I went through the whole of the long city and out of the gate to Stralow. I did not supsect that there my anaemic and languishing body would mature and acquire a robust strength.

A curtain had fallen, my holy of holies was rent asunder and new gods had to be installed. I left behind the idealism which, by the way, I had nourished with that of Kant and Fichte, and came to seek the idea in the real itself. If the gods had before dwelt above the earth, they had now become its centre.

I had read fragments of Hegel's philosophy, but I did not care for its grotesque and rocky melody. Once again I wanted to dive off into the sea, but with the firm intention of finding the nature of the mind as necessary, concrete and firmly established as that of physical nature, for I wanted to stop fencing and bring the pure pearls up to the sunlight.

I wrote a dialogue of about twenty-four pages entitled 'Cleanthes or the starting point and necessary progress of philosophy'. Here art and science, which had become completely separate regained to some extent their unity, and I vigorously set about the job itself, a philosophical and dialectical development of the divinity as it manifests itself as idea-in-itself, religion, nature and history. My last sentence was the beginning of Hegel's system, and this work for whose sake I had made some acquaintance with natural science, Schelling and history, which had caused me endless headaches and is written in so confused a manner (for it had actually to be a new logic) that I can now scarcely think myself back into it, this my dearest child, reared by moonlight, like a false siren delivers me into the arms of the enemy.

My vexation prevented me from thinking at all for several days and I ran like a madman around the garden beside the dirty waters of the Spree 'which washes souls and makes weak tea'. I even went on a hunting party with my landlord and rushed off to Berlin and wanted to embrace every street loafer I saw.

Soon afterwards I undertook only positive studies, the study of ownership by Savigny, Feuerbach and Grohlmann's *Criminal Law*, the

De Verhorum Significatione of Cramer, Wenning-Ingenheim's *System of Pandects*, Mühlenbruch's *Doctrina Pandectarum*, which I am still working through and finally a few titles from Lauterbach, *Civil Trials* and above all *Canon Law*, the first part of which—the *Concordia discordantium Canonum* of Gratian—I have read and excerpted almost entirely in the *corpus*, as also the supplement Lancelotti's *Institutiones*. Then I translated Aristotle's *Rhetoric* in part, read the *De Argumentis Scientiarum* of the famous Baco of Verulam, was very busy with Reimarus whose book *On the Instincts of Animals* I followed with delight, and also came across German law, though principally only in so far as I went through the capitularies of the Frankish kings and the letters that the Popes addressed to them. My vexation at Jenny's illness, my fruitless and failed intellectual endeavours and my consuming anger at having to make my idol a view that I hated, made me ill, as I have already written to you, dear father. When I recovered I burnt all my poems and sketches for novels, etc., fancying that I could be completely free from them, which has at least not yet been disproved.

During my illness I had got to know Hegel from beginning to end, together with most of his disciples. Through several gatherings with friends in Stralow I obtained entrance into a graduate club[1] among whose members were several university lecturers and the most intimate of my Berlin friends, Dr. Rutenberg. In the discussions here many contradictory views appeared and I attached myself ever more closely to the current philosophy that I had thought to escape, but all the rich harmonies were stilled and a veritable fit of irony came over me, as was quite natural after so much negation. To this was added Jenny's silence and I could not rest until I had acquired modernity and a contemporary scientific outlook through a few bad pieces like 'The Visit'.

If perhaps I have not here described clearly to you the whole of this last term, nor gone into all the details and slurred the nuances, let my excuse, dear father, be my desire to talk of the present.

Herr v. Chamisso sent me a highly insignificant note in which he informed me that 'he was very sorry that the Almanach could not make

---

[1] This was a club of Young Hegelian philosophers, mostly lecturers at the University and schoolteachers, who met for informal discussions. In 1842 it became more radical and gave itself the title of 'The Free Men'. It continued in existence until 1845.

use of my contributions because it had already been long in print'. I swallowed it in my anger. Wigand the bookseller has sent my plan to Dr. Schmidt, publisher of the Wunder firm that deals in good cheese and bad literature. I enclose his letter; the latter has not yet answered. Meanwhile I am by no means abandoning this plan, particularly because, through the agency of Bauer, who plays a leading role among them, and of my colleague Dr. Rutenberg, all the aesthetic celebreties of the Hegelian school have promised to contribute.

As regards the question of a financial career, my dear father, I have recently made the acquaintance of an assistant judge, Schmidthänner, who advised me to transfer after my third law examination, advice that I am all the more inclined to accept as I really prefer jurisprudence to any administrative studies. This gentleman told me that starting in the Münster Oberlandsgericht in Westphalen he himself and many others had been made assistant judges in three years, which, he said, was not difficult provided, of course, that one worked hard, as there the stages are not rigidly fixed as they are in Berlin and other places. If later, as an assistant judge, one obtains a doctorate, then there is also a much better prospect of being able to obtain the post of supplementary professor, as Herr Gärtner did in Berlin, who wrote a mediocre work on the legal books of the provinces and is otherwise known only for having joined the Hegelian school of jurists. But dear, dear father, would it not be possible to talk all over with you personally? Edward's condition, my darling mama's illness, your own indisposition (although I hope it is not serious), all this makes me wish, indeed makes it almost a necessity that I hasten to you. I would be already there did I not have definite doubts of obtaining your permission and consent.

Believe me, dearest father, it is no selfish consideration that impels me (although it would be bliss to see Jenny again), but rather a most insistent thought that I cannot express. It would even be a hard step for me from many points of view but, as my own sweet Jenny writes, these considerations have no place before duties that are sacred.

I ask you, dear father, whatever your decision, not to show this letter, or at least this page, to my angel of a mother. My sudden arrival might perhaps help that great and marvellous woman to recover.

The letter that I wrote to mama was completed long before the arrival of Jenny's dear letter and so, maybe unwittingly, I wrote too much of matters that are not completely fitting or perhaps hardly at all so.

In the hope that by and by the clouds that surround our family will retreat and that I may be allowed to suffer and weep with you and perhaps give you tangible proofs of the deep and sincere sympathy and immeasurable love that I can often only express so badly; in the hope, too, that you, dearly beloved father, will take into consideration the often very disordered state of my mind, and forgive where my heart has seemed to err, overcome by my fighting spirit, and that you will soon be completely restored to health so that I may myself press you to my heart and tell you all.

Your ever loving son

Karl

Forgive, dear father, the illegible handwriting and bad style; it is almost four o'clock. The candle is burnt right down and my eyes are sore; a real anxiety has come over me and I will not be able to quieten the ghosts I have roused until I am near you again. Please give my love to dear, wonderful Jenny. I have already read her letter twelve times and I still find new delights. It is in every particular, including that of style, the most beautiful letter that I can imagine written by a woman.

Dissertation and Preliminary Notes on the Difference between Democritus' and Epicurus' Philosophy of Nature

Written: Started at the end of 1839

First published: MEGA, I i (1) pp. 1–114
Reprinted: Frühe Schriften, pp. 18–106

Translated: Marx–Engels, *Sur La Religion,* ed. Badia et al., Paris, 1960, pp. 11–14 (i.e. Preface only). Easton and Guddat, *Writings of the Young Marx,* pp. 51–66

The Dissertation was presented to the University of Jena in April 1841. Pressure from Bruno Bauer, quarrels with his family, his engagement to Jenny v. Westphalen and the consequent need to obtain a job made Marx present it in a hurry. As the *Preface* shows it was meant to be part of a larger work. The extracts translated here form no part of the Dissertation as such, but are digressions interspersed among the quotations, notes and references, and presumably intended for incorporation in the larger work. Marx did intend publishing the Dissertation as it stood, but gave up the idea when he no longer had any prospect of an academic career.

Marx's starting-point is Hegel's philosophy of history which he intended to continue and correct. The Dissertation develops the problem raised by Marx's letter to his father: what was the philosopher's task after the seductive solution to the problem of the relationship of the real and the rational as offered by Hegel? Marx's answer was that Hegel had to be radically rethought and put on a new basis, a basis that would involve the disappearance of philosophy at the same time as its realization. For the function of philosophy was to criticize existing reality and to make the gap between the ideal and the real intolerable. The different notion of philosophy as a compensatory reflection of a deficient reality was not elaborated by Marx until 1843/44.

See further: Introduction, pp. 6 f., above; D. Baumgarten, 'Üeber den "verloren geglaubten" Anhang zu Karl Marx's Doktordissertation', in: *Gegenwartsprobleme der Soziologie,* ed. Eisermann, Potsdam, 1949; G. mende, *Karl Marx: Doktordissertation,* Jena, 1964; D. Livergood, *Marx's Philosophy of Action,* The Hague, 1967.

Preface

The form of this treatise would have been both more strictly scientific and also less pedantic in many of its developments had it not originally been intended to be a doctoral thesis. Extrinsic reasons have nonetheless persuaded me to have it printed in this form. Moreover, I think that I have here solved a problem in the history of Greek philosophy that has hitherto remained a mystery.

Specialists know that for the subject of this treatise there are no previous works that are at all useful. The blatherings of Cicero and Plutarch have been reproduced right up to the present time. Gassendi's exposition, which freed Epicurus from the interdict which the Church fathers and the Middle Ages, the period of unreason incarnate, had laid on him, is only an interesting stage. He tries to reconcile his Catholic conscience with his pagan science and Epicurus with the Church, which of course was a waste of effort. It is as though one wanted to put a Christian nun's habit on the serenely blooming body of a Greek Laïs. Gassendi has to learn too much philosophy from Epicurus for him to be in a position to teach us much about it.

This treatise should be considered as only the preliminary to a larger work in which I will describe in detail the cycle of Epicurean, Stoic and Sceptic philosophies in their relationship to the whole of Greek speculation. The deficiencies in the form and so on of the present treatise will then disappear.

Hegel has, it is true, by and large correctly described the general characteristics of these systems—but the admirably broad and bold plan of his history of philosophy, which really gave birth to the history of philosophy as a subject, made it impossible to enter into details; and also his conception of what he called 'speculative *par excellence*' prevented this giant of a thinker from recognizing the great importance that these systems have for the history of Greek philosophy and the Greek mind in general. These systems are the key to the true history of Greek philosophy. There are fuller indications concerning their connection with Greek life in the work of my friend Köppen entitled *Frederick the Great and his Opponents*.

The reason for adding a critique of Plutarch's polemic against Epicurus' theology as an appendix was that this polemic does not stand in isolation, but represents a *genre* in that it strikingly conveys the attitude of the theological mind to philosophy.

My critique does not discuss, among other things, how completely false Plutarch's whole approach is when he calls philosophy before the bar of religion. On this subject, let a passage from David Hume suffice instead of any argument:

'It is certainly a sort of insult for philosophy whose sovereign views should be recognized on all sides, when she is compelled on every occasion to defend herself because of her consequences and justify herself in the eyes of every art and science that is offended by her. One is put in mind of a king who is accused of high treason against his own subjects.'[1]

As long as a single drop of blood pulses in her world-conquering and totally free heart philosophy will continually shout at her opponents the cry of Epicurus:[2]

ἀσεβὴς δε οὐχ ὁ τοὺς τῶν πολλῶν θεοὺς ἀναιρῶν, ἀλλ ὁ τὰς τῶν πολλῶν δόξας θεοῖς προσάπτων. (The profane man is not the one who destroys the gods of the multitude but the one who foists the multitude's doctrines onto the gods.)

Philosophy makes no secret of it. The proclamation of Prometheus:[3]

ἁπλῷ λόγῳ τοὺς πάντας ἐχθαίρω θεούς (in a word, I detest all the Gods).

is her own profession, her own slogan against all the gods of heaven and earth who do not recognise man's self-consciousness as the highest divinity. There shall be none other beside it.

But to the pitiful cowards who rejoice over the apparently worsening social position of philosophy, she repeats what Prometheus said to the servant of the gods, Hermes:[4]

τῆς σῆς λατρείας τὴν ἐμὴν δυσπραξίαν, σαφῶς ἐπίστασ', οὐκ ἂν ἀλλάξαιμ' ἐγώ (Understand this well, I would not change my evil plight for your servility.)

---

[1] David Hume, *A Treatise of Human Nature*, ed. L. Selby-Bigge, Oxford, 1888, p. 250.

[2] Epicurus, Episcula ad Menoeceum, v. 123.

[3] Aeschylus, *Prometheus Bound*, v. 975.

[4] Ibid., vv. 966-70.

Prometheus is the foremost saint and martyr in the philosopher's calendar.

From the Notes to the Dissertation

Berlin, March 1841

[The world becomes philosophical, and philosophy becomes worldly]

As regards Hegel, too, it is pure ignorance on the part of his followers when they explain this or that aspect of his system as a compromise or something of the sort, i.e. when they pass a moral judgement on it. They forget that almost no time ago, as can plainly be shown them out of their own writings, they were fervent adherents to all aspects of his one-sidedness.

If they were really so seduced by the offer of ready-made knowledge that they accepted it fully with naïve, uncritical trust, then what a lack of conscience it shows to reproach the master with having a hidden intention behind his insights—the master for whom knowledge was no ready-made thing but a process whose outer limits were reached by the ferment of his intellectual originality. The attitude of these followers makes one rather suspect that it was they who were not serious before since they attack this former position of theirs by ascribing it to Hegel, but forget when doing so that he stands in immediate substantial relation to his system, while they have it only at second hand.

It is conceivable that a philosopher should be guilty of this or that inconsistency because of this or that compromise; he may himself be conscious of it. But what he is not conscious of is that in the last analysis this apparent compromise is made possible by the deficiency of his principles or an inadequate grasp of them. So if a philosopher really has compromised it is the job of his followers to use the inner core of his thought to illuminate his own superficial expressions of it. In this way, what is a progress in conscience is also a progress in knowledge. This does not involve putting the conscience of a philosopher under suspicion, but rather construing the essential characteristics of his views, giving them a definite form and meaning, and thus at the same time going beyond them.

Moreover, I consider this unphilosophical evolution of a large part of the Hegelian school as a phenomenon that will always accompany a transition from discipline to freedom.

It is a psychological law that once the theoretical intellect has achieved freedom within itself it turns into practical energy and, emerging from the shadow kingdom of Amenthes as will, directs itself against the exterior reality of the world. (But it is important from the philosophical point of view to elaborate on these pages because from the precise manner of this transition we can draw conclusions as to the immanent characteristics and historical character of a philosophy. We see here its *curriculum vitae* reduced, so to speak, to its simplest expression, its quintessence.) But the *praxis* of philosophy is itself theoretical. It is the sort of critique that measures individual existing things by their essence and particular realities by the Idea. But this immediate realization of philosophy is fraught with contradictions in its innermost essence and it is its essence that appears in the phenomena and imprints its seal on them.

So long as philosophy as will goes forth against the world of appearances, the system is degraded to an abstract totality, i.e. it has become one side of the world with another side over against it. Its relation to the world is one of reflection. Being inspired with the desire to realize itself, there is a tension between it and other things. Its inner self-sufficiency and perfection are destroyed. What was an inner light becomes a consuming flame that turns outwards. As a consequence, the world's becoming philosophical coincides with philosophy's becoming worldly, the realization of philosophy coincides with its disappearance, the exterior battles of philosophy are against its own inner deficiencies; in the struggle it acquires precisely those defects against which it is fighting, and so only eliminates them by making them its own. Philosophy's opposite and enemy is always the same as philosophy itself, but with the factors reversed.

This is one side of the matter, if we treat it purely objectively as immediate realization of philosophy. But there is also a subjective side which is merely a form of the same matter. This is the relationship of the philosophical system that is realized to the minds that think it, the individual self-conciousnesses in which its progress appears. The result of the relationship that exists *vis-à-vis* the world in the realization of philosophy is that these individual minds are always fighting on two fronts, one against the world and the other against philosophy. For what in the object appears to be a self-inverted relationship appears in them as a dual self-contradictory challenge to activity. Their liberation of the world from non-philosophy coincides with their own liberation from philosophy which fettered them with its own particular system. Because they are at first caught up in the energetic activity of immediate development, i.e. from the theoretical point of view have not yet got beyond that system, they only feel the contradiction with the plastic self-identity and don't see that, in so far as they turn against it, they are only realizing its individual stages.

In the end this duality of the philosophical mind produces two schools completely opposed to one another, one of which, the liberal party as we may loosely call it, lays most emphasis on philosophy as a concept and principle, while the other holds fast to what are not concepts, to the real. This second school is positive philosophy. The activity of the first takes the form of a critique, i.e. philosophy turning itself against the exterior world, the activity of the latter is an attempt to philosophize, i.e. philosophical introspection. The second school sees the deficiency as immanent to philosophy, whereas the first sees it as a deficiency of the world that it is trying to make philosophical. Each of these parties does exactly what the other aims at and what it does not itself intend. But the first, in spite of its inner contradictions, is in general aware of its principle and aim. In the second, the inversion, the craziness, so to speak, is manifested in all its purity. As regards content, it is only the liberal party, because it is the party of the concept, which makes any real progress, whereas positive philosophy is only capable of requirements and tendencies whose form contradicts their meaning.

Thus what first appears as an inverted relationship and an inimical rift between philosophy and the world becomes secondly a rift within the individual philosopher's mind and appears finally as an exterior division and duplication within philosophy as two opposed philosophical schools.

Naturally there also arises a crowd of inferior, whining, characterless versions which on occasion take cover behind some giant figure of the philosophical past—but the sheep is soon visible underneath the wolf's skin, the whimpering sound of some ephemeral nobody makes a comical contrast when it comes from behind the strong voice of an Aristotle sounding down the centuries whose mouthpiece they have unfortunately made themselves; it is as though a dumb man were to try to use an enormous megaphone to help himself speak—while on other occasions, armed with binoculars, some lilliputian or other stands on a part of the posterior of the giant, proclaims amazedly to the world what a surprising new view his vantage point affords, and makes ridiculous efforts to prove that he has found Archimedes' point, ποῦ στῶ, the fulcrum of the world, not in the swelling heart, but in the solid, tough dwelling on which he is standing. So there arise philosophers of hair, nails, toes, excrement and others who have to occupy an even worse position in the mystical world-man of Swedenborg. In conformity with their natures all these creatures divide easily into one of the two schools above mentioned. As far as the schools themselves are concerned, I will fully explain in another place both their relationship to each other, to the Hegelian philosophy and to the individual historical stages that represent this development.

Reason and the Proofs for the Existence of God

'Weak reason, however, is not that which does not recognize an objective God, but that which wants to.' Schelling in *Philosophical Letters on Dogmatism and Criticism* in *Philosophical Writings*, vol. 1, Landshut, 1803, p. 127, Letter II. Schelling should be given a word of advice: to return to the views of his earlier writings. Thus, for example, in the work on the self as the principle of philosophy we read: 'Let us suppose, for example, that God, in so far as he is a definite object, is the true ground of our being, then he enters, in so far as he is an object, into the sphere of our knowledge and so cannot be for us the final point on which the whole of this sphere depends' p. 5, loc. cit. We remind Schelling finally of the last words of his letter quoted before: 'It is high time to proclaim intellectual freedom to a better humanity and no longer tolerate that they bewail the loss of their chains.' p. 129 loc. cit. If it was already high time in 1795, what is it in 1841?

I take this opportunity to touch on a subject that has become almost notorious, that of the proofs for the existence of God. Hegel totally reversed, i.e. rejected, these theological proofs in order to justify them: strange clients that the barrister can only save from condemnation by striking them dead himself! Hegel interprets, for example, the argument from the world to God in this form: 'Because the contingent does not exist, then God or the Absolute does exist.' But the theological proof is the reverse: 'Because the contingent has true being, then God exists.' God is the guarantee of the contingent world. Naturally this also involves the opposite.

The proofs for the existence of God admit of two interpretations:

1. Either they are simply pure tautologies—for example the ontological proof merely amounts to this: 'What I really imagine is for me a real imagination' that reacts upon me and in this sense all gods, heathen as well as Christian, had a real existence. Did not Moloch reign in antiquity? Was not Delphic Apollo a real power in the life of the Greeks? Even Kant's *Critique* does not make any sense here. If someone imagines that he has one hundred pounds and if for him this is no arbitrary fancy, but he really believes in it then the one hundred imagined pounds have the same worth for him as one hundred real ones. He will, for example, contract debts on the strength of his imaginings, they will have an effect, as the whole of humanity has contracted debts on the strength of their gods. Kant's example could, on the contrary, have strengthened the ontological proof. Real pounds have the same existence as imagined gods. Surely there is no other place where a real pound can exist apart from the general, or rather collective, imagination of men. Take paper money into a land where the use of such money is not known and everyone will laugh at your subjective imagination. Go with your gods into another land where other gods hold sway and it will be proved to you that you are suffering from fanciful dreams. Rightly so. Anyone who brought a nomad god to the ancient Greeks would have the proof for the non-existence of this god. For he did not exist for the Greeks: what a particular land is for particular foreign gods, the land of reason is for God in general, an area in which his existence ceases.

2. Or else the proofs for the existence of God are nothing but proofs for the existence of an essentially human self-conciousness and logical elaborations of it. For example, the ontological proof. What being exists as soon as it is thought? Self-consciousness.

In this sense all the proofs for the existence of God are proofs of his non-existence, refutations of all conceptions of a God. The true proofs should be reversed and read: 'Since nature is badly constructed, God exists.' 'Because the world is irrational, God exists.' 'Because there is no thought, God exists.' But this merely means that God exists for anyone who finds the world irrational and thus is irrational himself. In other words, irrationality is the essence of God.

'If you presuppose the idea of an objective God, how can you speak of laws that reason independently creates, for autonomy can only be ascribed to an absolutely free being?' Schelling, loc. cit. p. 198.

'It is a crime against humanity to conceal principles that are communicable to everyone.' Loc. cit. p. 199.

Turning Points in the Development of Philosophy

Just as in philosophy there are turning points which in themselves rise to concreteness, gather its abstract principles into a totality and so break off the unilinear process, so are there also moments in which philosophy turns its eyes towards the outside world, no longer merely comprehends but, as a practical being, spins intrigues with the world without intermediary. It comes forth from the shadowy kingdom of Amenthes and throws itself on the breast of the worldly sirens. It is the shrovetide of philosophy. Let her dress up like a dog as the Cynic does, put on the robes of a priest like the Alexandrine, or the fragrant spring garment of the Epicurean. It is essential for philosophy at this stage to put on actors' masks. Just as in the story of the creation of mankind Deucalion threw stones behind him, so philosophy casts its eyes backwards (the bones of its mother are bright eyes), when its heart becomes strong enough to create a world; but like Prometheus who stole fire from heaven and began to build houses and settle on the earth, so philosophy, which has evolved so as to impinge on the world, turns itself against the world that it finds. So now the Hegelian philosophy.

Philosophy has isolated itself so as to become a complete and total world and the nature of this totality is conditioned by philosophy's own development as is also the form that is taken by its transition to a practical relationship to reality. Thus there is a rift running through the totality of the world, and indeed this rift has been widened as far as possible in that intellectual existence has become free and attained to the richness of the universal. The heart-beat has become in a concrete manner in itself the distinction which the whole organism is. The rift in the world is not causal if its two sides are totalities. So the world that is opposed by a philosophy that is complete in itself is one that is rent asunder. Therefore, the activity of this philosophy appears too to be rent asunder and contradictory; its objective universality returns into the subjective forms of the individual minds in which it has its life. Normal harps will sound beneath any hand; those of Aeolus only when the storm strikes them. But we should not let ourselves be misled by the storm that follows a great, a world-philosophy.

Someone who does not appreciate this historical necessity must consequently deny that man could continue to live at all after a total philosophy, or else treat the dialectic of quantity as such as the highest category of conscious minds and claim with some of our misguided Hegelians that mediocrity is the usual form in which absolute mind appears; but a mediocrity that gives itself out to be the normal appearance of the absolute has itself degenerated into boundlessness, namely a boundless pretension. Without this necessity it is impossible to understand how after Aristotle a Zeno, an Epicurus, even a Sextus Empiricus, how after Hegel the efforts of later philosophers, which are for the most part unmitigatedly deficient, could attain to the light of day.

In such times half-formed spirits have the opposite view to real commanders. They believe that they can make good their losses by reducing and dividing their forces and make a peace treaty with real needs, whereas Themistocles, when Athens was threatened with destruction, persuaded the Athenians to quit their city completely and found a new Athens on another element, the sea. Nor should we forget that the period that follows such catastrophes is an iron one, happy if it is marked by titanic struggles, lamentable if it is like the centuries that limp behind the great periods of art and busy themselves with imitating in wax, plaster and copper what sprang from Carrara marble like Pallas Athene from the head of Zeus, father of the gods. But those periods are titanic that follow a total philosophy and its subjective forms of development, for the division that forms its unity is gigantic. Thus the Stoic, Epicurean and Sceptic philosophies are followed by Rome. They are unhappy and iron for their gods are dead and the new goddess has as yet only the obscure form of fate, of pure light or of pure darkness. She still lacks the colours of the day. The root of the unhappiness, however, is that the soul of the period, the spiritual Monas, being sated with itself, shapes itself ideally on all sides in isolation and cannot recognize any reality that has come to fruition without it. Thus, the happy aspect of this unhappy time lies in the subjective manner, the modality in which philosophy as subjective consciousness conceives its relation to reality.

Thus, for example, the Stoic, and Epicurean philosophies were the happiness of their time; thus the night-butterfly, when the universal sun has sunk, seeks the lamplight of a private person.

There is another aspect which is more important for the writer of the history of philosophy: this reversal of the philosophers, their transubstantiation into flesh and blood, is always different according to the characteristics that an implicitly total and concrete philosophy carries in itself like a birthmark. It is at the same time a reply to those who, because Hegel held the condemnation of Socrates to be justified, i.e. necessary, because Giordano Bruno had to expiate the fire of his mind by the smoky fire of the stake, in their abstract and one-sided fashion draw the conclusion that the Hegelian philosophy pronounced judgement on itself. But it is important from the philosophical point of view to lay emphasis on this aspect because from the particular form of this reversal we can deduce the immanent nature and historical character of the progress of a philosophy. What before appeared as growth has now become definitive, and what was an implicit negativity has become negation. We see here at the same time its *curriculum vitae* reduced, so to speak, to its simplest expression, its quintessence, as one can draw conclusions as to the history of his life from the death of a hero. Since I conceive the Epicurean philosophy to hold such a place in Greek philosophy, I hope that this passage may serve as a justification for my approach. For instead of describing first the previous Greek philosophies and their influence on the nature of the Epicurean philosophy, I have rather gone backwards and illuminated them from Epicurus' philosophy and thus let it express in its own terms its own peculiar position.

Tasks for the Writer of a History of Philosophy

The writer of a history of philosophy has to interpret not so much the personality of the philosopher, even his intellectual personality, as the focus and form of his system, and even less to dwell upon psychological

E

minutiae and subtleties; he has rather to separate what is definite, the permanent and genuine crystallizations from the proofs, the debating points and the philosopher's own presentation, in so far as these are self-conscious; he has to separate the ever-advancing progress of true philosophical knowledge from the wordy exterior consciousness of the subject, a progress which manifests itself in so many forms and is the stuff and energy of those developments. It is precisely in this division of consciousness that this unity lies. In the presentation of a historical philosophy this critical stage is thoroughly necessary in order to reconcile the scientific presentation of a system with its historical existence, a reconciliation which is necessary just because its existence is a historical one but at the same time has a philosophical nature and thus develops according to its essence. At least, it is on authority and good faith that we have to rely in our supposition that any philosophy is a philosophy, even if the authority is a people and the faith centuries old. The proof can only be given by an exposition of its essence; everyone who writes a history of philosophy separates these two, essential and inessential, presentation and content, otherwise he would only have to copy, scarcely translate and even less allow himself to speak and amend. He would simply be the copyist of a copy.

Thus the question is rather: how does the concept of a person, a wise man, God and the particular characteristics of this concept enter into the system, how do they develop out of it?

Luther as Judge between Strauss
and Feuerbach[1]

Written: End of January 1842

First published: Anekdota zur neuesten deutschen Philosophie und Publicistik, ed. A.
Ruge, Zurich und Winterthur, 1843, vol. II, pp. 206–8

Reprinted: MEGA, i (1), pp. 174/5, *Frühe Schriften,* pp. 106–9

Translated: Easton and Guddatt, *Writings of the Young Marx,* pp. 93–5

This article was written for the *Deutsche Jahrbücher,* but held over because of the
censorship and published early in 1843 in Ruge's *Anekdota.* It was a reply to
previous articles in the *Deutsche Jahrbücher* that had compared Feuerbach
unfavourably with Strauss, who appeared to the more radical of the Young
Hegelians to be already outmoded. Here Marx declares for the first time his
support for Feuerbach's doctrines.

Strauss and Feuerbach! Which of the two is right in the debate that has
recently started on the concept of miracles?[2] Is it Strauss, who still
approaches the subject as a theologian, and thus prejudiced, or Feuerbach, who approaches it as a non-theologian, i.e. freely? Is it Strauss,
who views things as they appear in the eyes of speculative theology, or
Feuerbach, who sees them as they are? Is it Strauss, who cannot come
to any definite decision about miracles, who in a miracle still divines
some particular spiritual power independent of man's wishes—just as
though this spiritual or human power that Strauss guesses at were not
precisely man's wish, the wish, for example, to be free, the first act of
freedom!—or Feuerbach who makes short shrift and says: a miracle is
the realization of a natural or human wish in a supernatural manner?
Which of the two is right? Let Luther, a very good authority who
completely outweighs all protestant dogmatists because religion with

---

[1] See Introduction, p. xv; H–M. Sass, 'Feuerbach statt Marx', *International
Review of Social History,* 1967.

[2] Marx refers to an attack on Feuerbach by Strauss in the latter's *The Doctrines of
the Christian Faith,* Tübingen, 1840/41.

him was an immediate truth, second nature as it were, let Luther decide.

Luther says, for example, for it is possible to quote innumerable similar passages from him—concerning the resurrection of the dead in Luke 7:

'We should consider the works of our Lord Jesus Christ as something different and higher than the works of men, for they are written down for us also so that we should recognize by these same works what sort of a Lord he is, that is, a Lord and God who can help, otherwise no one could. Thus no man can mount so high or fall so low that God cannot help him, be the need ever so great.' 'What is impossible to our Lord God that we cannot be willing confidently to entrust it to Him? He has created the heaven and the earth and everything out of nothing. Every year he fills the trees with cherries, plums, apples and pears and needs no help. When in winter the snow is lying on the ground, none of us could bring a single cherry up out of the snow. But God is the person who can bring everything aright, who can bring to life what is dead and call into existence what is not, in short, something may fall as low as it likes, it is still not too low for our Lord God to be able to raise it up and set it aright. We should recognize these works of God and know that nothing is impossible for Him, so that when evil times come we may learn to have confidence in his omnipotence. If the Turk, or another evil, comes, then we can think that there is a helper and saviour there who has an almighty hand and can help. And that is the right and genuine faith.' 'A man should be confident in God and not despair. For God can do what lies outside the power of myself and other men. If I and other people can no longer help, then He can help me and even save me from death, as Psalm 68 says: we have a God who helps us, and the Lord God who saves us from death. So our heart should always be confident and of good cheer and hold fast to God. And the hearts that are undismayed and confident are those that serve God rightly and love Him.' 'We should be bold in God and His Son Jesus Christ. For what we cannot do, He can do; what we have not got, He has got. If we cannot help ourselves, then He can help us and will gladly and willingly do so as can be seen here.' (Luther's *Werke*, Leipzig, 1732, part XVI, pp. 442–45.)

In these few words you have a defence of the whole of Feuerbach's book, a defence of the definitions of providence, omnipotence, creation, miracle and faith as given in the book[1]. Shame on you, Christians, both high and lowly, learned and unlearned, shame on you that an anti-Christian had to show you the essence of Christianity in its true and unveiled form! And to you, speculative philosophers and theologians, I give you this advice: free yourselves from the concepts and prejudices of previous speculative philosophy if you also wish to attain to things as they are, that is, to the truth. And there is no other way for you to truth and freedom than through the Feuerbach.[2] Feuerbach is the purgatory of the present time.

No Berliner.[3]

[1] I.e. *The Essence of Christianity*.

[2] 'Feuer-bach' means literally in German 'river of fire'.

[3] In order to distinguish his article from two that had appeared in the *Deutsche Jahrbücher* signed respectively 'A Berliner' and 'Another Berliner' and which tried to minimize the differences between Strauss and Feuerbach.

Remarks on the latest Prussian Instruction on the Censorship[1]

BY A RHINELANDER

Written: Early February 1842

First published: Anekdota zur neuesten deutschen Philosophie und Publicistik, ed. A. Ruge, Zurich und Winterthur, 1843, vol. I, pp. 56–88

Reprinted: MEGA, I i (1), pp. 151–73. MEW, I, pp. 3–25

Translated: Molitor, I, pp. 121–61. Easton and Guddatt, *Writings of the Young Marx*, pp. 67–82

This article was originally written for the *Deutsche Jahrbücher* on the instigation of Marx's friend Köppen whom Ruge had urged to look out for new collaborators. Owing to the intensification of the Saxon censorship, it could not be published in the *Deutsche Jahrbücher* and was published (anonymously) a year later in *Anekdota*. It was occasioned by the censorship instruction of 24th December 1841 that appeared to be liberalizing the system. Marx, however, in the extract translated here, which forms the centre of the article, compared the new instruction unfavourably with the old one of 1819. In this and the subsequent articles Marx shows himself to be an intransigent liberal demanding that the state be founded on free reason without any religious influences.

In 1819 there still held sway the rationalism which in general understood by religion the so-called religion of reason. This rationalist point of view is also that of the edict on the censorship, although it is true that the edict is so illogical as to start from an irreligious point of view when its aim is the protection of religion. For it is contradictory to the general principles of religion to separate its general principles from its positive and particular content. For it is precisely because of its particular nature that every religion believes it is different from other imaginary religions and because of its particular character that it believes it is the true religion. The new instruction on censorship in its citation of article 2 leaves out the limiting clause whereby individual religious parties and sects were excluded from inviolability, but it does not leave the matter there and adds the following commentary:

[1] See introduction, p. xiv f.

'Anything directed in a frivolous or hostile manner against the Christian religion in general or against a particular point of doctrine cannot be tolerated.'

The previous edict on the censorship has no mention at all of the Christian religion; on the contrary, it distinguishes religion from all individual religious parties and sects. The new instruction on censorship not only changes religion into the Christian religion but also adds thereto particular doctrinal points. What a splendid product of our Christianized science! Who wants still to deny that it has forged new fetters for the press? Religion must not be attacked either in general or in particular. Or do you perhaps believe that the words 'frivolous' and 'hostile' make the new fetters into fetters of roses? How neatly put: frivolous, hostile! The adjective 'frivolous' is directed to the respectability of the citizen, it is the word for the outside world, whereas the adjective 'hostile' is whispered into the censor's ear, it is the legal interpretation of frivolity. We shall find in this instruction still more examples of this delicate tact that directs at the public a subjective word to bring blood to their cheeks and to the censor an objective word to drain the blood from the cheeks of the writer. In this manner *lettres de cachet* can be set to music.

And in what an extraordinary contradiction the instruction on the censorship has imprisoned itself! An incomplete attack that limited itself to individual facets of the phenomenon without being profound or serious enough to attain to the essence of the matter is frivolous and even dealing with a particular aspect as such is frivolous. So if a general attack on the Christian religion is forbidden, only a frivolous attack is permitted. Conversely an attack on the general principles of religion, or its essence or on a particular facet of it in so far as it is a manifestation of its essence is a hostile attack. Religion can only be attacked in a hostile or frivolous manner and there is no third course. This illogicality in which the instruction has imprisoned itself, is of course only an appearance for it rests on the impression that at least some sort of attack on religion was to be permitted; but it only requires an unprejudiced look to recognize this appearance as an appearance only. Religion must be attacked in neither a hostile nor a frivolous manner, neither in general nor in particular, thus religion must not be attacked at all.

Nevertheless, although the instruction puts the philosophical press in new chains in express contradiction of the edict on the censorship of 1819, yet it should at least be logical enough to free the religious press from the old chains. In fact it also makes it the aim of the censorship:

to oppose the fanatical transference of religious beliefs into politics and the confusion of concepts that this causes.

The new instruction is indeed clever enough not to mention this precision in its commentary, but it nevertheless takes it up in its citation of article 2. What is meant by fanatical transference of religious beliefs into politics? It means to allow the state to be ruled by the specific nature of religious beliefs, to make the specific nature of religion the measure of the state. The old edict on censorship could justifiably oppose this confusion of concepts because it submits the particular content of a particular religion to criticism. But the old edict based itself on the shallow, superficial rationalism that you yourselves despise so much. But how can you, who base the state even in particulars on faith and Christianity, and want a Christian state, still recommend the censorship to prevent this confusion of concepts?

The confusion of the political with the Christian-religious principle has even become an article of religious faith. I want to say a word to make this confusion clear. To speak only of Christianity as the recognized religion you have in your state both catholics and protestants. Both make the same claims of the state and have the same duties towards it. They disregard their religious differences and both wish that the state be the realization of political and legal reason. But you want a Christian state. But if your state is only of a Lutheran type, then for the Catholic it becomes a Church to which he does not belong, that he must reject as heretical and whose inner essence contradicts him; and the reverse is the same. Or if you are making the general spirit of Christianity into the particular spirit of your state, then your protestant education decides for you what the general spirit of Christianity is. You define what the Christian state is although recent times have shown you that individual state officials do not know how to draw the boundary between religion and the world, between state and church. It was not censors but diplomats who had, not to decide, but to negotiate about this confusion of concepts.[1] Finally you take up a heretical point of view when you reject particular dogmas as inessential. If you call your state Christian in general then you admit with a diplomatic expression that it is not Christian. So either forbid altogether the bringing of religion into politics—but you do not want that, since you wish to base the state not on free reason but on faith, and religion you regard as the general sanction of what exists—or permit also the fanatical transference of religion into politics. Let it be political in its own way, but you do not want that either: religion must support the secular power without the secular power being subject to religion. If you once bring religion into politics, it is an intolerable, even an irreligious, presumption to wish to delimit secularly how religion shall act inside politics. The man who binds himself to religion out of religiosity must allow it the deciding voice in all questions, or perhaps you mean by religion the cult of your own absoluteness and political wisdom?

The orthodoxy of the new instruction on the censorship conflicts in another way also with the rationalism of the old edict. This latter included in the aims of the censorship the suppression of 'what offends ethics and good morals'. The instruction mentions this passage as a citation from article 2. But while its commentary makes additions as regards religion, as regards morality it contains omissions. An offence against ethics and good morals becomes a violation of 'discipline, morals and exterior propriety'. It is plain: morality as morality, as the principle of a world that possesses its own laws, disappears and the place of its essence is taken by exterior phenomena like police respectability and conventional decency. Honour to whom honour is due, here we recognize true logic. The specifically Christian law-giver cannot recognize morality as a sphere sacred in itself and independent, for he vindicates its inner universal essence for religion. Independent morality violates the universal bases of religion and the particular concepts of religion are contrary to morality. Morality knows only its own universal and rational religion, and religion only its particular positive morality. Thus according to this instruction the censorship must reject the

---

[1] This refers to the Prussian diplomatists' negotiations with the Vatican following the imprisonment in 1837 of the Archbishop of Cologne for refusing to agree to the government's ruling on the religious upbringing of children of mixed marriages.

intellectual heroes of morality—Kant, Fichte, Spinoza, for example—as irreligious and violating discipline, morals and exterior respectability. And these moralists start from a contradiction in principle between morality and religion, for morality is based on the autonomy of the human mind whereas religion is based on its heteronomy.

The Philosophical Manifesto of the Historical School of Law[1]

Written: April 1842

First published: Rheinische Zeitung, 9th August 1842
Reprinted: MEGA, I i (1), pp. 251–9. *Frühe Schriften,* pp. 198–207

Translated: Molitor, I, pp. 109–20. Easton and Guddatt, *Writings of the Young Marx,* pp. 96–105

This article is one of the series that Marx promised Ruge in April 1842 for the *Anekdota,* and the only one actually to be written. It was prompted by the nomination of Savigny as Minister of Justice in February 1842. Savigny was well-known as a disciple of Gustav Hugo, the founder, in the beginning of the nineteenth century, of the Historical School of Law which maintained that the historical existence of laws was their only and complete justification. The extract below is the first half of the article, the second half consists mainly of quotations from Hugo's book.

Vulgar opinion views the historical school as a reaction against the frivolous spirit of the eighteenth century. The popularity of this view is in inverse proportion to its truth. The eighteenth century produced only one thing whose essential characteristic is frivolity and this one frivolous product is the historical school itself.

The shibboleth that the historical school has adopted is the study of sources, and they have carried this love of sources to such an extreme that they advise the captain not to sail his boat on the river but at its source. They will thus approve our returning to their sources, Hugo's natural law.[2] Their philosophy comes before their development, so we will look in vain for philosophy in their development itself.

A current fiction of the eighteenth century viewed the state of nature as the true state of man's nature. People wanted to see with their own

[1] See Introduction, p. xvii; H. Jaeger, 'Savigny et Marx', *Archives de Philosophie du Droit,* vol. 12, 1967, p. 65 ff.
[2] G. Hugo, *Lehrbuch eines civilistischen Cursus,* 4th ed., Berlin, 1819.

eyes the idea of man and created a natural man, Papagenos, whose naïvety went as far as their feathered skins. In the last decades of the eighteenth century, people imagined they could find traces of original wisdom in tribes in a state of nature and on all sides we heard bird catchers twittering the melodies of the Iroquois Indians, etc., thinking by these arts to lure the birds themselves into the trap. At the back of all these eccentricities lay the correct idea that crude natural circumstances are like naïve Dutch paintings of the true circumstances.

The natural man of the historical school as yet ungilded by any romantic culture is Hugo. His text book on natural right is the Old Testament of the historical school. Herder's view that men in a state of nature are poets and that the sacred books of tribes in a state of nature are poetic books poses no problem for us although Hugo writes the most trivial and insipid of prose, for, as every century has its own peculiar nature, so does it engender its own peculiar natural man. So even though Hugo is not composing poetry, he is still writing fiction and fiction is the poetry of prose which corresponds to the prosaic nature of the eighteenth century.

By treating Herr Hugo as ancestor and founder of the historical school we are dealing in its own terms, as the *Festschrift* of the most famous of the historical jurists on the occasion of Hugo's jubilee shows.[1] And by viewing Herr Hugo as a child of the eighteenth century we are even acting true to the spirit of Herr Hugo as he himself proves in that he gives himself out to be a follower of Kant and his natural law to be an offshoot of Kant's philosophy. We take up his Manifesto at this point.

Hugo misreads his master Kant by claiming that because we cannot know the true, we can consequently let the false, provided only that it exist, pass as quite valid. Hugo is a sceptic as regards the necessary essence of things only to become a complete optimist where their contingent existence is concerned. He does not therefore at all seek to prove that the positive is rational; he tries to prove that the positive is not rational. With self-satisfied industry he drags together from every corner of the world facts that will go to show that the central positive institutions like property, the constitution, marriage, are not a rational necessity and even that they contradict reason and that at most one

[1] F. K. Savigny, *Der Zehnte Mai 1788*, Berlin, 1838.

could idly argue for or against them. This method should by no means be ascribed to the character that he happens to have; it is rather the method of his principle, the open-hearted, naïve and reckless method of the historical school. If the positive is to have validity because it is positive, I must prove that the positive has no validity because it is rational, and how could I do this more plainly than by demonstrating that the irrational is positive and that the positive is not rational, that the positive does not exist through reason but in spite of it? If reason were the measure of the positive, the positive would not be the measure of reason. 'This may be madness, but it has method!' Thus Hugo profanes everything that is sacred to the legal, moral and political man, but he only destroys these saints in order to be able to worship their historical relics, he disgraces them in the eyes of reason, in order to honour them subsequently in the eyes of history, and also at the same time to honour historical eyes.

Hugo's arguments are as positive, i.e. uncritical, as his principles. He knows no distinctions. Any existing thing is an authority for him and he considers any authority a sufficient one. So in the same paragraph he quotes Moses and Voltaire, Richardson and Homer, Montaigne and Ammon, Rousseau's *Social Contract* and Augustine's *City of God*. His approach to peoples is equally levelling. The Siamese who considers it an eternal ordinance of nature that his king should sew up the mouth of a gossiper and slit open to the ears that of a clumsy orator, is, according to Hugo, as positive as the Englishman who counts it a political paradox if his king arbitrarily proclaims a tax of a penny. The shameless Conci who walk around naked and at most clothe themselves with mud are as positive as the Frenchman who not only clothes himself, but does it elegantly. The German who rears his daughter as the treasure of the family is not more positive than the Rajput who kills her in order to relieve himself of the trouble of bringing her up. In a word, the rash on the skin is as positive as the skin itself.

In one place this is positive, in another that, the one is as irrational as the other, so accept what is positive within your own four walls.

Thus Hugo is the complete sceptic. The scepticism of the eighteenth century with regard to the rationality of existence takes in him the form of scepticism as to the existence of reason. He adopts the Enlightenment, no longer sees anything rational in the positive, but only so as not to be obliged to see anything positive in the rational. He thinks that the appearance of reason has been removed from the positive in order to accept the positive without the appearance of reason; he thinks that the false flowers have been plucked from the chains in order to wear genuine chains without flowers.

Hugo's relationship to the other thinkers of the eighteenth-century enlightenment is rather like that of the disintegration of the French state at the disorderly court of the Regent[1] to the disintegration of the French state in the National Assembly. Dissolution on both sides! In the former it appears as disorderly frivolity which understands and mocks at the hollow intellectual bankruptcy of the contemporary scene, but only so as to be loosed from all rational and moral ties and carry on playing with the rotten ruins until it is itself driven into dissolution by the game. It is the putrefaction of its contemporary world which enjoys its own self. In the National Assembly, on the other hand, the dissolution has the appearance of a liberation of the new spirit from old forms which had no value any more and were no longer capable of containing it. It is the self-appreciation of the new life that smashes what is already smashed and throws away what has already been abandoned. Thus if it is correct to view Kant's philosophy as the German theory of the French Revolution, then Hugo's Natural Law is the German theory of the French *ancien régime*. We can recognize in him the complete frivolity of those *roués*, their universal scepticism which is insolent to ideas but very respectful to what is tangible and only perceives its own cleverness when it has killed off the spirit of the positive in order to possess the residue of the pure positive and be snug in its animal surroundings. Even if Hugo weighs carefully the relative grounds, he will with infallibly sure instinct find the rationality and morality of the institutions dangerous for reason. The only thing that appears to his reason not to be doubtful is what is animal.

---

[1] Philip II of Orleans.

The Proceedings of the Sixth Rhenish Parliament

BY A RHINELANDER

*First Article: Debates on the Freedom of the Press and
the Publication of the Parliamentary Proceedings*[1]

Written: April/May 1842

First published: Rheinische Zeitung, 5–19th May 1842

Reprinted: MEGA, I i (1), pp. 179–229. *Frühe Schriften,* pp. 110–73

This is Marx's first contribution to the *Rheinische Zeitung.* The Sixth Rhenish Parliament sat from 23rd May to 25th July 1841 and Marx discussed their proceedings in three articles: the following one was the first, the second was censored and the third, on the laws concerning stealing wood, was published in the *Rheinische Zeitung* in October 1842. The two extracts translated here, from the middle of the article, deal with religion and law.

Because the real situation of these gentlemen in the modern state bears no relation at all to the conception that they have of their situation; because they live in a world situated beyond the real world and because in consequence their imagination holds the place of their head and their heart, they necessarily turn towards theory, being unsatisfied with practice, but it is towards the theory of the transcendent, i.e. religion. However, in their hands religion acquires a polemical bitterness impregnated with political tendencies and becomes, in a more or less conscious manner, simply a sacred cloak to hide desires that are both very secular and at the same time very imaginary.

Thus we shall find in our Speaker that he opposes a mystical/religious theory of his imagination to practical demands . . . and that to what is reasonable from the human point of view he opposes superhuman

---

[1] See Introduction, p. xvii.

sacred entities and to the true sanctuary of ideas a vulgar point of view that is both arbitrary and unbelieving . . .

Thus so far from a law on the press being a repressive measure directed against the freedom of the press, simply a means to deter by penalties the repetition of a crime, the lack of a law dealing with the press should rather be seen as an exclusion of freedom of the press from the sphere of legal freedom, for legally recognized freedom exists in the state as law. Laws are as little repressive measures directed against freedom as the law of gravity is a repressive measure directed against movement, because although it keeps the heavenly bodies in perpetual motion yet it can also kill me if I wish to violate it and dance in the air. Laws are rather positive, bright and general norms in which freedom has attained to an existence that is impersonal, theoretical and independent of the arbitrariness of individuals. A people's statute book is its Bible of freedom.

The law on the press is therefore the legal recognition of the freedom of the press. It is law because it is the positive existence of freedom. Thus it must always be present, even when it is never applied, as in North America, while censorship, like slavery, can never become legal, though it were a thousand times present as law.

There are no preventive laws at the present time. Law only prevents by forbidding. It becomes active law as soon as it is transgressed for it is only true law when in it the unconscious natural law of freedom becomes the conscious law of the state. Where law is true law, i.e. where it is the existence of freedom, it is the true existence of the freedom of man. Thus the laws cannot prevent man's actions, for they are the inner laws of life of his action itself, the conscious mirror images of his life. Law thus retreats before man's life as a life of freedom and only when his behaviour has actually shown that he has ceased to obey the natural law of freedom, does the state law compel him to be free. Similarly physical law only appears alien to me when my life has ceased to be the life of these laws, when it is sick. Thus a preventive law is a meaningless contradiction.

The Leading Article in No. 179 of the Kölnische Zeitung[1]

Written: Early July 1842

First published: Rheinische Zeitung, 10–14th July 1842

Reprinted: MEGA, I i (1), pp. 232–50. *Frühe Schriften,* pp. 174–97

Translated: Marx–Engels, *Sur La Religion,* ed. Badia et al., Paris, 1960, pp. 15–40. Easton and Guddatt, *Writings of the Young Marx,* pp. 109–130

This article was a reply to an attack on the 'new philosophical school' by Karl Hermes, editor of the *Kölnische Zeitung,* who had accused the *Rheinische Zeitung* of intemperate discussion of religion. In the first of the extracts here Marx attacks Hermes's conception of religion as the foundation of the state, in the second, taken from the end of the article, he attacks the notion of a 'Christian state'.

The leading article calls fetishism the 'crudest form' of religion. It admits then, a fact accepted by all men of 'scientific research' even without its consent, that 'zoolatry' is a higher form of religion than fetishism; and does not zoolatry abase man below animals, does it not make the animal a god for man?

And now let us deal with fetishism! What a penny magazine type of learning! Fetishism is so far from raising man above his desires that it is precisely the 'religion of sensual desire'. Imagination born of desire gives to the fetish-worshipper the illusion that an 'inanimate object' is about to abandon its natural character and acquiesce in his lusts. Therefore the crude desire of the fetish-worshipper smashes the fetish when it ceases to be its docile servitor.

'In nations which have attained a superior historical importance, the apogee of their political life coincides with the full development of their religious feeling and the decadence of their grandeur and their power coincides with the decadence of their religious culture.'

[1] See Introduction, p. xvii.

Truth is attained by precisely reversing the author's claim; he has stood history on its head. Greece and Rome are, are they not, the countries of the highest 'historical civilization'. Greece's interior culmination is in the age of Pericles and her exterior culmination in the age of Alexander. In the age of Pericles, the sophists, Socrates (who can be called the incarnation of philosophy), art and rhetoric had banished religion. The age of Alexander was that of Aristotle who rejected the idea of the immortality of the 'individual' spirit and the God of the positive religions. And now Rome! Read Cicero! The Epicurean, Stoic or sceptical philosophies were the religion of the cultivated Romans, at the time when Rome had attained the culminating point of its history. If the fall of the states of antiquity entails the disappearance of the religions of these states, it is not necessary to go and look for another explanation, for the 'true religion' of the ancients was the cult of 'their nationality', of their 'State'. It is not the ruin of the ancient religions that entailed the fall of the states of antiquity, but the fall of the states of antiquity that entailed the ruin of the ancient religions. And someone as ignorant as the leading article shows itself to be nevertheless proclaims himself a 'legislator of scientific research' and writes 'decrees' for philosophy.

'The whole world of antiquity was condemned to disintegrate because with the progress that the peoples were making in their scientific knowledge there went necessarily in step the discovery of the errors on which their religious conceptions rested.'

Thus according to the leading article the whole of the ancient world disappeared because scientific research disclosed the errors of the ancient religions. Would not the ancient world have disappeared if research had passed over in silence the errors of the religions, if the works of Lucretius and Lucian had been recommended by the author of the leading article for censorship by the Roman authorities?

For the rest we allow ourselves to increase the erudition of Herr Hermes by adding a note.

At the very moment when the fall of the ancient world was imminent, there arose the Alexandrine school which tried at all costs to prove the 'eternal truth' of Greek mythology and its constant agreement with the results of scientific research. The Emperor Julian, too, belonged to this school which believed it was making the spirit of the time, whose dawn was breaking, disappear by closing their eyes so as not to see it. But let us pause at the result obtained by Hermes! In the ancient religions 'the vague presentiment of the divine has been overlayed by the thickest darkness of error' and so could not stand up to scientific discoveries. In Christianity it is just the opposite, as any thinking machine will affirm. And indeed, Hermes declares:

'Up till now the highest results of scientific research have only served to confirm the truths of the Christian religion.'

Apart from the fact that all the philosophies of the past without exception have been accused by theologians one after the other of apostasizing the Christian faith, even that of pious Malebranche and the inspired Jakob Boehme; apart from the fact that Leibinz was accused of being a good-for-nothing by the peasants of Brunswick and of being an atheist by the Englishman Clarke and the other followers of Newton; apart from the fact that, according to the most eminent and logical group of protestant theologians, there cannot be agreement between Christianity and reason because 'temporal' reason and 'spiritual' reason contradict each other, which Tertullian expressed in the following classic manner: *Verum est quia absurdum est*; apart from all that, how can one prove the agreement of scientific research and religion except by forcing scientific research to fuse with religion and religion follow its own path. Anyway, any other constraint could not be taken as proof.

Of course, if from the beginning you only recognize as scientific research what is merely your way of looking at things, it is easy for you to prophesy; but how is your affirmation more valid than that of the Indian Brahmin who proves the sanctity of the Vedas by reserving for himself alone the right to read them!

Hermes says well 'scientific research' but any research which contradicts Christianity 'stops halfway' or 'is misdirected'. Can proof be made any easier? . . .

The truly religious state is the theocratic one: in states of this sort the sovereign must either, as in the Jewish state, be the God of the religion, the Jehovah, or else, as in Tibet, the representative of God, the Dalai Lama or finally, as Görres in his latest work rightly demands of Christian states, all must submit themselves to a Church that must be infallible, for when, as in Protestantism, there is no supreme head of the church, the domination of religion is nothing but the religion of domination, the cult of the government's will.

As soon as a state embraces several denominations that have equal rights, a religious state is impossible without attacking the particular religious denominations, without being a church which condemns any member of a denomination as a heretic, which makes each bit of bread depend on faith, and which makes dogma the link between individuals and their existence as citizens. Ask the Catholic inhabitants of 'poor green Eire', ask the Huguenots before the French Revolution: they did not appeal to religion, for their religion was not the state religion, but to the 'rights of humanity'. These rights are interpreted by philosophy which asks that the state be the state of human nature.

But, says the half-hearted, narrow-minded rationalist who is as much unbeliever as theologian, it is the universal spirit of Christianity abstracted from denominational differences, which ought to be the spirit of the state! Here is the supreme irreligiousness. This is the supreme irreligiousness, the wantonness of secular reason to separate the universal spirit of religion from its positive forms; thus to separate religion from its dogmas and its institutions is the same as declaring that the universal spirit of the law should reign in the state irrespective of particular laws and positive legal institutions.

If you imagine that you can place yourself so far above religion that you are justified in separating its universal spirit from the positive institutions by which it defines itself, what have you to reproach philosophers with who push this separation to the end and do not stop half-way when they say that the universal spirit of religion is not the spirit of Christianity but the spirit of humanity?

Christians live in states with different constitutions, some in republics, others under an absolute monarchy, others finally under a constitutional monarch. Christianity does not decide how far the constitutions are good, for it knows no difference betweeen constitutions. It teaches, as religion ought to teach: be submissive to authority, for all authority is from God. So it is not by starting from Christianity, but from nature itself and the essence of the state that you ought to decide whether con-situations are just, not starting from the nature of Christian society but from the nature of human society.

The Byzantine state was the religious state *par excellence*, for dogmas there were affairs of state, but the Byzantine state was the worst of states. The states of the *ancien régime* were the most Christian states but they were nevertheless the states where reigned 'the good pleasure of the court'.

There exists a contradiction that 'common sense' cannot cope with.

Either the Christian state corresponds to the concept of a state which is to be a realization of liberty according to reason, and in that case the only condition for a state's being Christian is that it should be rational, and then it is sufficient to deduce the state from the rational character of human relationships, which is the job of philosophy. Or the state of rational freedom cannot be deduced from Christianity and in that case you will yourselves admit that this deduction is not included in the attitude of Christianity for it cannot wish for a bad state and a state that is not a realization of rational freedom is a bad state.

You can answer this dilemma however you like, you will have to agree that the construction of the state ought not to start from religion but from the rational character of freedom. Only the crassest ignorance would hold that this theory of the autonomous character that belongs to the concept of the state is the sudden fantasy of modern philosophers.

Philosophy has done with regard to politics what physics, mathematics, medicine and each science has done in its respective sphere. Bacon of Verulam declared that theological physics was a virgin consecrated god and sterile: he emancipated physics from theology and it became fertile. No more than you ask the doctor whether he is a believer should you put this question to the politician. In the period that proceeds and immediately follows the great discovery by Copernicus of the true solar system, the law of gravity of the state was also discovered. Its centre of gravity was found to be in itself and the different European governments tried to apply this discovery, with the superficiality of every first practical trial, in the system of the balance of powers. Similarly, first Machiavelli and Campenella, then later Hobbes, Spinoza, Hugo Grotius, through to Rousseau, Fichte and Hegel began to consider the state through human eyes and deduced its natural laws from reason and experience and not from theology, just like Copernicus who disregarded the fact that Joshua had ordered the sun to stop on Gabaon and the moon above the valley of Ajalon.

Modern philosophy has only continued work that Heraclitus and Aristotle had already begun. Therefore your polemics are not against the reason of modern philosophy, they are against the ever new philosophy of reason. Of course, the ignorance which discovered for the first time yesterday or the day before in the *Rheinische Zeitung* or the *Kölnische Zeitung* the very old ideas on the state, this ignorance regards the ideas of history as sudden fantasies of isolated individuals because to it they are new and arrived over-night. This ignorance forgets that it assumes itself the old role of the doctor of the Sorbonne who thought it his duty publicly to accuse Montesquieu for having had the frivolity to declare that the supreme civic quality was political virtue and not religious virtue; it forgets that it assumes the role of Joachim Lange who denounced Wolff on the pretext that his doctrine of predestination would lead to the desertion of soldiers and thus the relaxation of a military discipline and in the end the dissolution of the state; finally it forgets that the Prussian civil code comes precisely from the philosophical school of that same 'Wolff' and the Code Napoléon not from the Old Testament but from the ideas of Voltaire, Rousseau, Condorcet, Mirabeau, Montesquieu and the French Revolution. Ignorance is a demon, it is to be feared that it may yet play many a tragedy. The greatest Greek poets were right to represent it in terrible dramas of the royal families of Mycenae and Thebes in the form of a tragic destiny.

But if the previous professors of constitutional law have constructed the state from instincts either of ambition or sociability or even from reason, but from the individual's reason and not social reason, the profounder conception of modern philosophy deduces the state from the idea of the all. It considers the state as the great organism in which juridical, moral and political liberties must be realized and in which each citizen, by obeying the laws of the state, only obeys the natural laws of his own reason, human reason. *Sapienti sat.*

In conclusion we address ourselves to the *Kölnische Zeitung* once again with a philosophical word of farewell. It was reasonable on its part to annex for itself a liberal of the old school. One can be at the same time liberal and reactionary in a most convenient manner: it is sufficient simply to be clever enough always to address oneself to the liberals of the most recent past who know no other dilemma than that of Vidocq's 'prisoner or jailer'. It was even more reasonable that the liberal of the most recent past should attack the liberals of today. Without parties there is no evolution and without separation no progress. We trust that the editorial of the 179th edition inaugurates for the *Kölnische Zeitung* a new era, the era of character.

Communism and the Augsburger Allgemeine Zeitung[1]

Written: Early October 1842

First published: Rheinische Zeitung, 16th October 1842

Reprinted: MEGA, I i (1), pp. 260–4. MEW, I, pp. 105–8

Translated: Easton and Guddatt, *Writings of the Young Marx*, pp. 131–5

Marx's first article as editor of the *Rheinische Zeitung*

The *Augsburger Allgemeine Zeitung* had accused the *Rheinische Zeitung* of communist sympathies. Moses Hess had been responsible for the paper's reprinting an article on workers' housing from a journal of Wilhelm Weitling and reporting the speeches of followers of Fourier delivered at a recent congress at Strasbourg. The article is particularly interesting for the light that it sheds on Marx's first reactions to French socialism.

Cologne, 15th October. The 248th number of the *Augsburger Allgemeine Zeitung* is so gauche as to discover a Prussian communist in the *Rheinische Zeitung*; no genuine communist, it is true, but still a person who in her imagination flirts with communism and ogles it platonically.

The reader shall decide when we have brought forward the pretended evidence whether these rude fantasies of the Augsburg paper spring from self-interest, and whether this idle juggling of its fevered imagination is consistent with speculation and diplomatic affairs.

It is said that the *Rheinische Zeitung* included in its supplement a communist article on workers' housing estates in Berlin[2] and added the following remark: this information 'should be interesting for the history of these important contemporary problems'. It then follows, according to Augsburg logic, that the *Rheinische Zeitung* 'has served up

---

[1] See Introduction, p. xviii f.

[2] This refers to a correspondence printed in Weitling's journal *The Young Generation* and reprinted in the *Rheinische Zeitung*.

this sort of unwashed stuff with its own recommendation'. So when I say, for example, 'the following information from *Mephistopheles*[1] about the inner household of the *Augsburger Zeitung* should be interesting for the history of this bumptious lady', do I thereby recommend the dirty 'stuff' from which the Augsburg lady sews together her gaudy wardrobe? Or should we consider communism as no important question simply because it is no question for a lady's salon, because it wears dirty linen and is not perfumed with rose water?

But the Augsburg paper bears a justifiable grudge against our misunderstanding. The importance of communism does not consist in its being an extremely important question for France and England. Communism has a European importance in that it has been used by the *Augsburger Zeitung* to compose phrases with. One of its Paris correspondents, a convert who treats history as a confectioner does botany, has just had a brainwave: the monarchy must in its own way assimilate socialist–communist ideas. Imagine the dejection of the Augsburger who will never forgive us for having revealed communism to the public in its unwashed nakedness; understand the sour irony which shouts at us: 'so you recommend communism which once possessed the fortunate elegance of forming a phrase for the *Augsburger Zeitung*!'

The second reproach directed against the *Rheinische Zeitung* concerns the conclusion of a report from Strasbourg on the communist speeches delivered at the congress there,[2] for the two half-sisters had so divided the booty that the Rhenish paper reported the proceedings and the Bavarian paper the meals of the Strasbourg scholars. The passage under attack runs as follows: 'Today the middle class is in the same position as the nobility in 1789; then the middle class laid claim to the privileges of the nobility and obtained them, today the class that possesses nothing desires to share the wealth of the middle classes who are now in power. Today the middle class has taken better precautions against a surprise attack than the nobility in 1789 and it is to be expected that the problem will find a peaceful solution.'

Bülow-Cummerov, the late *Berliner politische Wochenblatt*, Dr.

[1] A short-lived contemporary journal.
[2] The Tenth Congress of French Intellectuals was held in Strasbourg from 28th September to 9th October 1842. Disciples of Fourier were among those present and publicized his doctrines.

Kosegarten and all feudal writers admit with the most sad indignation that Sieyès' prophecy has come true and that the Third Estate has become everything and intends to be everything. That the class that today possesses nothing desires to share the riches of the middle classes is a fact which, quite apart from the speeches at Strasbourg and the silence at Augsburg is plain to anyone who goes around the streets of Manchester, Paris and Lyons. Can the Augsburg paper believe that her displeasure and silence alter the facts of the age? The Augsburg paper is impertinent even in retreat. It bolts off in fright at the insidious phenomena of our time and believes that the dust that it throws up behind and the anxious abuses that it murmurs between its teeth when fleeing will blind and confuse both the uncomfortable phenomena and the comfortable reader.

Or does the Augsburg paper begrudge the expectation of our correspondent that the undeniable collision will be solved 'in a peaceful manner'? Or do they reproach us with not having straightaway prescribed a proven recipe and conjured out of thin air to put in the pocket of the astonished reader a report that is clear as daylight on the unsatisfactory solution of the problem? We do not possess the art of resolving with one phrase problems that two peoples are working to overcome.

But, dearest and best Augsburger, you give us to understand à *propos* of communism that Germany is now so poor in men of independent means that nine-tenths of our more educated youth begs its future bread from the state, that our rivers are neglected, our shipping declining, that our commercial cities, previously so blooming, have lost their former splendour, that free institutions are only just beginning to be slowly obtained in Prussia, that our superfluous population wanders abroad helplessly to lose its Germanity in foreign nationalities, and that for all these problems there is not a single recipe, no attempt to be 'clear over the means to accomplish' the great deed that shall free us from all these sins! Or do you expect no peaceful solution? Another article in the same number sent from Karlsruhe almost seems to imply this when even concerning the Customs Union the insidious question is directed at Prussia: 'is it thought that such a crisis would pass by like a squabble about smoking in the zoo?' The reason that you advance for your unbelief is a communist one. 'This would mean letting loose an industrial crisis, losing millions of capital and depriving thousands of workers of their bread'. Our 'peaceful expectation' came at a most inconvenient time, for you had already decided to let a bloody crisis loose. Therefore, presumably in your article on Great Britain, according to your own logic you approve of the demagogic Doctor M'Dougall who emigrated to America because 'there was nothing doing with this royal race'.

Before we take our leave of you, we would like also in passing to point out to you your own wisdom. Your style makes it inevitable that here and there without doing any harm you should not indeed have a thought, but at least express one. You think that the polemic of Herr Hennequin from Paris against the parcelling out of landed properties brings him into surprising harmony with the autonomous nobility. Surprise, says Aristotle, is the beginning of philosophizing. You have ended with the beginning. Otherwise how could you have failed to notice the surprising fact that communist principles are spread in Germany not by liberals but by your own reactionary friends?

Who speaks of Trade Unions? The reactionaries. They say the working class is forming a state inside a state. Do you find it astonishing that the modern expression of such thoughts should be: 'the state should be transformed into the working-class'? But if the workers' class is to become the state and if the modern worker, like every modern man, by the state understands and can only understand the sphere that he has in common with all his fellow citizens, how can you synthesize both thoughts if not in a *workers' state*? Who polemicizes against the parcelling out of landed property? The reactionaries. One feudalistic work which has recently appeared (Kosegarten on Parcelling)[1] went so far as to call private property a prerogative. That is Fourier's fundamental principle. As soon as one is agreed over principles, is there not room for disagreement on their consequences and application?

The *Rheinische Zeitung* does not even concede theoretical validity to communist ideas in their present form, let alone desires their practical realization, which it anyway finds impossible, and will subject these ideas to a fundamental criticism. If she had aims and capacities beyond well-polished phrases the Augsburger would have perceived

[1] W. Kosegarten, *Betrachtunger über die Veraüsserlichkeit und Teilbarkeit des Grundbesitzes*, Bonn, 1842.

that books like those of Leroux and Considérant and above all the acute work of Proudhon cannot be criticized by superficial and transitory fancies but only after consistent and probing study. We have to take such theoretical works all the more seriously as we cannot agree with the Augsburger which finds the reality of communist ideas not in Plato but in its obscure acquaintance who, though being gifted in several lines of scientific research, sacrificed all the money he could lay his hands on and washed his comrades' plates and cleaned their boots according to the will of Father Enfantin. We are firmly convinced that the true danger does not lie in the practical attempt to carry out communist ideas but in their theoretical development; for practical attempts, even by the masses, can be answered with a cannon as soon as they become dangerous, but ideas that have overcome our intellect and conquered our conviction, ideas to which reason has riveted our conscience, are chains from which one cannot break loose without breaking one's heart; they are demons that one can only overcome by submitting to them. Yet the *Augsburger Zeitung* has never got to know the crisis of conscience caused by the rebellion of man's subjective desires against the objective insights of his own reason, for it has neither reason of its own, nor insights, nor even conscience.

Proceedings of the Sixth Rhenish Parliament

BY A RHINELANDER

Third Article: Debates on the Law on Thefts of Wood[1]

Written: October 1842

First published: Rheinische Zeitung, 25th October–3rd November 1842

Reprinted: MEGA, I i (1), pp. 266–304. *Frühe Schriften*, pp. 208–57

The third of the series of articles on the Sixth Rhenish Parliament: see comment on the first. In it Marx deals directly for the first time with socio-economic problems.

If every violation of property without differentiation or further definition is theft, would not private property be theft? Through my private property do I not exclude a third party from this property? And do I not thus violate his right to property? When you deny the distinction between essentially different types of the same crime, then you deny the crime as distinct from the law and you do away with the law itself, for every crime has a facet that is in common with the law. It is thus a fact as historical as it is rational that an undifferentiated harshness destroys all the effects of punishment for it has destroyed punishment as a consequence of the law. . . .

But we unpractical men lay claim, on behalf of the masses of the poor who have no political or social possessions to what the learned and docile servants of the so-called historians found to be the true wise man's stone which could form any impure pretension into the pure gold of right. We reclaim for poverty the right of custom, and moreover a right of custom which is not a local one but which is that of poverty in all lands. We go further and affirm that customary right by

---

[1] See further: Introduction, p. xviii; K. Löwith, 'Self-alienation in the Early Writings of Karl Marx', in *Social Research*, 1954.

its nature can only be the right of the lowest and elementary mass of propertyless people.

Among the so-called customs of the privileged are understood customs against the law. The date of their birth falls in the period when the history of mankind formed a part of natural history and the Egyptian legend was proved true when all the gods concealed themselves in the form of animals. Mankind appears as disintegrated into particular animal races who are held together not by equality but by an inequality that regulates the laws. A universal lack of freedom requires laws that lack freedom, for whereas human law is the existence of freedom, animal law is the existence of a lack of freedom. . . .

The rights of aristocratic custom run counter by their content to the form of general law. They cannot be formed into laws because they are formulations of lawlessness. The fact that these customary rights are through their content in conflict with the form of law, i.e. its universality and necessity, proves that they are unjust customs and that, instead of being enforced in opposition to the law, they should be abrogated because of this opposition and even on occasion be punished. For no one stops behaving unjustly simply because this way of behaving is a custom, any more that the thieving son of a thief is excused by his family's idiosyncracies. If a man behaves unjustly intentionally, then his intention should be punished, and if he behaves unjustly out of custom, then his custom should be punished as being a bad one. In an age of general law rational customary rights are nothing but the custom of legal rights, for rights do not cease to be customary once they have constituted themselves as law, but they do cease to be purely customary. For the law-abiding man law becomes his own custom whereas the man who does not abide by the law is constrained by it even though it is not his custom. Rights no longer depend on the chance of whether custom is rational for custom becomes rational, because rights are legal, because custom has become the custom of the state. . . .

It is unwillingly that we have followed this boring and stupid debate, but we thought it our duty to use an example to show what can be expected of an estates assembly motivated by particular interests were it ever really called upon to legislate.

We repeat once again that our estates have fulfilled their position as estates, but we are far from wishing to justify them thereby. The Rhinelander would have to triumph in them over the representative, and the man over the owner of the woods. Even in law it is not only the representation of particular interests but also the representation of the interest of the province that has been entrusted to them. However contradictory both these tasks may be, one should not hesitate in the case of a confrontation to sacrifice the representation of particular interests to that of the province. The feeling for right and law is the most important provincial characteristic of the Rhinelander; but it is self-evident that particular interests know no fatherland and no province either, no cosmopolitanism and no parochialism either.

Those imaginative writers who are pleased to find in romantic idealism a bottomless depth of character and a most fruitful source of peculiarly individual types of attitude in a representation of particular interests are quite wrong: such a representation destroys all natural and spiritual differences in that it enthrones in their place an immoral, foolish and spiritless abstraction of limited content which is slavishly subordinate to a narrow consciousness.

Letter to Arnold Ruge[1]

Written: 30th November 1842

First published: MEGA, I i (2), pp. 285–7

This letter explains in detail the reasons for Marx's break with the *Freien*. He had been getting increasingly estranged from his former colleagues in Berlin whose extremism did not permit them to appreciate the difficulties involved in editing a Rhineland newspaper.

Cologne, 30th Nov. 1842

Dear Friend,

My letter today will be only about 'troubles' with the 'Free Men'.

You already know that the censorship daily mutilates us so pitilessly that often the paper can scarcely appear. A mass of articles by the 'Free Men' came to grief that way. I took the liberty of myself striking out just as much as the censor, for Meyen and company sent us heaps of scrawls pregnant with world revolution and empty of ideas written in a slovenly style with a bit of atheism and communism (which the gentlemen have never studied) mixed in. Rutenberg's complete lack of judgement, independence and capability had made them accustomed to treat the *Rheinische Zeitung* as their own spineless organ, but it seemed to me that I ought no longer to tolerate this dishwater in the previous manner. Thus this omission of some invaluable production of 'freedom', a freedom whose principal object is 'to be free from all thoughts' was the first reason for a darkening of the Berlin sky.

Rutenberg, who had already been removed from editing the German articles (where his chief activity consisted in punctuation), who had only been given the French section through my influence, Rutenberg had the luck to be counted as dangerous by the enormous stupidity of our state's Providence although he was never more dangerous to anyone than to the *Rheinische Zeitung* and himself. Rutenberg's dismissal was forcefully demanded. The Prussian authorities, this Prussian despotism,

---

[1] See Introduction, p. xviii ff.

the most hypocritical and the most treacherous, spared the director an unpleasant scene, and the new martyr who already knows how to convey the attitudes of a martyr in physiognomy, behaviour and speech with some virtuosity, exploits this opportunity and writes the world over and to Berlin that he is the exiled principle of the *Rheinische Zeitung* which is now changing its position *vis-à-vis* the government. It is self-evident. On this subject, too, there came demonstrations from the freedom heroes on the banks of the Spree, 'the dirty water that washes souls and thins tea'.

Finally there was in addition the relationship of yourself and Herwegh to the Free Men to fill up the measure of the angry Olympians.

A few days ago I received a letter from little Meyen whose favourite category, and quite rightly, is 'ought', in which there was talk of my relationship: (1) to you and Herwegh; (2) to the Free Men; and (3) of the new principles of editing and the position *vis-à-vis* the government. I replied immediately and gave him my frank opinion of the deficiencies of their work which finds freedom more in a licentious, sansculottish and thus convenient form than in a free, i.e. independent and profound content. I called for them to show less vague reasoning, finesounding phrases, conceited self-admiration and more precision, more detail on concrete circumstances and more knowledge of the subject. I explained that I held the smuggling into incidental theatre reviews etc. of communist and socialist dogmas, that is of a new world-view, be unsuitable and indeed immoral, and that I desired quite a different and more profound discussion of communism if it were to be discussed at all. I then asked that religion should be criticized more within a critique of the political situation than the political situation within a critique of religion, because this approach fits better the nature of a newspaper and the education of the public, for religion has no content of its own and does not live from heaven but from earth and falls automatically with dissolution of the inverted reality whose theory it is. Finally I wished that, if philosophy were to be spoken of, there should be less trifling with the slogan 'atheism' (which looks like children who assure anyone who will listen to them that they are not afraid of an ogre) and more presenting its content to the people. That's all.

Yesterday I got an insolent letter from Meyen, who had not yet received this one and asks me about everything possible and then: (1) I must explain what my position is in their dispute with Bauer about which I have not heard a word; (2) why I did not let this and this through; am threatened with conservatism; (3) the newspaper should not temporize, but must do its utmost, i.e. give way peacefully to the police and censorship instead of holding to its post in a struggle that may be hidden from the public but is nevertheless stubborn and compels loyalty. Finally there was abusive comment on Herwegh's engagement, etc. etc.

There is evident in all this a frightful dose of conceit that does not understand how, in order to save a political organ, one can sacrifice some Berlin bragging and that thinks of absolutely nothing but its own cliquish gossip. Thereupon the little fellow swelled up like a peacock, beat on his breast and put on his sword with high protestation, let some words drop about 'his' party, threatened me with disgrace, declaimed like the Marquis Posa, only a bit worse, and so on. From morning to night we have to put up with the most frightful torments from the censorship, ministerial rescripts, presidential complaints, outcries in the provincial parliament, screams from the shareholders etc. etc., and I only remain at my post because I feel myself bound as far as I can to frustrate the realization of the intentions of the powers that be. So you can imagine that I am somewhat irritated and gave Meyen rather a rough answer. So it is probable that the 'Free Men' will withdraw for a moment. Therefore I ask you urgently both to support us yourself with contributions and to encourage your friends to do so . . .

Yours,
Marx

On the Estates Committees in Prussia

Written: December 1842

First published: Rheinische Zeitung, 11–31st December 1842

Reprinted: MEGA, I i (1), pp. 321–35

Marx attacks an article in the *Augsburger Allgemeine Zeitung* that was in favour of the institution of the Estates Committees (national advisory committees whose membership was chosen on the basis of Estates) as represented in the Provincial Parliaments. Frederick William IV had decided on their institution as an attempt to meet demands for popular representation. The excerpt below is from the very end of the article and gives Marx's own interpretation of what 'representation' should mean.

For further details on the Estates Committees see: E. Huber, *Deutsche Verfassungsgeschichte*, Stuttgart, 1960, vol. 2, pp. 488 ff.

From what we have said it is self-evident that not only can we not agree with complaints about the narrow standing orders of the committees but on the contrary feel compelled to protest earnestly against any enlargement of them as being contrary to the interests of the state. Just as misguided is the liberalism that wishes to see intelligence represented in the provincial parliament. Intelligence is not only no particular element of representation, it is no element at all but a principle that cannot take part in a composition of elements but only create an organization out of itself. You cannot talk of intelligence as a part to be integrated into the whole but only of it as the organizing soul. There is no question here of completion but of opposition. The question is: representation of intelligence or representation by estates. The question is whether particular interests should represent the political intelligence or whether the political intelligence should represent particular interests. Political intelligence will order landed property, for example, according to the laws of the state, but it will not order the laws of the state according to landed property. It will give landed property not the force of its private egoism but that of its political nature, it will not determine the universal essence according to the particular essence but will determine the particular according to the universal. Representative landed property, on the other hand, does not regulate itself by intelligence, it regulates intelligence by itself, like the clock-maker who did not want to regulate his clock by the sun, but the sun by his clock. The question can be summed up in a few words: shall landed property criticize and dominate political intelligence or the reverse?

For intelligence there is no exterior, it is the inner determining soul of everything, while in reverse for a determinate element, like landed property, everything is exterior that is not itself. Therefore not only the composition, but also the proceedings of the provincial parliament are mechanical for it must treat all general interests and even particular interests that are separate from its own as something alien and foreign. Everything particular, like landed property, is in itself limited, and therefore as such must be governed by a general power that stands above it which it cannot govern according to its own needs.

The peculiar constitution of the provincial parliaments makes them nothing but a society of particular interests who have the privilege of enforcing their delimiting characteristics against the state and who are thus an authorized self-constitution of anti-state elements within the state. Thus their very essence makes them ill-disposed to the state, for the particular in its isolated activity is always an enemy of the whole, since it is precisely this whole that gives it the feel of its limitations and thus of its nothingness.

If this political self-reliance of particular interests were a necessity in the state, this would only be a symptom of its inner disease, just as the laws of nature say that an unhealthy body must break out in spots. One must opt for one of two points of view, either that the particular interests overstrain themselves, become alienated from the political spirit of the state and wish to limit the state, or the state concentrates itself in the government alone, and grants the limited spirit of the people as a recompense simply a sphere to ventilate its particular interests. Finally one could make a synthesis of both views. So if the desire for a representation of intelligence is to be meaningful, then we must interpret it as the desire for the conscious representation of the people's intelligence not in order to enforce individual needs against the state but to realize that its highest need is to make the state really its own creation, its own state. To be represented is in general something to be suffered; only the material, spiritless, dependent, insecure need representation; but no element in the state should be material, spiritless, dependent, insecure. Representation should not be conceived of as the representation of some stuff that is not the people itself, but only as its self-representation, as an action of state that only distinguishes itself by the universality of its content from the other manifestations of its political life. Representation must not be looked upon as a concession to defenceless weakness and powerlessness but as the self-conscious vitality of the strongest force. In a true state there is no landed property, no industry, no material stuff that can, as such elements, strike a bargain with the state, there are only spiritual powers and it is only in their resurrection in the state, in their political rebirth that natural powers are capable of having a political voice. The state has spiritual nerves throughout the whole of nature, and it must appear at every point that not matter but form, not nature without the state but political nature, not the unfree object, but the free man dominates.

Letter to Arnold Ruge

Written: 13th March 1843
First published: MEGA, I i (2), pp. 306–8

In this letter Marx gives his views on the projected *Deutsch-französische Jahr-bücher* and then talks about his impending marriage. The postscript contains interesting remarks on his attitude to Bruno Bauer and to the local Jewish Community.

Cologne, 13th March 1843

Dear Friend,

As soon as it is in any way possible I will fly direct to Leipzig. I have just promised this to Stucke who seems to be strongly impressed by most of the men of state in Berlin. Dr. Stucke is a very good-natured man.

Now as regards our plan, I will tell you what my conviction provisionally is. When Paris was conquered some suggested the government be entrusted to Napoleon's son with a regency, others to Bernadotte, others finally to Louis Philippe. But Talleyrand answered: Louis XVIII or Napoleon. That is a principle: all the rest is intrigue.

And similarly I would like to qualify almost anything else apart from Strasbourg (or at most Switzerland) as not a matter of principle but of intrigue. Books of more than twenty pages are no writing for the people. The most one can risk there is a monthly journal.

Now if the *Deutsche Jahrbücher* were permitted again, then the most we could achieve would be a feeble copy of the holy dead and nowadays that is no longer enough. On the other hand, Franco-German annals would be a principle, an event of consequence, an undertaking which could arouse one's enthusiasm. Of course, I am only giving you my own humble opinion and in all else am subject to the eternal power of fate.

Finally—and business for the paper compels me to finish—I will also inform you of what my private plans are. As soon as we have completed the contract, I want to go to Kreuznach and get married and stay there a month or more with my bride's mother because in any case before we get to work we shall have to have some pieces of work ready. So it would be all the more possible for me, if necessary, to stay some weeks in Dresden because all the preliminary business, promulgations etc. take up a lot of time.

I can assure you without any romanticism that I am head over heels in love in all earnestness. I have already been engaged for over seven years and my bride has fought the hardest of fights for me that have almost undermined her health, partly with her pietist-aristocratic relations for whom 'the Lord in heaven' and 'the Lord in Berlin' are alike objects of reverence, partly with my own family in which some parsons and other enemies of mine have settled. I and my bride have thus fought through years of more unnecessary and exhausting conflicts than many others who are three times as old as we are and continually speak of their 'experience of life' (the favourite word of our *juste milieu*).

By the way, we have received an anonymous reply to Prutz's adverse report on the new *Tubinger Jahrbücher*.[1] I recognize the handwriting as Schwegler's. You are characterized as a highly-strung creature of unrest, Feuerbach as a flippant scoffer, and Bauer as a thoroughly uncritical person! The Swabians! That will make a fine mixture!

For your fine and really popular essay of complaint[2] we have used a superficial essay of Pfutzner (of which I have excised half) for want of a better review and more time. The fellow never goes deep enough into the matter and the small capers that he cuts make his own self more of an object of ridicule than that he makes his enemy ridiculous.

Yours
Marx

I have taken care of the books for Fleischer. Your exchange of letters at the beginning is interesting.[3] Bauer on Ammon is splendid. 'The

---

[1] Entitled *Jahrbücher de Gegenwart*, ed. A. Schwegler. They appeared 1843–48 and provided a platform for Strauss's followers.

[2] A complaint to the Saxon parliament on the suppression of the *Deutsche Jahrbücher* that Ruge published in *Anekdota*.

[3] All the writings that Marx refers to in his postscript were published in *Anekdota*: The 'exchange of letters' was between Ruge and the censorship

Joys and Sorrows of the theological consciousness' seems to me to be a not quite successful translation from the section of the Phenomenology entitled 'The unhappy consciousness'. Feuerbach's aphorisms only seem to be amiss in one point in that he refers too much to nature and not enough to politics. Nevertheless that is the only link by which present philosophy can become a reality. Yet it will no doubt be like the sixteenth century when there was a series of state enthusiasts to match the enthusiasts of nature. What pleased me most was the review of the good *Literarische Zeitung*.[1]

You will already have read Bauer's self-defence.[2] In my opinion he has never written so well.

As far as the *Rheinische Zeitung* is concerned, I would not remain under any conditions. It is impossible for me to write under Prussian censorship or live in Prussian air.

Just now the president of the Israelites here came to see me and asked my support for a petition to the provincial parliament on behalf of the Jews, and I will give it. Although I find the Isrealite faith repugnant, yet Bauer's opinions seem to me to be too abstract. The point is to punch as many holes in the Christian state as possible and to smuggle in the rational as far as we can. At least that is what we must try to do— and the bitterness grows with every petition that is rejected with a protest.

authorities concerning the *Deutsche Jahrbücher*; the two essays by Bruno Bauer are a review of Ammon's *History of the Life of Jesus* and *Sorrows and Joys of the Theological Consciousness*; the 'aphorisms' are Feuerbach's *Preliminary Theses on the Reform of Philosophy*.

[1] An essay of Ruge's in the *Anekdota* attacking the semi-official *Berliner Literarische Zeitung*.

[2] *The Good Cause of Freedom*, written on his dismissal from the University of Bonn.

Critique of Hegel's Philosophy of Right[1]

Written: March–August 1843

First published: MEGA, I i (1), pp. 401–553; *Frühe Schriften*, pp. 258–426

Translated: Molitor, IV, pp. 17–259; Easton and Guddatt, *Writings of the Young Marx*, pp. 152–202

A paragraph by paragraph commentary on §§ 261–313 of Hegel's *Principles of the Philosophy of Right*. The first few pages are missing. The essence of Marx's criticism of Hegel is contained in the first extract below; the other three deal with Marx's views on democracy, bureaucracy and private property. Letters of Marx to Ruge indicate that Marx may have begun work on this manuscript as early as 1841, intending to publish it as an article.

'The actual idea is spirit which separates itself into the two ideal spheres of its concept, family and civil society, which are its finite phase, in order to leave its ideality and become explicit as infinite actual spirit. Thus it is to these spheres that spirit bestows the material of this its finite actuality, i.e. human beings as a mass so that the function assigned to any given individual is visibly mediated by circumstances, his caprice and his personal choice of his station in life.'[2]

If we translate this sentence into prose then we get this result: The ways and means by which the state mediates itself with the family and civil society are through 'circumstances, caprice and personal choice of station in life'. Thus the rational basis of the state has nothing to do with the splitting up of the stuff of the state into family and civil society. The state arises from them in an unconscious and arbitrary way. The family and civil society are the dark natural background from which the light of the state is kindled. The business of the state, the family and civil society, are understood to be part of the stuff of the state in so far as they form parts of the state, take part in the state as such.

---

[1] See further: Introduction, pp. xix ff; S. Avineri, 'The Hegelian Origins of Marx's Political Thought', *Review of Metaphysics*, 1967; J. Hyppolite, 'La Conception Hégélienne de l'Etat et sa Critique par Karl Marx', *Cahiers Internationaux de Sociologie*, 1947.

[2] Hegel, *Philosophy of Right*, trans. T. M. Knox, Oxford, 1942, p. 162.

This development is remarkable from a double point of view:
1. Family and civil society are viewed as conceptual spheres of the state,
and indeed as the spheres of its finiteness, as its finiteness. It is the state
that divides itself into them, that presupposes them and indeed it does
this 'in order to leave its ideality and become explicit as finite actual
spirit'. 'It separates in order to. . . . It bestows on these spheres the
material of its actuality so that this assignment to the individual
appears as mediated.' The so-called 'actual Idea' (spirit as infinite, actual)
is presented as though it behaved according to a particular principle and
with a particular intention. It separates itself into finite spheres, and it
does this 'in order to return back into itself, to become explicit', and it
does this indeed so that things shall be as they really are.

At this point the logical, pantheistic mysticism appears very clearly.

The real relationship is: 'that the attribution of the material of the
state to individuals seems to be mediated by circumstances, caprice
and his personal choice of his station in life'. This fact, this real relationship is pronounced by speculation to be an appearance, a phenomenon. These circumstances, this caprice, this choice of a station in
life, this real mediation are only the appearance of a mediation, which
the actual idea undertakes with itself and which takes place behind the
scenes. Reality is not expressed as itself but as another reality. The
ordinary empirical world does not have its own spirit as a lawgiver, but
an alien one, whereas the actual idea does not have as its existence a
reality developed from itself but that of the ordinary empirical world.

The idea is made subjective and the true relationship of the family
and civil society to the state is conceived of as their inner imaginary
activity. The family and civil society are the presuppositions of the
state; they are its properly active elements. But in speculation the
relationship is inverted. When the idea is made a subject, the real
subjects, the civil society, the family, 'circumstances, caprice etc.'
become unreal objective phrases of the idea and have a completely
different significance.

The attribution of the material of the state 'to individuals through
circumstances, caprice and choice of one's station in life' is not simply
declared to be the genuine, the necessary, the completely justified; they
are not declared as such to be rational; but on the other hand, they are
declared so, but only in such a way that they are said to be an apparent

mediation, that they are left as they are yet at the same time receive the significance of being a definition of the idea, a result, a product of the idea. The difference is not in the content but in the way it is treated and spoken of. There is a dual history, an esoteric and an exoteric one. The content lies in the exoteric part. The interest of the esoteric is always to rediscover in the state the history of the logical concept. But it is on the exoteric side that the true development occurs.

Rationally expressed, Hegel's sentences would only amount to this: The family and civil society are parts of the state. The stuff of the state is divided among them by 'circumstances, caprice and the choice of one's station in life'. Citizens are members of families and memers of civil society.

'The actual idea is Spirit which separates itself into the two ideal spheres of its concept, the family and civil society, which are its finite phase'—thus the separation of the state into family and civil society is ideal, i.e. necessary, is part of the essence of the state; the family and civil society are real parts of the state, real spiritual instances of will, they are the modes of being of the state; family and civil society make themselves into the state. They are the initiators. According to Hegel, they are, on the contrary, created by the actual idea; it is not their own life-process that unites them to the state, it is the life-process of the idea that has distinguished them from itself; indeed they are the finite phase of this idea; they owe their existence to another spirit than their own. They are definitions posited by a third party, not self-definitions. Therefore they too are defined as 'finiteness', as the 'actual idea's' own finitude. The aim of its being is not this being itself, for the idea separates off these presuppositions 'in order to leave its ideality and become explicit as finite actual spirit', that is, the political state cannot exist without the natural basis of the family and the artificial basis of civil society: they are its *conditio sine qua non*. However, the condition is put in the position of the conditioned, the determining of the determined and the producer is in the position of the product of what it has itself produced. The actual idea only lowers itself to the 'finitude' of the family and civil society so as to transcend them and enjoy and produce its own infinity; thus (in order to attain its aim) it is to these spheres that spirit bestows the material of this its finite actuality (this? which? these spheres are its 'finite actuality', its 'material') i.e. human beings as a mass (the material of the state is here 'individuals, the mass', 'the state is composed by them', this composition is here expressed as an act of the idea, as an attribution that it performs with its own material; the fact is that the state originates in the mass as it exists as members of the family and civil society; speculation expresses this fact as an act of the idea, not as the idea of the mass, but as the act of a subjective idea, distinct from the fact itself), 'so that the function assigned to any given individual' (before only the assigning of individuals to the spheres of family and civil society was spoken of) 'is visibly mediated by circumstances, caprice etc.' Thus empirical reality is taken as it is; it is also declared to be rational, but it is rational not because of its own reason but because the empirical fact in its empirical existence has a meaning other than its own. The fact that served as a beginning is not conceived of as such but as a mystical result. The real becomes an appearance, but the idea has no other content than this appearance. Also the idea has no other aim than the logical one 'to become explicit as infinite actual spirit'. In this paragraph is set down the whole mystery of the philosophy of law and of Hegel's philosophy in general. . . .

On Democracy

Democracy is the truth of monarchy, monarchy is not the truth of democracy. Monarchy is necessarily democracy as an inconsequence against itself, whereas the monarchical element in democracy is no inconsequence. Monarchy cannot, as democracy can, be understood in its own terms. In democracy none of its elements gets a different meaning from its own. Each is merely an element of the whole people. In monarchy one part determines the character of the whole. The whole constitution must modify itself in relation to the fixed point. Democracy is the constititution of the species. Monarchy is a variety and a bad one at that. Democracy is content and form. Monarchy ought only to be form, but it falsifies the content.

In monarchy the whole, the people, is subsumed under one of its modes of being, the political constitution; in democracy the constitution itself appears as only one determination, and the self-determination of the people at that. In monarchy we have the people of the constitution; in democracy we have the constitution of the people.

Democracy is the solution to the riddle of all constitutions. Here the constitution is constantly, not only in itself and essentially but also in its existence and reality, brought back to its real basis, the real man, the real people, and set up as its own work. The constitution appears as what it is, the free product of man; one could say that this is valid in certain respects for constitutional monarchy also, but the specific difference of democracy is that in it the constitution is nothing more than one element in the being of the people, that the political constitution does not explicitly form the state.

Hegel starts from the state and makes man into the subjective aspect of the state; democracy starts from man and makes the state into objectified man. Just as religion does not make man, but man makes religion, so the constitution does not make the people, but the people makes the constitution. In a certain respect democracy has the same relation to all the other forms of state as Christianity has to all other forms of religion. Christianity is the religion *par excellence*, the essence of religion, deified man as a particular religion. Similarly democracy is the essence of all constitutions of the state, socialized man as a particular constitution of the state; it has the same relationship to other constitutions as the species has to its types, only that in this case, the species itself appears as a particular existence and thus over against existences that do not correspond to the essence, it appears as a particular type. Democracy is the Old Testament in relation to other political forms. Man is not there for the benefit of the law, but the law for the benefit of man, it is a human existence, whereas in other political forms man has only a legal existence. That is the fundamental character of democracy.

All other constructions of the state are a certain, definite and particular form of the state. In democracy the formal principle is at the same time the material principle. Thus it is first the true unity of universal and particular. In a monarchy, for example, or in a republic, as merely a particular form of the state, political man has his particular existence beside the unpolitical, private man. Property, contract, marriage, civil society appear here (as Hegel develops it quite correctly for these abstract forms of the state, only that he thinks he is developing the idea of the state) as particular modes of being alongside the political state. They appear as the content, to which the political state has the relationship of organizing form, in fact merely a reason that is without content in itself, determining and limiting, now confirming, now denying. In democracy as the political state puts itself beside this content and distinguishes itself from it, it is itself only a particular content and a particular mode of existence of the people. In the monarchy, for instance, this particular element, the political constitution, has the significance of a universal that dominates and determines all particulars. In democracy the state as a particular is only a particular and as a universal is a real universal, i.e. is no particular characteristic distinguished from the rest of the content. The manner in which the most recent French thinkers have conceived of this is that in a true democracy the political state disappears. This is correct in so far as *qua* political state and constitution, it is no longer valid for the whole.

In all states that are not democracies, the state, the law, the constitution is the dominant factor without really dominating, i.e. materially penetrating all the other spheres that are not political. In a democracy the constitution, the law and the state itself are only a self-determination of the people and a particular content of them in so far as it is a political constitution.

It is self-evident, moreover, that all forms of state have democracy as their truth and therefore that they are untrue in as far as they are not democracies.

In the old states the political state formed the content of the state and excluded the other spheres; the modern state is a compromise between the political and the non-political state.

In democracy, the abstract state has ceased to be the dominant element. The struggle between monarchy and republic is itself still only a struggle inside the abstract form of the state. The *political* republic is democracy inside the abstract form of the state. The abstract political form of democracy is therefore a republic; but here it ceases being only a political constitution.

Property and so on, in short the whole matter of law and the state is with little modification the same in North America as in Prussia. Thus there, a republic is merely a form of the state as here the monarchy is. The content of the state lies outside its constitution. So Hegel is right when he says: the political state is the constitution, that is, the matter of the state is not political. There is only an exterior identity here, a mutual determination. It would be very difficult to construct the political state and the constitution from the different elements of the people's life. It developed itself as universal reason over against the other spheres, as something beyond them. The historical task consisted then in their re-vindication, but the particular spheres did not realize here that their private essence coincides with the other-worldly essence of the constitution or the political state, and that its other-wordly being is nothing but the affirmation of their own alienation. The political constitution was formerly the religious sphere, the religion of the people's life, the heaven of its universality over against the earthly and real existence. The political sphere was the only state sphere in the state, the only sphere in which the content as well as the form was a content of the species[1] and the genuine universal; but at the same time this was in such a manner that, because this sphere stood over against the others, its content too became a formal and particular one. Political life in the modern state is the scholasticism of the people's life. Monarchy is the perfected expression of this alienation. Republicanism is its negative inside its own sphere. It is evident that the political constitution as such can only be elaborated where the private spheres have obtained an independent existence. Where trade and landed property are not free and have not yet been made independent, the political constitution also is unfree and still not independent. The Middle Ages was the democracy of unfreedom.

The abstraction of the state as such belongs only to the modern time, because the abstraction of private life also belongs only to modern times. The abstraction of the political state is a modern product.

In the Middle Ages there were serfs, feudal property, corporations of trade and of learned men etc. This means that in the Middle Ages property, trade, society and men were political; the material content of the state was delimited by its form; each private sphere had a political

---

[1] The term 'species' (*Gattung*) was often used by Marx during the years 1843/44 either on its own or in phrases like 'species-life', 'species-consciousness'. Marx borrowed the word from Feuerbach who had used it particularly in *Das Wesen des Christentums*. According to Feuerbach, the distinguishing characteristic of man was that he was not only conscious of himself as an individual, but also as a member of a species united by the possession of a common 'essence'.

character or was a political sphere or politics formed the character of the private sphere. In the Middle Ages the political constitution was the constitution of private property but only because the constitution of private property was the political constitution. In the Middle Ages the people's life and the state's life were identical. Man was the real principle of the state, but it was unfree man. So it is the democracy of unfreedom, perfected alienation. The abstract, reflected opposition only begins with the modern world. The Middle Ages is the real dualism and the modern time the abstract dualism. . . .

On Bureaucracy

'Bureaucracy' is the 'state formalism' of civil society. It is the 'state's consciousness', the 'state's will', the 'state's power' as a corporation and thus a particular, closed society within the state. (The 'general interest' can only maintain itself as a 'particular' vis-à-vis particulars, so long as the particular maintains itself as a 'general' vis-à-vis the general. Bureaucracy must thus safeguard the imaginary universality of the particular interest, the spirit of the corporation, in order to safeguard the imaginary particularity of the general interest, its own spirit. The state must be a corporation as long as the corporation wishes to be a state.) But bureaucracy wishes the corporation to be an imaginary power. Of course the individual corporation has this same desire for its particular interest against bureaucracy, but it desires bureaucracy against the other corporations, against other particular interest. Therefore bureaucracy, being the completion of the corporation, has the victory over the corporation which is the incomplete bureaucracy. It degrades this latter to an appearance or desires to degrade it to an appearance, but it desires that this appearance exist and believe in its own existence. The corporation is the attempt of civil society to become a state; but bureaucracy is the state that has really made itself into a civil society.

The 'state formalism' that bureaucracy is, is the 'state as formalism' and Hegel has described it as such a formalism. Because this 'state formalism' constitutes itself as a real power and comes to have a material content of its own, then it is self-evident that 'bureaucracy' is a web of 'practical illusions' or the 'illusion of the state'. The bureaucratic spirit is through and through a Jesuitical, theological spirit. The bureaucrats are the Jesuits and theologians of the state. Bureaucracy is the republic as priest.

Since it is of the essence of bureaucracy to be the 'state as formalism', so its aim implies this also. The real aim of the state thus appears to bureaucracy as an aim against the state. The spirit of bureaucracy is therefore the 'formal spirit of the state'. Thus it makes the 'formal spirit of the state' or the real lack of spirit by the state into a categorical imperative. Bureaucracy counts in its own eyes as the final aim of the state. Because it makes its 'formal' ends into its content, it enters into conflict everywhere with 'real' ends. It is therefore compelled to claim the formal for its content and its content as the formal. The aims of the state are transformed into the aims of the bureaux and the aims of the bureaux into the aims of the state. Bureaucracy is a circle from which no one can escape. Its hierarchy is a hierarchy of knowledge. The apex entrusts the lower circles with insight into the individual while the lower circles leave insight into the universal to the apex, so they deceive each other reciprocally.

Bureaucracy constitutes an imaginary state beside the real state and is the spiritualism of the state. Thus every object has a dual meaning, a real one and a bureaucratic one, just as knowledge is dual, a real and a bureaucratic (it is the same with the will). But the real thing is treated according to its bureaucratic essence, its otherworldly spiritual essence. Bureaucracy holds in its possession the essence of the state, the spiritual essence of society, it is its private property. The general spirit of bureaucracy is secret, mystery, safeguarded inside itself by hierarchy and outside by its nature as a closed corporation. Thus public political spirit and also political mentality appear to bureaucracy as a betrayal of its secret. The principle of its knowledge is therefore authority, and its mentality is the idolatry of authority. But within bureaucracy the spiritualism turns into a crass materialism, the materialism of passive obedience, faith in authority, the mechanism of fixed and formal behaviour, fixed principles, attitudes, traditions. As far as the individual bureaucrat is concerned, the aim of the state becomes his private aim, in the form of a race for higher posts, of careerism. Firstly he considers the real life as a material one, for the spirit of this life has its own separate existence in bureaucracy. Bureaucracy must therefore make it its job to render life as material as possible. Secondly for himself life becomes

H

material, i.e. in as far as it becomes an object of bureaucratic procedure, for his spirit is laid down for him, his aim lies outside himself and his existence is the existence of the bureaucratic. The state only continues to exist as separate fixed spirits of bureaux whose connection is subordination and passive obedience. Real knowledge appears as devoid of content, as real life appears as dead, for this imaginary knowledge and this imaginary life count as essential. . . .

Independence and self-reliance in the political state . . . are achieved by private property whose apogee appears as inalienable landed property. Thus political dependence does not spring from the inner nature of the political state, it is no gift of the political state to its members, it is not the spirit that gives the state a soul. For the members of the political state receive their independence from a thing unconnected with the essence of the political state, a thing of abstract private law, from abstract private property. Political dependence is an accident of private property, not the substance of the political state. The political state and in it the legislative power, as we have seen, is the revealed mystery of the true worth and essence of the elements in the state. The significance that private property has in the political state is its essential, its true significance; the significance that difference in class has in the political state, is the essential significance of difference of class. Similarly the essence of princely power and of government appears in the 'legislative power'. It is here in the sphere of the political state, that the individual elements of the state relate to themselves as to the being of their species, their 'species-being';[1] for the political state is the sphere of their universal determination, their religious sphere. The political state is the mirror of truth for the different elements of the concrete state. . . .

On Primogeniture and Private Property

Hegel describes private right as the right of the abstract personality or as abstract right. And truth compels it to be developed as the abstraction of right and thus as the illusory right of the abstract personality, as the morality developed by Hegel is the illusory existence of abstract

[1] See note on p. 67.

subjectivity. Hegel develops private right and morality as abstractions of this nature, but he does not conclude that the state and customary morality, which presupposes them, can be nothing but the society (social life) of these illusions: on the contrary he concludes that they are subordinate elements of this life of customary morality. But what are private right and morality other than the right and morality of these subjects of the state? or rather the person of private right and the subject of morality are the person and subject of the state. Hegel has repeatedly been attacked for his development of morality. All he has done is to develop the morality of the modern state and modern private right. People have wanted to separate morality more from the state, to emancipate it more. What has this proved? That the separation of the present-day state from morality is moral, that morality is not political and that the state is immoral. Yet it is a great, though in one respect (namely that Hegel claims that the state that has such an ethic as its presupposition is the real idea of customary morality) unconscious service of Hegel to have assigned its true position to modern morality.

In constitutions where the right of primogeniture is guaranteed, private property is the guarantee of the political constitution. This appears in the right of primogeniture in such a way that a particular type of private property is this guarantee. The right of primogeniture is just a particular example of the general relationship of private property and political state. The right of primogeniture is the political meaning of private property, private property in its political significance, i.e. in its general significance. Thus the constitution is here the constitution of private property.

Where we meet with the right of primogeniture in its classical form, in the German peoples, we also find the constitution of private property. Private property is the universal category, the universal bond of state. Even general functions appear as private property now of a corporation, now of a class.

The more detailed aspects of trade and commerce are the private property of particular corporations. Court honours, jurisdiction etc. are the private property of particular classes. The different provinces are the private property of different princes. Service owed for land etc. is the private property of the lord. Intellect is the private property of the clergy. My dutiful activity is the private property of another, as my right is again a particular private property. Sovereignty, here the nation, is the private property of the emperor.

It has often been said that in the Middle Ages every form of right, freedom and social life appears as a privilege, as an exception to the rule. It is impossible to overlook here the empirical fact that these privileges all appear in the form of private property. What is the general reason for this coincidence? Private property is the species-existence of privilege, of right as an exception. . . . .

A Correspondence of 1843[1]

Written: March, May and September 1843 (and probably slightly altered later for publication)

First published in: Deutsch-französische Jahrbücher, February 1844

Reprinted: MEGA, I i (1), pp. 557, 561–6, 572–5; *Frühe Schriften*, pp. 427–8, 432–8, 446–50

Translated: La Nouvelle Critique, December 1954, VII, no. 60, pp. 1–13; Easton and Guddatt, *Writings of the Young Marx*, pp. 203–15

The following three letters are taken from a correspondence between Marx, Ruge, Bakunin and Feuerbach. There is a pessimistic letter from Ruge in between Marx's first two and letters from Bakunin, Feuerbach and Ruge before Marx's third letter, which closes the correspondence. The letters were published at the beginning of the *Deutsch-französische Jahrbücher* to show the aims of the journal.

I

Holland, March 1843

I am at present travelling in Holland. So far as I can see from the local papers and French ones, Germany has got very bogged down and will become even more so. I assure you, even though one may be the very oppostie of patriotic, yet one can be ashamed for one's country, even in Holland. The least Dutchman is still a citizen in comparison with the greatest German. And what foreigners think of the Prussian Government! A frightful unanimity reigns, for no-one is any longer decieved about the stark nature of the system. So the new school has after all served some purpose. The parade cloak of liberalism has fallen and the most perverse despotism stands in its total nakedness before the eyes of the world.

This is also a revelation, though an inverted one. It is a truth that at least teaches us to realize the emptiness of our patriotism, the monstrosity of our state and to veil our faces. You smile at me and ask me: What

[1] See Introduction, p. xxii.

is gained thereby? One cannot make a revolution out of shame. I answer: Shame is already a revolution. It is really the victory of the French Revolution over the German patriotism that conquered it in 1813. Shame is a sort of anger directed against oneself and if a whole nation were really ashamed of itself then it would be like the lion who recoils to spring. I concede that even shame is not yet present in Germany; on the contrary, the wretches are still patriots. But what system could drum the patriotism out of them if not the ridiculous one of our new knight?[1] The comedy of despotism in which we are the actors is as dangerous for him as tragedy once was for the Stuarts and the Bourbons. And even if the true nature of this comedy were not realized for a long time, yet it would still already be a revolution. The state is too important a thing to be turned into a harlequinade. You could probably let a ship full of fools run before the wind for a good while, but it would run into its fate just because the fools did not believe in it. This fate is the revolution which stands before us.

II

Cologne, May 1843

Your letter, my dear friend, is a good elegy, a choking dirge; but it is definitely not political. No people despairs, and though merely from stupidity it may merely hope for the very long time, yet after many years, it gets a rush of cleverness and fulfills all its pious wishes.

Yet you have infected me, your theme is not yet exhausted, I will add the finale and when all is at an end, then give me your hand so that we may begin again from the beginning. Let the dead bury and mourn their dead. In contrast, it is enviable to be the first to go alive into the new life; and this shall be our lot.

It is true that the old world is in the possession of the philistine. But we should not treat him as a scarecrow and turn back frightened. We must rather look him straight in the eye. It is worthwhile studying this lord of the world.

Of course he is only lord of the world providing that he fills it with his own society as worms do a corpse, the society of these lords needs nothing further than a number of slaves and the owners of the slaves do

[1] i.e. Frederick William IV.

not need to be free. Although their ownership of land and men gives them the title of lord in the highest sense of the word they are not therefore less philistine than their people.

Human beings are beings with minds, are republicans. The narrow-minded bourgeois want neither of these. What is left for them to be and wish?

Their desires to exist and procreate (and none of them, says Goethe, gets any further) are the same of those of animals, and the most a German politician would add is that man knows that he desires this and the German is prudent enough to desire nothing further.

First we would have to arouse in the breasts of these men that feeling of human freedom that characterizes a man. It is only this feeling, which left the earth with the Greeks, and with Christianity disappeared into the blue vapours of heaven, that can turn the society of men into a community for the realization of their highest end, a democratic state.

Men on the other hand who do not feel themselves to be men grow up for their masters like a breed of slaves or horses. This whole society is geared to the hereditary lords. This world belongs to them. They take it as it is and feels itself to be. They take themselves as they find themselves and stand where their feet grew: on the necks of these political animals, who know no other vacation than to be 'subject, devoted and obedient' to them.

The philistine world is the world of political animals, and if we have to recognize its existence, we have no alternative but simply to accept the *status quo* as justified. Barbaric centuries begot and reared this world and now it stands as a consistent system whose principle is the de-humanized world. Thus our Germany, the most perfectly philistine world, had to be far behind the French Revolution which restored the idea of man; and a German Aristotle who wanted to write his Politics with our political situation as his source would adopt as his motto 'Man is a social but completely unpolitical animal'. And he could not give a more accurate definition of the state than Herr Zopfl, the author of *Konstitutionelle Staatsrecht in Deutschland* has already done. It is, according to him, a 'union of families' which (let us continue further) belongs as a hereditary possession to a highest family that one calls dynasty. The more fruitful the families show themselves, the happier the people are, the greater the state and the more powerful the dynasty.

Even in the standard despotism of Prussia, a reward of £50 is fixed for the seventh child.

The Germans are such prudent realists that none of their wishes and loftiest thoughts go beyond their own bare lives. And this state of affairs, neither more nor less, is accepted by their lords. These people, too, are realists: they may be professional officers and land-owners, far removed from any thought on human greatness, but they are not mistaken, they are right, they are perfectly well equipped and adequate as they are to exploit and rule over this animal kingdom. For lordship and exploitation are the same concept here as everywhere. When they allow homage to be paid to themselves and look over the swarming heads of these brainless beings, what thought comes more readily to their mind than that of Napoleon on the banks of the Beresina? It is said of him that he pointed down to the throng of those drowning and called to his followers: 'look at those toads!' This is probably a lying slander, but it nevertheless has its truth. The one thought of despotism is to despise men, to de-humanize them, and this thought has the advantage of many others that it is at the same time fact. The despot always sees men as bereft of any worth. For him they sink before his eyes into the slime of vulgar life from which like toads they continually emerge. If such a view forces itself even upon men who were capable of great aims like Napoleon before his foolhardy ideas of wanting to found a dynasty, how could a completely normal king in such circumstances be an idealist?

The general principle of a monarchy is the despised, despicable, de-humanized man; and Montesquieu was very wrong to say that this principle is honour. He has to resort to the distinction between monarchy, despotism and tyranny. But these are words for a single concept, or at most different attitudes to the same principle. Where the monarchical principle is in the majority, men are in the minority and where it is in no doubt, men do not exist. Now why should a man like the king of Prussia, who has no proof that his position is in question, not follow his whim? And if he does so, what is the result? Contradictory aims? Fine, that means that they will result in nothing. Impotent politics? These are still the only political realities. Shame and embarrassment? There is only one shame and one disgrace, leaving the throne. As long as the whim remains in its place, it is right. It can be as fickle, brainless and contemptible as it likes, it is still good enough to rule a people that has never known any law apart from the arbitrary will of its king. I do not say that the brainless system and loss of respect at home and abroad will be without consequences; I would not insure the ship of fools; but I affirm that the king of Prussia will remain a man of his time so long as the inverted world is the real one.

You know that I have a lot to do with this man. Already when he only had the *Berliner Politisches Wochenblatt* as his organ, I recognized his worth and his character. Even at the Allegiance Ceremony in Königsberg he justified my suspicion that the question would now become a purely personal one. He declared that his heart and soul would in the future serve as the fundamental law of the Prussian domain, his state; and in fact in Prussia the king is the system. He is the only political person. It is his personality that gives this or that character to the system. What he does or is made to do, what he thinks or what people put into his mouth, that is in Prussia what the state thinks or does. So the present king has rendered a genuine service in explaining this so plainly.

The only mistake that people made for ages was to think it important what wishes and thoughts the king would bring forth. This could make no practical difference, the material that the monarchy works in is philistinism and the monarch is always merely the king of philistines; he cannot make either himself or his people free and genuine men, so long as both sides remain as they are.

The king of Prussia tried to change the system with a theory, a thing his father never possessed. The fate of this attempt is well known. It was a complete failure, and quite naturally so. If you have once arrived in politics at an animal world then the only regression possible is to return to it and the only progress is to abandon its basis and change to the human world of democracy.

The old king did not wish for anything extravagant. He was a philistine and laid no claim to intellect. He knew that the sole desire of the lackey state that he owned was a prosaic, tranquil existence. The young king was bolder and more awake and had much bigger ideas about the omnipotence of the monarch whose only limits are his own heart and intellect. The old ossified state of lackeys and slaves disgusted him. He wanted to give it life and impregnate it completely with his own wishes, feelings and thoughts and he, in the state that was his property, could require that, provided only that it was possible. Hence his liberal speeches and outpourings. Not the dead law but the heart of the king overflowing with life was to rule all his subjects. He wished to move all hearts and minds in favour of his own heartfelt wishes and long-nurtured plans. A movement followed. But the other hearts did not beat as his, and the subjects could not open their mouths without talking of the abrogation of the old forms of authority. The idealists, who are brazen enough to want to make humanity human, spoke up and while the king indulged his old German imagination, thought that they could philosophize in a new German manner. Of course this was unheard of in Prussia. For a moment the old order of things seemed to be stood on its head, things even began to change into men. There were even men with names, even though it was forbidden to mention names in the state parliaments. But the servants of the old despotism soon put an end to these un-German instincts. It was not difficult to bring the wishes of the king who is in love with a great past full of priests, knights and serfs, into conflict with the aims of the idealists who merely wish to draw the consequences of the French Revolution, that is in the last analysis of course a republic and an order of free men instead of one of dead things.

When this conflict had become sharp and uncomfortable enough and the quick anger of the king was sufficiently aroused, then the servants who had previously managed affairs so easily went to him and explained that the king did ill to mislead his subjects into useless speeches, for they would not be able to rule a race of speech-makers. Even the lord of all the backward Russians was uneasy about the movements in the heads of the forward Prussians and demanded the restoration of the previous tranquil state of affairs. And there followed a new version of the previous prescription of man's wishes and ideas about human rights and duties, regression to the old, ossified lackey state in which the slave serves in silence and the owner of land and people rules as silently as possible, entirely through his well-trained, obedient servants. Neither can say what they want, neither the former that they want to become men nor the latter that he cannot afford to have men in his country. So silence is the only way out:

Muta pecora, prona et ventri oboedientia.

This is the unhappy attempt to transcend the philistine state while retaining its very basis: and the additional result is that he has made clear to all the world that despotism necessarily involves brutality and is incompatible with humanity. A brutal relationship can only be sustained by brutality. I have thus finished with our common task of getting a clear picture of the philistine and his state. You will not say that I value the present too highly and if I nevertheless do not despair of it, it is only its own desperate situation that fills me with hope. I am not alluding to the incapacity of the lords and the indolence of the servants and subjects who let everything happen as God pleases; and yet both together would already be sufficient to bring about a catastrophe. I merely draw your attention to the fact that the enemies of philistinism, i.e. all men who think and suffer, have arrived at an understanding that was impossible before owing to lack of means and that even the passive system of reproduction of the old subjects daily wins recruits for the service of the new humanity. But the system of profit and commerce, of property and human exploitation leads much quicker than increase of population to a rift inside contemporary society that the old society is incapable of healing, because it never heals or creates, only exists and enjoys. The existence of a suffering humanity which thinks and a thinking humanity which is oppressed must of necessity be disagreeable and unacceptable for the animal world of philistines who neither act nor think but merely enjoy.

On our side the old world must be brought right out into the light of day and the new one given a positive form. The longer that events allow thinking humanity time to recollect itself and suffering humanity time to assemble itself the more perfect will be the birth of the product that the present carries in its womb.

III

Kneuznach, September 1843

I am pleased that you have decided to turn your thoughts away from looking back at the past and forward to a new undertaking. In Paris, therefore. The old school of philosophy (*absit omen!*) and the new capital of the new world. What is necessary always happens. So I do not doubt that all obstacles, whose importance I do not underestimate, will be overcome.

The enterprise may or may not come to fruition; in any case I shall be in Paris at the end of this month for the air around here enslaves one and I see no scope at all in Germany for free activity.

In Germany everything is suppressed by force, there is intellectual anarchy, a government of pure stupidity has installed itself and Zurich obeys the orders of Berlin. So it becomes increasingly clear that we must look for a new rallying point for independent minds who can really think. I am convinced that our plan will meet a real need, and real needs must be really satisfied. So I have no reserves concerning the undertaking provided that we are serious about it.

The interior difficulties almost seem to be even greater than the exterior ones. For even though the 'whence' is not in doubt, yet all the more confusion reigns over the 'whither'. It is not only that a general anarchy has burst out among the reformers. Everyone will have to admit to himself that he has no exact view of what should happen. However, that is just the advantage of the new line that we do not anticipate the world dogmatically but wish to discover the new world by criticism of the old. For before, philosophers had the answer to all riddles lying in their desks and the stupid exterior world had only to open its mouth for the roasted pigeons of absolute knowledge to fly into it. Philosophy has become secularized and the most striking proof of this is that the philosophical mind itself is not merely in an exterior way drawn into the painful struggle but also in its inner nature. If our job is not building a future that will last for all ages, what we do have to accomplish now is all the more certain, I mean the reckless critique of all that exists, reckless in the sense that the critique is neither afraid of its own results nor of conflicting with the powers that be.

I am therefore not in favour of raising a dogmatic banner, on the contrary. We must try and help the dogmatists to understand their own principles. Thus communism in particular is a dogmatic abstraction, though by this I do not mean any imaginable and possible communism but the really existing communism, that Cabet, Dezamy, etc. teach. This communism is itself only a peculiar presentation of the humanist principle infected by its opposite private individualism. The abolition of private property and communism are therefore by no means identical, and it is no chance that communism has seen other socialist doctrines like those of Fourier, Proudhon, etc. necessarily arise opposite, since it is itself only a particular one-sided realization of the socialist principle.

And again the whole socialist principle is only one facet of the true reality of the human essence. We have just as much to take into account the other facet, the theoretical existence of man, and make religion, science, etc. the object of our critique. Moreover, we wish to have an effect on our contemporaries, and more particularly on our German contemporaries. The question is how to go about it. Two facts cannot be denied. Religion and politics are the twin subjects in which contemporary Germany is chiefly interested. We must start from these subjects in whatever state they are, and not oppose them with some ready-made system, like, for example, the *Voyage en Icarie*.[1]

The reason has always existed, but not always in a rational form. Thus, the critic can start from any form that man's mind has taken, theoretical or practical, and develop out of the actual forms of existing reality the true reality as what it ought to be, that which is its aim. Now, as regards actual life, the political state, even where it is not yet consciously impregnated with socialist principles, contains in all its modern forms the demands of reason. Nor does it stop there. It presupposes everywhere the realization of reason. But in this way its ideals come into conflict everywhere with its real suppositions.

Thus, the social truth emerges everywhere out of this conflict of the political state with itself. As religion is the table of contents of the theoretical battles of mankind, so is the political state of its practical ones. So inside its republican form the political state expresses all social struggles, needs and truths. We do not, therefore, sacrifice any of our principles when we make the exclusively political questions—for example, the difference between the estates and the representative system—the object of our critique. For this question really expresses in a political manner the difference between the lordship of man and the lordship of private property. Thus, the critic not only can but also must go into these political questions which, in the opinion of the crass socialists, are beneath all value. In that he develops the advantages of a

[1] Etienne Cabet, *Voyage en Icarie*, Paris, 1842. The book was a description of a communist Utopia.

representative system over one of the estates, he interests a large party in a practical manner. In that he raises the representative system from its political form to a universal one and thus gives force to its true and fundamental meaning, he compels this party to go beyond itself, for its victory implies its dissolution.

So there is nothing to stop us from making a critique of politics the starting point of our critique, from taking part in party politics and so identifying ourselves with real battles. We do not then set ourselves opposite the world with a doctrinaire principle, saying: 'Here is the truth, kneel down here!' It is out of the world's own principles that we develop for it new principles. We do not say to her, 'Stop your battles, they are stupid stuff. We want to preach the true slogans of battle at you.' We merely show it what it is actually fighting about, and this realization is a thing that it must make its own even though it may not wish to.

The reform of consciousness consists solely in letting the world perceive its own consciousness by awaking it from dreaming about itself, in explaining to it its own actions. Our whole and only aim consists in putting religious and political questions in a self-conscious, human form, as is also the case in Feuerbach's critique of religion.

So our election cry must be: reform of consciousness not through dogmas, but through the analysis of mystical consciousness that is not clear to itself, whether it appears in a religious or political form. It will then be clear that the world has long possessed the dream of a thing of which it only needs to possess the consciousness in order really to possess it. It will be clear that the problem is not some great gap between the thoughts of the past and those of the future but the completion of thoughts of the past. Finally, it will be clear that humanity is not beginning a new work, but consciously bringing its old work to completion.

So we can summarize the tendency of our journal in one word: self-understanding (equals critical philosophy) by our age of its struggles and wishes. This is a task for the world and for us. It can only be the result of united forces. What is at stake is a confession, nothing more. To get its sins forgiven, humanity only needs to describe them as they are.

Letter to Ludwig Feurbach[1]

Written: 20th October 1843

First published: Ludwig Feuerbach in seinem Briefwechsel und Nachlass, ed. K. Grün, Leipzig–Berlin, 1874, pp. 360–1

Reprinted: MEGA, I i (2), 316–17

Translated: Maximilen Rubel, *La Nef,* June 1948, V, no. 43, pp. 65–6

This letter, written to persuade Feuerbach to contribute to the *Deutsche-Französische Jahrbücher*, indicates the importance that Marx attached to Feuerbach's co-operation.

Kreuznach, 20th October 1843

Dear Sir,

On his journey of a few months ago Dr. Ruge informed you of our plan to produce Franco-German annals and at the same time asked you for your co-operation. The affair is now so far forward that Paris is the place of printing and publication and the first monthly issue is to appear at the end of November.

I seem to be able to gather from your Preface to the second edition of *The Essence of Christianity*, that you are busy with a detailed work on Schelling or, at least have a lot in store concerning this windbag. You see, that would be a wonderful beginning.

How cleverly has Herr Schelling understood how to seduce the French, first the feeble, eclectic Cousin and later even the genius Leroux. For Pierre Leroux and his like, Schelling still counts as the man who replaced transcendental idealism with rational realism, replaced abstract thought with the thought of flesh and blood and departmentalized philosophy with a philosophy of the world! To the French romantics and mystics he calls: 'I am the unity of philosophy and theology', to the French materialists: 'I am the unity of flesh and idea', to the French sceptics: 'I am the destroyer of dogmatism', in a word 'I am Schelling!'

[1] See Introduction, p. xxii.

You would thus render our enterprise, and still more, truth, a great service if right in the first number you could contribute a profile of Schelling. You are just the man for that, for you are the reverse of Schelling. For the realization of the sincere—we ought to believe the best of our adversary—ideas of his youth, Schelling had no means but imagination, no energy but vanity, no drive except opium and no quality except the irritability of a feminine power of sensitivity. But these sincere youthful ideas which, with Schelling, remained an imaginative dream of his youth, have with you become truth, reality and virile earnestness. Schelling is therefore an anticipatory caricature of you, and as soon as the reality appears opposite the caricature it must dissolve into dust or fog. Thus I consider you the necessary and natural opponent of Schelling, summoned by their majesties nature and history. Your struggle with him is the struggle of the imagination of philosophy with philosophy itself. . . .

Yours very sincerely,

Dr. Marx

On the Jewish Question[1]

Written: End of 1843

First published: Deutsch-französische Jahrbücher, February 1844, pp. 182–214

Reprinted: MEGA, I i (1), pp. 576–606, *Frühe Schriften,* pp. 451–87

Translated: Molitor, I, pp. 163–214; Karl Marx, *Early Writings,* ed. T. B. Bottomore, London, 1963, pp. 3–40; Easton and Guddatt, *Writings of the Young Marx,* pp. 216–48

This is a review article of Bruno Bauer's two essays on the Jewish question. It represents the first reasonably extended and coherent picture of Marx's views on the state and society. With its commentary on the constitution of the French Revolution and the American constitution it contains Marx's most accessible critique of the fundamental political principles of classical liberalism. Marx also develops his views on the analogy between religious and political alienation; he considers (speculative) philosophy as an alienation to be rejected on the same footing as religious alienation; finally he advocates the social reduction of all these alienations, religious, philosophical and political, and their absorption by human society.

I

Bruno Bauer, *The Jewish Question,* Brunswick, 1843

The German Jews seek emancipation. What sort of emancipation do they want? Civil, political emancipation. Bruno Bauer answers them: No one in Germany is politically emancipated. We ourselves are not free. How then could we liberate you? You Jews are egoists if you demand a special emancipation for yourselves as Jews. You ought to work as Germans for the political emancipation of Germany, and as men for the emancipation of mankind, and consider your particular sort

---

[1] See further: Introduction, pp. xxv ff., S. Avineri, 'Marx and Jewish Emancipation', *Journal of the History of Ideas,* 1964; J. Gebhardt, 'Karl Marx und Bruno Bauer', in, *Politische Ordnung und Menschliche Existenz,* Munich, 1962.

of oppression and ignominy not as an exception to the rule but rather as a confirmation of it.

Or do the Jews want to be placed on an equal footing with Christian subjects? But in that case they recognize the Christian state as justified, and acquiesce in a regime of general enslavement. Why are they not pleased with their particular yoke when they are pleased with the general yoke? Why should the German interest himself in the emancipation of the Jews if the Jew does not interest himself in the liberation of the German?

The Christian state is only acquainted with privileges. In it the Jew possesses the privilege of being a Jew. As a Jew, he has rights that the Christian does not have. Why does he wish for rights that Christians enjoy and he does not have?

The wish of the Jew to be emancipated from the Christian state entails a demand that the Christian state should give up its religious prejudice. But does the Jew give up his own religious prejudice? Does he then have the right to demand of another that he foreswear his religion? It is the very nature of the Christian state that prevents it from emancipating the Jew; but, adds Bauer, it is also the nature of the Jew that prevents his being emancipated. As long as the state is Christian and the Jew Jewish, the one is as incapable of bestowing emancipation as the other is incapable of receiving it.

The Christian state can only have its typical, i.e. privileged relationship to the Jew by permitting the separation of the Jew from the other subjects, but at the same time subjecting him to a pressure from the other separated spheres that is all the heavier since the Jew stands in religious opposition to the dominant religion. But likewise the Jew can only have a Jewish relationship to the state and treat it as alien to himself, for he opposes his own imaginary nationality to actual nationality, and his own imaginary law to actual law, fancies himself justified in separating himself from humanity, as a matter of principle takes no part in the movement of history and waits on a destiny that has nothing in common with the destiny of mankind as a whole. He considers himself a member of the Jewish people and the Jewish people as the chosen people.

On what grounds then do you Jews seek emancipation? On account of your religion? But it is the mortal enemy of the state religion. As citizens? There are no citizens in Germany. As men? You are not men any more than those to whom you appeal.

After a critical review of the way the question of Jewish emancipation was previously formulated and solved, Bauer frames the question in a new way. How, he asks, are they constituted, the Jew who is to be emancipated and the Christian state which is to do the emancipating? His answer consists in a critique of the Jewish religion, he analyses the religious opposition between Judaism and Christianity and explains the nature of the Christian state in a way that is bold, acute, witty and thorough, and in a style as precise as it is pithy and energetic.

What, then, is Bauer's solution to the Jewish question and what is the result? To formulate a question is already to solve it. The critique of the Jewish question is the answer to it. Here is a resumé:

We must emancipate ourselves before we can emancipate others.

The most flexible form of the opposition between Christian and Jew is the religious opposition. How is an opposition to be done away with? By making it impossible. How does one make a religious opposition impossible? By abolishing religion. As soon as Jew and Christian recognize their opposed religions as merely different stages in the development of the human spirit, as different snake skins that history has cast off and recognize man as the snake that used the skins for covering, then they will no longer be in religious opposition but only in a critical, scientific, human opposition. Science is thus their unity, and contradictions in science are solved by science itself.

The German Jew in particular suffers from the general lack of political emancipation and the pronounced Christianity of the state. In Bauer's opinion, however, the Jewish question has a general significance that is independent of specifically German circumstances. It is the question of the relationship of religion to the state, of the opposition between religious prejudice and political emancipation. Emancipation from religion is laid down as a precondition both for the Jew who desires to be politically emancipated and for the emancipating state which itself needs emancipation.

'Fine, people say (the Jew himself included), the Jew is not to be emancipated as a Jew, because he is a Jew, because he has universal human moral principles that are so outstanding; rather his Jewishness will take second place to his citizenship and he will be a citizen in spite of his being and remaining a Jew. In other words he is and remains a Jew in spite of his being a citizen and living in a condition similar to other men. For his narrow Jewish nature always in the end triumphs over his human and political obligations. The prejudice remains even though it is overcome by universal principles. But if it does remain then it would be more correct to say that it is the prejudice that overcomes everything else.

'The Jew would only be able to remain a Jew in the life of the state in a sophistical sense, that is, in appearance only; so if he wished to remain a Jew, the appearance would become what was essential and gain the upper hand. This means that his life in the state would become only an appearance or a momentary exception to the rule governing the real nature of things' ('The Capability of Present-day Jews and Christians for Liberation', *Twenty-One Sheets*, p. 57).

Let us listen, on the other hand, to how Bauer formulates the task of the state: 'France' it runs 'has recently (Debate of the Chamber of Deputies for the 26th December 1840) given us apropos of the Jewish question a glimpse of a free life, as she does continually in all other political questions since the July Revolution. But she has revoked her freedom by law, thus declaring it to be a sham and on the other hand she has contradicted her free law by her actions' (*The Jewish Question*, p. 64).

'Universal freedom has not yet been established by law in France and the Jewish question still not solved because legal freedom, which consists in the equality of all citizens, is limited in practice since life is still dominated and divided by religious privileges and this lack of freedom reacts on the law and forces it to agree to the division of citzens who are in principle free, into oppressors and oppressed' (p. 65).

When, therefore, would the Jewish question in France be solved?

'The Jew, for example, would have had to cease being a Jew if he were to refuse to let his law stop him from fulfilling his duties to the state and his fellow citizens, for example, going to the Chamber of Deputies on the Sabbath and taking part in public debates. Any religious privilege at all, including, therefore, the monopoly of a privileged church, must be abolished and if some or many or even the overwhelming majority still believe themselves bound to fulfil their religious duties, then this must be allowed them as a purely private affair' (p. 65). 'Religion no longer exists when there is no longer a privileged religion. Take from religion its power of exclusion and it ceases to exist' (p. 66). 'Herr Martin du Nord was of the opinion that the proposal to omit the mention of Sunday in the law was equivalent to a motion declaring that Christianity had ceased to exist: a declaration that the abolition of the Sabbath law for the Jews would be equivalent to a proclamation of the dissolution of Judaism would be just as perfectly justified' (p. 71).

So Bauer requires on the one hand that the Jew give up Judaism and man in general give up religion in order to achieve civil emancipation. On the other hand it follows that for him the political abolition of religion is the equivalent of the abolition of all religion. The state that presupposes religion is not yet a true and real state. 'Of course religious ideas afford the state guarantees. But what state? What sort of state?' (p. 97).

It is here that Bauer's one-sided approach to the Jewish question appears.

It is in no way sufficient to enquire: Who should emancipate? Who should be emancipated? A proper critique would have a third question—*what sort of emancipation* is under discussion? What preconditions are essential for the required emancipation? It is only the critique of political emancipation itself that would be the final critique of the Jewish question and its true resolution into 'the general problems of the age'.

Bauer falls into contradictions because he does not formulate the question at this level. He poses conditions that are not grounded in the nature of political emancipation itself. He raises questions not contained within the problem and solves problems that leave his questions unanswered. Bauer says of the opponents of Jewish emancipation: 'Their one fault was that they presupposed the Christian state as the only true one and did not subject it to the same critique to which they subjected Judaism' (p. 3). Here Bauer's fault lies in the fact that he subjects only the Christian state to his critique, not 'the state as such'. That he does not investigate the relationship of political to human emancipation and thus poses conditions that are only explicable by supposing an uncritical confusion of political emancipation and universal human emancipation. Bauer asks the Jews: Does your standpoint give you the right to seek political emancipation? But we ask the reverse question: Has the standpoint of political emancipation the right to require from the Jews the abolition of Judaism and from all men the abolition of religion?

The Jewish question always presents itself differently according to the state in which the Jew lives. In Germany, where there is no political state, no state as such, the Jewish question is a purely theological one. The Jew finds himself in religious opposition to the state which recognizes Christianity as its foundation. This state is a professed theologian. Criticism is here criticism of theology, a two-sided criticism of Christian and of Jewish theology. But we are still always moving inside theology however critically we may be moving.

In France, which is a constitutional state, the Jewish question is a question of constitutionalism, a question of the incompleteness of political emancipation. Since here the appearance of a state religion is retained although in an empty and self-contradictory formula, namely that of the religion of the majority, the relationship of the Jew to the state contains the appearance of a religious or theological opposition.

It is in the North American states—or at least a part of them—that the Jewish question loses its theological importance for the first time and becomes a really *secular* question. It is only where the political state exists in its complete perfection that the relationship of the Jew and of the religious man in general to the political state, and thus the relationship of religion to the state, can stand out in all its peculiarities and purity. The criticism of this relationship ceases to be a theological criticism as soon as the state ceases to have a theological attitude to religion, as soon as it adopts the attitude of a state towards religion, i.e. a political attitude. Criticism then becomes a criticism of the political state. At this point, where criticism ceases to be theological, Bauer's criticism ceases to be critical. 'There is in America neither state religion nor a religion declared to be that of the majority, nor pre-eminence of any one way of worship over another. The state is stranger to all forms of worship' (G. de Beaumont, *Mary or Slavery in the U.S. . . .*, Paris, 1835, p. 214).[1] There are even some North American states where 'the constitution does not impose religious belief and practice as a condition of political rights' (loc. cit., p. 225). And yet 'people in the U.S. do not

[1] English translation (abridged): Barbara Chapman, Stanford, 1958.

believe that a man without religion can be an honest man' (loc. cit., p. 224). Yet North America is the land of religiosity *par excellence* as Beaumont, Tocqueville and the Englishman Hamilton[1] all aver with one voice. But the North American states are serving here only as an example. The question is: what is the relationship of complete political emancipation to religion? The fact that even in the land of completed political emancipation we find not only the existence of religion but a living existence full of freshness and strength, furnishes us with the proof that the existence of religion does not contradict or impede the perfection of the state. But since the existence of religion is the existence of a defect, the source of this defect can only be sought in the nature of the state itself. Religion for us no longer has the force of a basis for secular deficiencies but only that of a phenomenon. Therefore we explain the religious prejudice of free citizens by their secular prejudice. We do not insist that they must abolish their religious limitation in order to abolish secular limitations. We insist that they abolish their religious limitations as soon as they abolish their secular limitations. We do not change secular questions into theological ones. We change theological questions into secular ones. History has for long enough been resolved into superstition: we now resolve superstition into history. The question of the relationship of political emancipation to religion becomes for us a question of the relationship of political emancipation to human emancipation. We criticize the religious weakness of the political state by criticizing the secular construction of the political state without regard to its religious weaknesses. We humanize the opposition of the state to a particular religion, Judaism for example, into the opposition of the state to particular secular elements, and the opposition of the state to religion in general into the opposition of the state to its own presuppositions in general.

The political emancipation of the Jew, the Christian and religious man in general, implies the emancipation of the state from Judaism, Christianity and religion in general. The state as state emancipates itself from religion in the manner peculiar to its own nature by emancipating itself from the state religion, i.e. by not recognizing, as a state, any religion, by affirming itself simply as a state. Political emancipation is not the completed and consistent form of religious emancipation

[1] Thomas Hamilton, *Men and Manners in North America*, Edinburgh, 1833.

because political emancipation is not the completed and consistent form of human emancipation.

The limitations of political emancipation are immediately evident in the fact that a state can liberate itself from a limitation without man himself being truly free of it and the state can be a free state without man himself being a free man. Bauer himself tacitly admits this when he poses the following condition for political emancipation: 'Every single religious privilege, including the monopoly of a privileged church, must be abolished. If several or more or even the overwhelming majority of people still felt obliged to fulfil their religious duties, this practice should be left to them as a completely private matter.' Therefore the state can have emancipated itself from religion, even when the overwhelming majority of people is still religious. And the overwhelming majority does not cease to be religious simply because its religion is private.

But the attitude of the state, especially the free state, to religion is merely the attitude of the men who make up the state to religion. It follows from this that man liberates himself from an impediment through the medium of the state and politically by entering into opposition with himself and getting round this impediment in an abstract, limited and partial manner. It follows also that when man liberates himself politically, he liberates himself by means of a detour, through the medium of something else, however necessary that medium may be. It follows finally that man, even when he proclaims himself an atheist through the intermediary of the state, i.e. when he proclaims the state to be atheist, still retains his religious prejudice, just because he recognizes himself only by a detour and by the medium of something else. Religion is precisely the recognition of man by detour through an intermediary. The state is the intermediary between man and his freedom. As Christ is the intermediary onto whom man unburdens all his divinity, all his religious bonds, so the state is the mediator onto which he transfers all his Godlessness and all his human liberty.

The political elevation of man above religion shares all the deficiencies and all the advantages of political elevation in general. The state as state annuls private property for example as soon as man declares in a political manner that private property is abolished, as soon as he abolishes the requirement of a property qualification for active and passive participation at elections, as has happened in many North American states. Hamilton interprets this fact from the political standpoint quite correctly: 'the masses have thus gained a victory over the property owners and monied classes'. Is private property not abolished ideally speaking when the non-owner has become the law giver for the owner? The census is the last political form of recognizing private property.

And yet the political annulment of private property has not only not abolished private property, it actually presupposes it. The state does away with difference in birth, class, education and profession in its own manner when it declares birth, class, education and profession to be unpolitical differences, when it summons every member of the people to an equal participation in popular sovereignty without taking the differences into consideration, when it treats all elements of the people's real life from the point of view of the state. Nevertheless the state still allows private property, education and profession to have an effect in their own manner, that is as private property, as education, as profession, and make their particular natures felt. Far from abolishing these factual differences, its existence rests on them as a presupposition, it only feels itself to be a political state and asserts its universality by opposition to these elements. Therefore Hegel defines the relationship of the political state to religion quite rightly when he says: 'In order for the state to come into existence as the self-knowing ethical actuality of spirit, it is essential that it should be distinct from the form of authority and of faith. But this distinction emerges only in so far as divisions occur within the ecclesiastical sphere itself. It is only in this way that the state, above the particular churches, has attained to the universality of thought—its formal principle—and is bringing this universality into existence.'[1] Of course! only thus does the state build its universality over and above its particular elements.

The perfected political state is by its nature the species-life of man in opposition to his material life. All the presupposition of this egoistic life continue to exist in civil society outside the sphere of the state, but as proper to civil society. When the political state has achieved its true completion, man leads a double life, a heavenly one and an earthly one,

[1] See Hegel, *Principles of the Philosophy of Right*, trans. T. M. Knox, Oxford 1942, p. 173.

not only in thought and consciousness but in reality, in life. He has a life both in the political community, where he is valued as a communal being, and in civil society where he is active as a private individual, treats other men as means, degrades himself to a means and becomes the plaything of alien powers. The political state has just as spiritual an attitude to civil society as heaven has to earth. It stands in the same opposition to civil society and overcomes it in the same manner as religion overcomes the limitations of the profane world, that is, it must likewise recognize it, reinstate it and let itself once more be dominated by it. Man in the reality that is nearest to him, civil society, is a profane being. Here where he counts for himself and others as a real individual, he is an illusory phenomenon. In the state, on the other hand, where man counts as a species-being, he is an imaginary participant in an imaginary sovereignty, he is robbed of his real life and filled with an unreal universality.

The conflict with his citizenship and with other men as members of the community in which man as an adherent of a particular religion finds himself can be reduced to the secular division between political state and civil society. For man as a bourgeois[1] 'life in the state is only an apparent and momentary exception to the essential rule'. Of course the bourgeois, like the Jew, only remains in the life of the state sophistically speaking, just as the citizen only sophistically remains a Jew or bourgeois; but this sophism is not a personal matter. It is a sophism of the political state itself. The difference between the religious man and the citizen is the difference between the trader and the citizen, between the labourer and the citizen, between the property owner and the citizen, between the living individual and the citizen. The opposition to the political man in which the religious man finds himself is the same opposition in which the bourgeois finds himself to the citizen and the member of civil society to his political lion's skin.

This secular strife to which the Jewish question can in the last analysis be reduced—the relationship of the political state to its presuppositions, whether these be material elements like private property or intellectual like education, religion, the conflict between general and private interests, the rift between the political state and the civil society—these

---

[1] In this passage Marx uses 'bourgeois' to mean a member of civil society, and 'citizen' to mean an individual with political rights.

secular oppositions are left intact by Bauer while he polemicizes against their religious expressions. 'It is precisely the same need which is the basis of civil society, ensures its continued existence and guarantees its necessity that also exposes its existence to perpetual dangers, sustains an unsure element within it, produces the continuing oscillating mixture of wealth and poverty, need and superfluity, and in general creates change' (p. 8).

Compare the whole section entitled 'Civil Society' (pp. 8–9), which is drafted from the main points of Hegel's philosophy of right. Civil society in its opposition to the political state is recognized as necessary because the political state is recognized as necessary.

Political emancipation is of course a great progress. Although it is not the final form of human emancipation in general, it is nevertheless the final form of human emancipation inside the present world order. It is to be understood that I am speaking here of real, practical emancipation.

Man emancipates himself politically from religion by banishing it from the field of public law and making it a private right. Religion is no longer the spirit of the state where man behaves, as a species-being in community with other men albeit in a limited manner and in a particular form and a particular sphere: religion has become the spirit of civil society, the sphere of egoism, the *bellum omnium contra omnes*. Its essence is no longer in community but in difference. It has become the expression of separation of man from his common essence, from himself and from other men, as it was originally. It is still only the abstract recognition of a particular perversion, private whim and arbitrariness. For example, the infinite splintering of religion in North America already gives it the exterior form of a purely individual affair. It is shoved away into the crowd of private interests and exiled from the common essence as such. But we should not be deceived about the limitations of political emancipation. The separation of man into a public and a private man, the displacement of religion from the state to civil society is not a stage but the completion of political emancipation, which thus does not abolish or even try to abolish the actual religiosity of man.

The decomposition of man into Jew and citizen, protestant and citizen, religious man and citizen, this decomposition is no trick played upon political citizenship, no avoidance of political emancipation. It is political emancipation itself, the political manner of emancipating oneself from religion. Of course, in times when the political state is born violently as such out of civil society, when man's self-liberation tries to complete itself in the form of political self-liberation, the state must go as far as abolishing, destroying religion, but only in the same way as it goes as far as abolishing private property, at the most, by declaring a maximum, by confiscation or a progressive tax, or in the same way as it abolishes life, by the guillotine. In moments of particular self-cons-ciousness political life tries to suppress its presuppositions, civil society and its elements, and to constitute itself as the real, harmonious life of man. However, this is only possible through violent opposition to its own conditions, by declaring the revolution to be permanent. The political drama therefore ends necessarily with the restoration of reli-gion, private property and all the elements of civil society, just as war ends with peace.

Indeed, it is not the so-called Christian state, the one that recognizes Christianity as its basis, as the state religion and thus adopts an exclusive attitude to other religions, that is the perfected Christian state, but rather the atheist state, the democratic state, the state that downgrades religion to the other elements of civil society. If the state is still a theologian, makes an official confession of the Christian faith and does not yet dare to declare itself a state, then it has not yet succeeded in expressing its human basis, of which Christianity in the transcendental expression, in a secular, human form, in its reality as a state. The so-called Christian state is quite simply the non-state because it is only the human background of Christianity and not Christianity itself that can be translated into real human achievements.

The so-called Christian state is the Christian negation of the state, but in no way the state realization of Christianity. The state that still recognizes Christianity in the form of a religion, does not yet recognize it in a political form because it still has a religious attitude to religion, that is, it is not the real elaboration of the human basis of religion because it still accepts the unreal, the imaginary form of this human kernel. The so-called Christian state is the imperfect state and the Christian religion serves as a supplement and a sanctification of its imperfection. Religion therefore necessarily becomes a means for the state, and the state is one of hypocrisy. There is a great difference between the perfect state counting religion as one of its presuppositions because of the deficiencies in the general essence of the state, and the imperfect state declaring religion to be its foundation because the deficiences in its particular existence make it a deficient state. In the latter case religion becomes imperfect politics. In the former the imperfection of even a perfect politics shows itself in religion. The so-called Christian state needs the Christian religion in order to complete itself as a state. The democratic state, the true state, does not need religion for its political completion. Rather it can abstract from religion, because it realizes the human foundations of religion in a secular manner. The so-called Christian state, on the other hand, has a political attitude towards religion and a religious attitude towards politics. When it degrades the forms of the state to an appearance, then it degrades religion just as surely to an appearance.

In order to explain this opposition, we shall examine Bauer's model the Christian state, a model that derives from a study of the Christian Germanic state.

'In order to prove', says Bauer, 'the impossiblity or non-existence of a Christian State, people have often recently pointed to the sayings in the Gospel which the present state does not only not follow, but cannot even begin to follow if it does not wish to bring about its complete dissolution as a state'. 'But the matter is not dealt with so easily. What do those sayings in the Gospel demand? Supernatural self-denial, subjection to the authority of revelation, disregard of the state, abolition of secular relationships. But the Christian state demands and performs all this. It has made the spirit of the Gospel its own, and if it does not repeat it in the same words that the Gospel uses, that is only because it expresses this spirit in political forms, that is, in forms that are certainly borrowed from the nature of the state and this world but which, in the religious rebirth that they must experience, are degraded to an appearance. Its disregard of the state is realized and completed through the political institutions' (p. 55).

Bauer now further develops the theme of how the people in a Christian state are merely non-people, have no more will of their own and have their true existence in their leader to whom they are subject and who is nevertheless alien to them in origin and nature since he is

God-given and arrived at without their own co-operation; Bauer also explains how the laws of this people are not their own work but direct revelations; how the supreme leader needs privileged intermediaries with his own people and the masses; how the masses themselves disintegrate into a number of particular groups formed and defined by chance which differentiate themselves through their interests, particular passions and prejudices, and obtain as a privilege the permission mutually to exclude each other, etc. (p. 56).

But Bauer himself says: 'Politics, if it is to be nothing but religion, cannot be politics; any more than dishwashing, if it has the force of a religious practice, should be treated as a household matter' (p. 108). In the Christian Germanic state however religion is a 'household matter' just as 'household matters' are religious. In the Christian Germanic state the dominance of religion is the religion of dominance.

The separation of the 'spirit of the Gospel' from the 'letter of the Gospel' is an irreligious act. The state which lets the Gospel speak political words, in words different from the Holy Spirit, commits sacrilege in its own religious eyes if not in the eyes of men. The state that recognizes Christianity as its highest norm and the Bible as its Magna Carta must be met with the words of the Holy Scripture for every word of Scripture is holy. Both this state and the dregs of humanity on which it is based arrive at a painful contradiction that is insurmountable from the point of view of religious consciousness, if it has pointed out to it those sayings of the Gospel with which it 'does not conform and cannot conform unless it wishes to dissolve itself entirely'. And why does it not wish to dissolve itself entirely? It can give neither itself nor others an answer to this question. In its own consciousness the Christian state is an ideal whose realization is unattainable. It can only convince itself of its own existence by lies and so remains for ever an object of self-doubt, an insufficient, problematic object. Thus criticism is fully justified when it forces the state that appeals to the Bible into a crazed state of mind where it no longer knows whether it is an imagination or a reality, where the infamy of its worldy ends for which religion serves as a cloak arrives at an insoluble conflict with the honesty of its religious consciousness which views the final aim of the world as religion. This state can only pacify its inner uneasiness by becoming a myrmidon of the Catholic Church. In face of the Catholic Church, which declares secular powers to be its bondsmen, the state is as powerless as is the secular power which affirms itself to be dominant over the religious spirit.

In the so-called Christian state it is alienation that is important, not man himself. The man who is important, the king, is a being specifically differentiated from other men (which is itself a religious conception) who is in direct contact with heaven and God. The relationships that hold sway here are ones of faith. The religious spirit is thus not yet really secularized.

But the religious spirit can never really be secularized. For what is it but the unsecular form of a stage in the development of the human spirit? The religious spirit can only be secularized in so far as the stage in the development of the human spirit whose religious expression it is, emerges and constitutes itself in its secular form. This happens in the democratic state. The foundation of this state is not Christianity but the human foundation of Christianity. Religion remains as the ideal, unsecular consciousness of its members, because it is the ideal form of the stage of human development that is realized in this state.

What makes the members of the political state religious is the dualism between their individual and their species-life, between life in civil society and political life, their belief that life in the state is the true life even though it leaves untouched their individuality. Religion is here the spirit of civil society, the expression of separation and distance of man from man. What makes a political democracy Christian is the fact that in it man, not only a single man but every man, counts as a sovereign being; but it is man as he appears uncultivated and unsocial, man in his accidental existence, man as he comes and goes, man as he is corrupted by the whole organization of our society, lost to himself, sold, given over to the domination of inhuman conditions and elements—in a word, man who is no longer a real species-being. The fantasy, dream and postulate of Christianity, the sovereignty of man, but of man as an alien being separate from actual man, is present in democracy as a tangible reality and is its secular motto.

The religious and theological consciousness has all the more religious and theological force in the complete democracy as it is without political significance and earthly aims. It is the affair of minds that are shy of the world, the expression of a limited understanding, the product of arbitrariness and fantasy, a really other-worldly life. Christianity achieves here the practical expression of its significance of a universal religion in that it groups together the most different opinions in the form of Christianity and even more because it does not lay on others the requirements of Christianity, but only a religion in general, any religion (compare the above mentioned work of Beaumont). The religious consciousness revels in richness of religious opposition and religious diversity.

Thus we have shown that political emancipation from religion leaves religion intact even though it is no longer a privileged religion. The contradiction with his citizenship in which the adherent of a particular religion finds himself is only a part of the general secular contradiction between the political state and civil society. The perfect Christian state is the one that recognizes itself as a state and abstracts from the religion of its members. The emancipation of the state from religion is not the emancipation of actual man from religion.

So we do not say to the Jews, as Bauer does: you cannot be emancipated politically without emancipating yourselves radically from Judaism. Rather we say to them: because you can be politically emancipated without completely and consistently abandoning Judaism, this means that political emancipation itself is not human emancipation. If you Jews wish to achieve political emancipation without achieving human emancipation, then the incompleteness and contradiction does not only lie in you, it lies in the nature and category of political emancipation. If you are imprisoned within this category, then you are sharing in something common to everyone. Just as the state is evangelizing when it, although a state, has a Christian attitude to Jews, so the Jew is acting politically when he, although a Jew, requests civil rights.

But if a man, although a Jew, can be politically emancipated and acquire civil rights, can he claim and accept human rights? Bauer denies it.

The question is whether the Jew as such, i.e. the Jew who himself admits that his true nature compels him to live in eternal separation from others, is capable of accepting universal human rights and bestowing them on others.

The concept of human rights was first discovered by the Christian world in the previous century. It is not innate in man, but won in a struggle against the historical traditions in which man has hitherto been educated. Thus human rights are not a gift of nature, no dowry but the prize of the struggle against the accident of birth and against privileges that history transmitted from generation to generation up to the present time. They are the result of culture and only to be possessed by the man who has won and merited them.

Can the Jew really take possession of them? As long as he is a Jew the limited nature which makes him a Jew must gain the upper hand over the human nature that should bind him as a man to other men and must separate him off from non-Jews. He declares through this separation that the particular nature that makes him a Jew is his true and highest nature, before which his human nature must give way.

In the same way, the Christian as Christian cannot grant human rights (pp. 19, 20).

According to Bauer man must sacrifice the 'privilege of belief' in order to be able to receive general human rights. Let us discuss for a moment the so-called human rights, human rights in their authentic form, the form they have in the writings of their discoverers, the North Americans and French! These human rights are partly political rights that are only exercised in community with other men. Their content is formed by participation in the common essence, the political essence, the essence of the state. They fall under the category of political freedom, under the category of civil rights, which, as we have seen, in no way presuppose the consistent and positive abolition of religion, nor, consequently, of Judaism. It remains to discuss the other part of human rights, the rights of man, in so far as they differ from the rights of the citizen.

Among them are freedom of conscience, the right to exercise a chosen religion. The privilege of belief is expressly recognized either as a human right, or as a consequence of one of the human rights, freedom.

Declaration of the Rights of Man and of the Citizen, 1791, Article 10: 'No one should be molested because of his opinions, not even religious ones'. In the first section of the constitution of 1791 'the liberty of every man to practice the religion to which he adheres' is guaranteed as human right. *The Declaration of the Rights of Man . . . 1793* counts among human rights, in Article 7: 'the free exercise of religious practice'. Indeed, concerning the right to publish one's thoughts and opinions, to hold assemblies and practice one's religion, it goes as far

K

as to say: 'the necessity of announcing these rights supposes either the present or the recent memory of despotism'. Compare the constitution of 1795, Section 14, Article 354.

Constitution of Pennsylvania, Article 9, Paragraph 3: 'All men have a natural and indefeasible right to worship Almighty God according to the dictates of their own consciences: no man can of right be compelled to attend, erect or support a place of worship, or to maintain any ministry, against his consent; no human authority can, in any case whatever, control or interfere with the rights of conscience.'

Constitution of New Hampshire, Articles 5 & 6: 'Among the natural rights, some are in their very nature unalienable. . . . Of this kind are rights of conscience' (Beaumont loc. cit., pp. 213, 214).

The incompatibility of religion with the rights of man is so far from being evident in the concept of the rights of man, that the right to be religious, to be religious in one's own chosen way, to practice one's chosen religion is expressly counted as one of the rights of man. The privilege of faith is a universal right of man.

The rights of man are as such differentiated from the right of the citizen. Who is the 'man' who is different from the 'citizen?' No one but the member of civil society. Why is the member of civil society called 'man', simply man, and why are his rights called the rights of man? How do we explain this fact? From the relationship of the political state to civil society, from the nature of political emancipation.

Above all we notice the fact that the so called rights of man, the rights of man as different from the rights of the citizen are nothing but the rights of the member of civil society, i.e. egoistic man, man separated from other men and the community. The most radical constitution, the constitution of 1793, can say:

Declaration of the Rights of Man . . . , Article 2. These rights etc. (natural and imprescriptable rights) are: equality, liberty, security, property.

What does liberty consist of?

Article 6: 'Liberty is the power that belongs to man to do anything that does not infringe on the right of someone else' or according to the declaration of the rights of man of 1791 'liberty consists in the power of doing anything that does not harm others'.

Thus freedom is the right to do and perform what does not harm others. The limits within which each person can move without harming others is defined by the law, just as the boundary between two fields is defined by the fence. The freedom in question is that of a man treated as an isolated monad and withdrawn into himself. Why is the Jew, according to Bauer, incapable of receiving the rights of man? 'So long as he is a Jew the limited nature that makes him a Jew will get the upper hand over the human nature that should unite him as a man to other men and will separate him from the non-Jew.' But the right of man to freedom is not based on the union of man with man, but on the separation of man from man. It is the right to this separation, the rights of the limited individual who is limited to himself.

The practical application of the rights of man to freedom is the right of man to private property.

What does the right of man to property consist in?

Article 16 (Constitution of 1793): 'The right of property is the right which belongs to all citizens to enjoy and dispose at will of their goods and revenues, the fruit of their work and industry.'

Thus the right of man to property is the right to enjoy his possessions and dispose of the same arbitrarily, without regard for other men, independently from society, the right of selfishness. It is the former individual freedom together with its latter application that forms the basis of civil society. It leads man to see in other men not the realization but the limitation of his own freedom. Above all it proclaims the right of man 'to enjoy and dispose at will of his goods, his revenues and fruits of his work and industry'.

There still remain the other rights of man, equality and security.

Equality, here in its non-political sense, is simply the counterpart of the liberty described above, namely that each man shall without discrimination be treated as a self-sufficient monad. The constitution of 1795 defines the concept of this equality, in conformity with this meaning, thus:

Article 3 (Constitution of 1795): 'Equality consists of the fact that the law is the same for all, whether it protects or punishes.'

And security?

Article 8 (Constitution of 1793): 'Security consists in the protection afforded by society to each of its members for the conservation of his person, rights and property.'

Security is the highest social concept of civil society, the concept of the police. The whole of society is merely there to guarantee to each of its members the preservation of his person, rights and property. It is in this sense that Hegel calls civil society the 'state of need and of reason'.

The concept of security does not allow civil society to raise itself above its egoism. Security is more the assurance of egoism.

Thus none of the so-called rights of man goes beyond egoistic man, man as he is in civil society, namely an individual withdrawn behind his private interests and whims and separated from the community. Far from the rights of man conceiving of man as a species-being, species-life itself, society, appears as a framework exterior to individuals, a limitation of their original self-sufficiency. The only bond that holds them together is natural necessity, need and private interest, the conservation of their property and egoistic person.

It is already paradoxical that a people that is just beginning to free itself, to tear down all barriers between different sections of the people and form a political community, should solemnly proclaim (Declaration of 1791) the justification of egoistic man separated from his fellow men and the community. Indeed, this proclamation is repeated at a moment when only the most heroic devotion can save the nation, and is therefore peremptorily demanded, at a moment when the sacrifice of all the interests of civil society is raised to the order of the day and egoism must be punished as a crime (*Declaration of the Rights of Man . . . 1793*). This fact appears to be even more paradoxical when we see that citizenship, the political community, is degraded by the political emancipators to a mere means for the preservation of these so-called rights of man, that the citizen is declared to be the servant of egoistic man, the sphere in which man behaves as a communal being is degraded below the sphere in which man behaves as a partial being, finally that it is not man as a citizen but man as a bourgeois who is called the real and true man.

'The aim of every political association is the conversation of the natural and imprescriptible rights of man' (*Declaration of the Rights of Man . . . 1791*, Article 2). 'Government is instituted to guarantee man the enjoyment of his natural and imprescriptible rights' (*Declaration of the Rights of Man . . . 1791*, Article 1). So even in the moments of youthful freshness and enthusiasm raised to fever pitch by the pressure of circumstances, political life is declared to be a mere means whose end is the life of civil society. It is true that its revolutionary practice is in flagrant contradiction with its theory. While, for example, security is declared to be a right of man the violation of the privacy of correspondence is publicly inserted in the order of the day. While the 'unlimited freedom of the press' (Constitution of 1793, Article 122) is guaranteed as a consequence of the right of man to individual freedom, the freedom of the press is completely destroyed, for 'the liberty of the press must not be permitted when it compromises public liberty' ('The Young Robespierre' in Buchez and Roux, *Parliamentary History of the French Revolution*, vol. 28, p. 159). This means then that the right of man to freedom ceases to be a right as soon as it enters into conflict with political life, whereas, according to the theory, political life is only the guarantee of the rights of man, the rights of individual man, and so must be given up as soon as it contradicts its end, these rights of man. But the practice is only the exception and the theory is the rule. Even though one were to treat the revolutionary practice as the correct version of the relationship, the riddle still remains to be solved of why, in the minds of the political emancipators, the relationship is turned upside down and the end appears as the means and the means as the end. This optical illusion of their minds would always be the same riddle, although it would then be a psychological and theoretical riddle.

The riddle has a simple solution.

Political emancipation is at the same time the dissolution of the old society on which rests the sovereign power, the essence of the state alienated from the people. Political revolution is the revolution of civil society. What was the character of the old society? One word characterizes it. Feudalism. The old civil society had a directly political character. The elements of civil life, like, for example, property or the family or the type and manner of work, were, in the form of seignorial right, estates and corporations, raised to the level of elements of state life. They defined in this form the relationship of the single individual to the state as a whole, that is, his political relationship, the relationship of separation and exclusion from the other parts of society. For this sort of organization of the people's life did not turn property or work into social elements but completed their separation from the state as a whole, and made them into particular societies within society. But the vital functions and conditions of life in civil society was still political even though political in the feudal sense, that is, they excluded the individual from the states as a whole. They turned the particular relationship of the corporation to the totality of the state, into his own general relationship to the life of the people, as it turned his particular civil occupation into his general occupation and situation. As a consequence of this organization the unity of the state—the mind, will and authority of this state unity, the power of the state in general—equally appears necessarily as the particular affair of a lord and servants who are cut off from the people.

The political revolution overthrew this feudal power and turned state affairs into affairs of the people; it turned the state into a matter of general concern, i.e. into a true state; it necessarily destroyed all estates, corporations, guilds, privileges which were so many expressions of the separation of the people from the community. The political revolution thus abolished the political character of civil society. It shattered civil society with its simple parts, on the one hand into individuals, on the other hand into the material and spiritual elements that make up the life experience and civil position of these individuals. It unfettered the political spirit that had, as it were, been split, cut up and drained away into the various cul-de-sacs of feudal society. The political revolution collected this spirit together after its dispersion, freed it from its confusion with civil life and set it up as the sphere that was common to all, the general affair of the people in ideal independence from the other particular elements of civil life. Particular professions and ranks sank to a merely individual importance. They were no longer the relationship of individuals to the state as a whole. Public affairs as such became the general affair of each individual and politics was a general occupation.

But the perfection of the idealism of the state was at the same time the perfection of the materialism of civil society. The shaking off of the political yoke entailed the shaking off of those bonds that had kept the egoistic spirit of civil society fettered. Political emancipation entailed the emancipation of civil society from politics, from even the appearance of a general content.

Feudal society was dissolved into its basis, into man. But into the man that was its true basis, egoistic man. This man, the member of civil society, is the basis, the presupposition of the political state. He is recognized by it as such in the rights of man.

But the freedom of egoistic man and the recognition of this freedom is the recognition of the unimpeded movement of the spiritual and material elements that go to make up its life.

Man was therefore not freed from religion; he received freedom of religion. He was not freed from property; he received freedom of property. He was not freed from the egoism of trade; he received freedom to trade.

The formation of the political state and the dissolution of civil society into independent individuals, who are related by law just as the estate and corporation men were related by privilege, is completed in one and the same act. Man as member of civil society, unpolitical man, appears necessarily as natural man. The rights of man appear as natural rights, because self-conscious activity is concentrated upon political action. Egoistic man is the passive, given result of the dissolved society, an object of immediate certainty and thus a natural object. Political revolution dissolves civil life into its component parts, without revolutionizing and submitting to criticism these parts themselves. Its attitude to civil society, to the world of need, to work, private interests, private law is that they are the foundation of its existence, its own presupposition that needs no further proof, and thus its natural basis. Finally, man as a member of civil society counts for true man, for man as distinct from the citizen, because he is man in his sensuous, individual, immediate existence, while political man is only the abstract fictional man, man as an allegorical or moral person. This man as he actually is, is only recognized in the form of the egoistic individual, and the true man only in the form of the abstract citizen.

The abstraction of the political man is thus correctly described by Rousseau: 'He who dares to undertake the making of a people's institutions ought to feel himself capable, so to speak, of changing human nature, of transforming each individual, who is by himself a complete and solitary whole, into part of a greater whole from which he in a manner receives his life and being; of altering man's constitution for the purpose of strengthening it; and of substituting a partial and moral existence for the physical and independent existence nature has conferred on us all. He must, in a word, take away from man his own resources and give him instead new ones alien to him, and incapable of being made use of without the help of other men.'[1]

All emancipation is bringing back man's world and his relationships to man himself.

Political emancipation is the reduction of man, on the one hand to a member of civil society, an egoistic and independent individual, on the other hand to a citizen, a moral person.

The actual individual man must take the abstract citizen back into himself and, as an individual man in his empirical life, in his individual work and individual relationships become a species-being; man must recognize his own forces as social forces, organize them and thus no longer separate social forces from himself in the form of political forces. Only when this has been achieved will human emancipation be completed.

II

The Capacity of present Day Jews and Christians
to Become Free
By Bruno Bauer (*Twenty-one Sheets*, pp. 56–71)

This is the form that Bauer gives to the question of the relationship of the Jewish and Christian religions to each other and to criticism. Their relationship to criticism is their relationship to 'the capacity to become free'.

The conclusion is: 'the Christian has only one barrier to surmount, his religion, in order to give up religion altogether', and thus to become free; 'the Jew, on the other hand, has not only to break with his Jewish nature but also with the development and completion of his religion, a development that has remained alien to him' (p. 71). So Bauer here turns the question of Jewish emancipation into a purely religious question. The theological problem of who has the better prospect of getting to heaven, Jew or Christian, is repeated in the enlightened form: which of the two is more capable of emancipation? And the question is no longer: which gives freedom, Judaism or

---

[1] J–J. Rousseau, *The Social Contract and Discourses*, book II, chapter VII, trans. Cole, London, 1955, p. 32.

Christianity? It is rather the reverse: which gives more freedom: the negation of Judaism or the negation of Christianity.

If they wish to become free, then the Jew should not profess Christianity, but the dissolution of Christianity, the general dissolution of religion, i.e. the Enlightenment, criticism and its result, free humanity (p. 70).

It is still a profession that is in question for the Jews, but no longer the profession of Christianity but of the dissolution of Christianity.

Bauer demands of the Jews that they break with the essence of the Christian religion, a demand that, as he admits himself, does not proceed from the development of the Jewish essence.

It was to be predicted that when Bauer at the end of his *The Jewish Question* conceived of Judaism as merely the crude religious criticism of Christianity and thus only saw in it a religious significance, that the emancipation of the Jews would turn into a philosophico-theological act.

Bauer understands the ideal, abstract essence of the Jew, his religion, to be his whole essence. He concludes therefore quite rightly: 'The Jew contributes nothing to humanity when he neglects his limited law,' when he abolishes the whole of his Judaism (p. 65).

According to this, the relationship of Jews and Christians is as follows: the sole interest of Christians in Jewish emancipation is a general human and theoretical interest. Judaism is a fact that must offend the religious eye of the Christian. As soon as his eye ceases to be religious then this fact ceases to offend. The emancipation of the Jew is in itself no task for the Christian.

The Jew on the other hand, has not only his own task in order to achieve his liberation but also the Christian's task, the 'Critique of the Synoptics' and 'The Life of Jesus' etc., to get through.[1]

They must look to it themselves: they will create their own destiny; but history does not allow itself to be mocked (p. 71).

We attempt to break the theological conception of the problem. The question of the Jews' capacity for emancipation is changed for us into the question what particular social element needs to be overcome in

[1] Marx refers to: Bruno Bauer, *Kritik der evangelischen Geschichte der Synoptiker*, Leipzig, 1841; D. F. Strauss, *Das Leben Jesu*, Tübingen, 1935/6.

order to abolish Judaism? For the fitness of the present day Jew for emancipation is bound up with the relationship of Judaism to the emancipation of the contemporary world. And this relationship stems necessarily from the position of Judaism in the contemporary enslaved world.

Let us discuss the actual secular Jew not the sabbath Jew, as Bauer does, but the everyday Jew.

Let us look for the secret of the Jew not in his religion, but let us look for the secret of religion in the actual Jew.

What is the secular basis of Judaism? Practical need, selfishness.

What is the secular cult of the Jew? Haggling. What is his secular god? Money.

Well then, an emancipation from haggling and money, from practical, real Judaism would be the self-emancipation of our age.

An organization of society that abolished the presupposition of haggling and thus its possibility, would have made the Jew impossible. His religious consciousness would dissolve like an insipid vapour into the real live air of society. On the other hand: if the Jew recognizes this practical essence of his as null and works for its abolition, he is working for human emancipation with his previous development as a basis and turning himself against the highest practical expression of human self-alienation.

Thus we recognize in Judaism a general contemporary anti-social element which has been brought to its present height by a historical development which the Jews zealously abetted in its harmful aspects and which now must necessarily disintegrate.

In the last analysis the emancipation of the Jews is the emancipation of humanity from Judaism.

The Jew has already emancipated himself in a Jewish manner.

The Jew who in Vienna, for example, is only tolerated, controls through the power of his money the fate of the whole empire. The Jew who may be without rights in the smallest of the German states, decides the destiny of Europe. While the corporations and guilds turn a deaf ear to the Jew or do not yet favour him, their bold and selfish industry laughs at medieval institutions (Bruno Bauer, *The Jewish Question*, p. 114).

This is no isolated fact. The Jew has emancipated himself in a Jewish

manner not only annexing the power of money but also because
through him and also apart from him money has become a world
power and the practical spirit of the Jew has become the practical spirit
of the Christian people. The Jews have emancipated themselves in so
far as the Christians have become Jews.

'The pious and politically free inhabitant of New England', Captain
Hamilton informs us, 'is a sort of Laocoon, who does not even make the
least effort to free himself from the snakes that enlace him'.

Mammon is their idol, they adore him not with their lips alone but with all of
the strength of their body and soul. In their eyes the world is nothing but a
Stock Exchange and they are convinced that here on earth their only vocation
is to become richer than other men. The market has conquered all their other
thoughts, and their one relaxation consists in bartering objects. When they
travel they carry, so to speak, their wares or their display counter about with
them on their backs and talk of nothing but interest and profit. If they lose sight
for a moment of their own business, this is merely so that they can pry into
someone else's.

Indeed, the practical dominance of Judaism over the Christian world
has reached its unambiguous, normal expression in North America.
Here even the announcing of the gospel, the Christian pulpit, has
become an article of trade and the bankrupt gospel merchant becomes
like the evangelist who has become rich in business.

A man such as you see at the head of a respectable congregation began by being
a merchant—his trade fell off, so he became a minister—another began as a
priest, but as soon as he had a certain sum of money at his disposal, he left the
pulpit for business. In the eyes of many, the religious ministry is a real industrial
career (Beaumont loc. cit. pp. 185–6).

According to Bauer it is a hypocritical state of affairs when in theory
political rights are denied the Jew while in practice he possesses a
monstrous power and exercises on a large scale a political influence that
is limited on a small scale (*The Jewish Question*, p. 114).

The contradiction between the practical political power of the Jew
and his political rights is the general contradiction between politics and
the power of money. Whereas the first ideally is superior to the second,
in fact it is its bondsman.

Judaism has maintained itself alongside Christianity not only as a
religious critique of Christianity, not only as an incarnate doubt about

the religious provenance of Christianity, but just as much because the practical Jewish spirit, Judaism or commerce,[1] has maintained itself, and even reached its highest development, in Christian society. The Jew who is a particular member of civil society is only the particular appearance of the Judaism of civil society.

Judaism has maintained itself not in spite of, but because of, history.

From its own bowels civil society constantly begets Judaism.

What was the implicit and explicit basis of the Jewish religion? Practical need, egoism.

The monotheism of the Jew is therefore in reality the polytheism of many needs, a polytheism that makes even the lavatory an object of divine law. Practical need, or egoism, is the principle of civil society and appears as such in all its purity as soon as civil society has completely given birth to the political state. The god of practical need and selfishness is money.

Money is the jealous god of Israel before whom no other god may stand. Money debases all the gods of man and turns them into commodities. Money is the universal, self-constituted value of all things. It has therefore robbed the whole world, human as well as natural, of its own values. Money is the alienated essence of man's work and being, this alien essence dominates him and he adores it.

The god of the Jews has been secularized and has become the god of the world. Exchange is the actual god of the Jew. His god is only the illusion of exchange.

The view of nature that has obtained under the domination of private property and money is the actual despising and degrading of nature. It does really exist in the Jewish religion, but only in imagination.

In this sense Thomas Münzer declares it intolerable 'that all creation has been made into property: the fish in the water, the bird in the air, the off-spring of the earth—creation, too, must become free'.

What lies abstract in the Jewish religion, a contempt for theory, art, history, man as an end in himself, is the actual, conscious standpoint, the virtue of the money man. The species relationship itself, the relationship of man to woman, etc., becomes an object of commerce! Woman is bartered.

---

[1] This is a pun, as the word *Judentum* was also used to mean 'commerce'.

The imaginary nationality of the Jew is the nationality of the merchant, of the money man in general.

The baseless and irrational law of the Jew is only the religious caricature of morality and law in general, the purely formal rights with which the world of selfishness surrounds itself.

Here, too, the highest relationship of man is the legal relationship, the relationship to laws that are not valid for him because they are the laws of his own will and essence, but because they are the masters and deviations from them are avenged.

Jewish Jesuitry, the same practical Jesuitry that Bauer points out in the Talmud, is the relationship of the world of selfishness to the dominant laws whose crafty circumvention forms the chief art of this world.

If the affairs of the world were to be conducted within the limits of its laws, this would entail the continual supersession of these laws.

Judaism could not develop itself any further theoretically as a religion because the attitude of practical need is narrow by nature and exhausted in a few traits.

The religion of practical need could, by its nature, find its completion not in theory but in practice for this latter is its true form.

Judaism could not create a new world; it could only draw the new creations and relationships of the world into the sphere of its own industry, because practical need whose spirit is selfishness is passive and does not really extend itself, but finds itself extended by the progress of social circumstances.

Judaism reaches its apogee with the completion of civil society; but civil society first reaches its completion in the Christian world. Only under the domination of Christianity which made all national, natural, moral and theoretical relationships exterior to man, could civil society separate itself completely from the life of the state, tear assunder all the species-bonds of man, put egoism and selfish need in the place of these species-bonds and dissolve man into a world of atomistic individuals with hostile attitudes towards each other.

Christianity had its origin in Judaism. It has dissolved itself back into Judaism.

The Christian was from the beginning the theorizing Jew, the Jew is therefore the practical Christian, and the practical Christian has become the Jew again. Christianity has overcome real Judaism in appearance only. It was too gentlemanly, too spiritual, to remove the crudeness of practical need other than by raising into the blue heavens.

Christianity is the sublime thought of Judaism, Judaism is the vulgar practical application of Christianity. But this practical application could only become universal after Christianity as the perfect religion had completed, in a theoretical manner, the self-alienation of man from himself and from nature.

Only then could Judaism attain general domination and make externalized man and externalized nature into alienable, saleable objects, a prey to the slavery of egoistic need and the market.

Selling is the practice of externalization. As long as man is imprisoned within religion, he only knows how to objectify his essence by making it into an alien, imaginary being. Similarly, under the domination of egoistic need he can only become practical, only create practical objects by putting his products and his activity under the domination of an alien entity and lending them the significance of an alien entity—money.

In its perfected practice the Christian egoism concerning the soul necessarily changes into the Jewish egoism concerning the body, heavenly need becomes earthly, and subjectivism becomes selfishness. We explain the tenacity of the Jew not by his religion, but by the human basis of his religion, practical need, egoism.

Because the true essence of the Jew has been realized and secularized in civil society, it could not convince the Jew of the unreality of his religious essence which is merely the ideal perception of practical need. Thus it is not only in the Pentateuch or the Talmud that we find the essence of the contemporary Jew: we find it in contemporary society, not as an abstract but as a very empirical essence, not as the limitation of the Jew but as the Jewish limitations of society.

As soon as society manages to abolish the empirical essence of Judaism, the market and its presuppositions, the Jew has become impossible, for his mind no longer has an object, because the subjective basis of Judaism, practical need, has become humanized and because the conflict of man's individual, material existence with his species existence has been superseded.

The social emancipation of the Jew implies the emancipation of society from Judaism.

Towards A Critique of Hegel's Philosophy of Right[1]
Introduction

Written: End of 1843–beginning of 1844

First published: Deutsch-französische Jahrbücher, February 1844, pp. 71–85

Reprinted: MEGA, I i (1), pp. 607–21; *Frühe Schriften*, pp. 488–505

Translated: Marx–Engels, *Sur La Religion*, ed Badia et al., Paris, 1960, pp. 41–58. Karl Marx, *Early Writings*, ed. T. B. Bottomore, London, 1963, pp. 41–58; Easton and Guddatt, *Writings of the Young Marx*, pp. 249–64

Originally intended as an introduction to the *Critique of Hegel's Philosophy of Right* translated above, this article has something of the power of synthesis, the incision and the certitude of the *Communist Manifesto*. It begins with Marx's famous epigrams on religion and then takes up the themes of the realization and abolition of philosophy already sketched out in the *Dissertation*. Marx points out the distinction between a political revolution, such as that of 1789, and a social revolution, such as the one that he predicted for Germany. This distinction runs through all Marx's writings in 1844.

As far as Germany is concerned, the criticism of religion is essentially complete, and the criticism of religion is the presupposition of all criticism.

The profane existence of error is compromised as soon as its heavenly *oratio pro aris et focis* is refuted. Man has found in the imaginary reality of heaven where he looked for a superman only the reflection of his own self. He will therefore no longer be inclined to find only the appearance of himself, the non-man, where he seeks and must seek his true reality.

The foundation of irreligious criticism is this: man makes religion, religion does not make man. Religion is indeed the self-consciousness and self-awareness of man who either has not yet attained to himself or has already lost himself again. But man is no abstract being squatting

---

[1] See Introduction, pp. xxvi f.

outside the world. Man is the world of man, the state, society. This state, this society, produces religion's inverted attitude to the world, because they are an inverted world themselves. Religion is the general theory of this world, its encyclopaedic compendium, its logic in popular form, its spiritual *point d'honneur*, its enthusiasm, its moral sanction, its solemn complement, its universal basis for consolation and justification. It is the imaginary realization of the human essence, because the human essence possesses no true reality. Thus, the struggle against religion is indirectly the struggle against that world whose spiritual aroma is religion.

Religious suffering is at the same time an expression of real suffering and a protest against real suffering. Religion is the sigh of the oppressed creature, the feeling of a heartless world and the soul of soulless circumstances. It is the opium of the people.

The abolition of religion as the illusory happiness of the people is the demand for their real happiness. The demand to give up the illusions about their condition is a demand to give up a condition that requires illusion. The criticism of religion is therefore the germ of the criticism of the valley of tears whose halo is religion.

Criticism has plucked the imaginary flowers from the chains not so that man may bear chains without any imagination or comfort, but so that he may throw away the chains and pluck living flowers. The criticism of religion disillusions man so that he may think, act and fashion his own reality as a disillusioned man come to his senses; so that he may revolve around himself as his real sun. Religion is only the illusory sun which revolves around man as long as he does not revolve around himself.

It is therefore the task of history, now the truth is no longer in the beyond, to establish the truth of the here and now. The first task of philosophy, which is in the service of history, once the holy form of human self-alienation has been discovered, is to discover self-alienation in its unholy forms. The criticism of heaven is thus transformed into the criticism of earth, the criticism of religion into the criticism of law, and the criticism of theology into the criticism of politics.

The following exposition[1]—a contribution to this task—does not

---

[1] Marx intended to write a critical study of Hegel's *Philosophy of Right* and this article was to serve as its Introduction. The *Critique of Hegel's Philosophy* and

deal with the original but with its copy, the German philosophy of the state and law. The only reason is that it is dealing with Germany.

If we wanted to start with the German *status quo* itself, the result would still be an anachronism even if one did it in the only adequate way, i.e. negatively. Even the denial of our political present is already a dusty fact in the historical lumber room of modern peoples. Even if I deny powdered wigs, I still have unpowdered wigs. If I deny the situation in the Germany of 1843, I am according to French reckoning, scarcely in the year 1789, still less at the focal point of the present.

Indeed, German history can congratulate itself on following a path that no people in the historial firmament have taken before it and none will take after. For we have shared the restorations of the modern peoples, without sharing their revolutions. We have had restorations, firstly because other peoples dared to make a revolution, and secondly because other peoples suffered a counter-revolution; once because our masters were afraid and once because they were not afraid. With our shepherds at our head, we always found ourselves in the company of freedom only once—on the day of its burial.

There is a school that justifies the abjectness of today by the abjectness of yesterday, a school which declares every cry of the serf against the knout to be rebellious as long as the knout is an aged, historical knout with a pedigree, a school to which history, like the God of Israel to his servant Moses, only shows its *a posteriori*. This school, the Historical School of Law,[1] would have invented German history had it not been itself an invention of that history. It is a Shylock, but a servile Shylock that for every pound of flesh cut from the heart of the people swears upon its bond, its historical, Christian–Germanic bond.

Easy-going enthusiasts, on the other hand, Germanophiles by blood and liberal by reflection look for the history of freedom beyond our history in the primeval Teutonic forests. But how is the history of our freedom different from the history of the wild boar's freedom if it is only to be found in the forests? Moreover, it is well known that the forest echoes back the same words that are shouted into it. So peace to the primeval German forests!

the *Economic and Philosophical Manuscripts of Right,* may be two preliminary drafts of this study.

[1] On the Historical School of Law, see pp. xvii ff.

But war on the situation in Germany! Of course. It is below the level of history and below any criticism, but it remains an object of criticism just as the criminal, though below the level of humanity, yet remains an object of the executioner. In its struggle against this situation criticism is no passion of the head, it is the head of passion. It is no anatomical knife, it is a weapon. Its object is its enemy that it does not aim to refute, but to annihilate. For the spirit of this situation is refuted already. In itself it is not an object worthy of thought but an existence as despicable as it is despised. Criticism does not itself need to arrive at an understanding with this object for it is already clear about it. It no longer pretends to be an end in itself but only a means. The essential feeling that animates it is indignation, its essential task is denunciation.

The point is to describe the counter-pressures of all social spheres, a general passive discontent, a narrowness that both recognizes and yet misconceives itself, all contained in the framework of a government that lives from the preservation of all mediocrities and is itself nothing but mediocrity in government.

What a charade! Society is infinitely divided into a multiplicity of races which stand opposed to each other with petty antipathies, bad consciences and a brutal mediocrity. It is precisely the ambivalent and suspicious attitude to each other that leads their masters to treat them all without distinction, although with different formalities, as persons whose existence has been granted as a favour. And even the fact that they are dominated, ruled and possessed they must recognize and profess as a favour of heaven! And on the other side are the masters themselves whose greatness is in inverse proportion to their number.

The criticism that tackles this state of affairs is engaged in a hand to hand battle and in a hand to hand battle it does not matter whether the opponent is equally noble, well born and interesting, the point is to hit him. The point is not to allow the Germans a moment of self-deceit or resignation. We must make the actual oppression even more oppressive by making them conscious of it, and the insult even more insulting by publicizing it. We must describe every sphere of German society as the disgrace of German society, we must force these petrified relationships to dance by playing their own tune to them! So as to give them courage, we must teach the people to be shocked by themselves. We are thus fulfilling an inevitable need of the German people and the needs that spring from the true character of a people are the final bases of its satisfaction.

Even for modern peoples this struggle against the narrow content of the German *status quo* is not without interest; for the German *status quo* is the unabashed consummation of the *ancien régime* and the *ancien régime* is the hidden deficiency of the modern state. The struggle against the German political present is the struggle against the past of modern peoples and they are still burdened with reminiscences from this past. It is instructive for them to see the *ancien régime*, that played tragedy in their history, play comedy as a German ghost. Its history was tragic so long as it was the established power in the world and freedom was a personal fancy; in a word, so long as it believed and had to believe in its own justification. So long as the *ancien régime*, as the existing world order, was struggling with a world that was just beginning, then there was on its part a universal historical error, but not a personal one. Its demise was therefore tragic.

The present German regime, on the other hand, an anachronism in flagrant contradiction to all generally recognized axioms, the nullity of the *ancien régime* exhibited for all the world to see, only imagines that it believes in itself and requires this imagination from the rest of the world. If it believed in its own nature, would it try to hide it under the appearance of an alien nature and seek its salvation in hypocrisy and sophistry? The modern *ancien régime* is only the comedian of a world order whose real heroes are dead. History is thorough and passes through many stages when she carries a worn out form to burial. The last stage of a world-historical form is its comedy. The gods of Greece who had already been mortally wounded in the *Prometheus Bound* tragedy of Aeschylus, had to die once more a comic death in the dialogues of Lucian. Why does history follow this course? So that mankind may take leave of its past joyfully. It is this joyful political function that we vindicate for the political powers of Germany.

But as soon as modern socio-political reality is submitted to criticism, as soon, that is, as criticism raises itself to the level of truly human problems, it finds itself outside the German *status quo*, or it would conceive of its object at a level below its object. An example: the relationship of industry and the world of wealth in general to the political world is one of the chief problems of modern times. In what form does this problem begin to preoccupy the Germans? Under the form of protectionism, a system of prohibitions and a national economy. German chauvinism has left men for matter and so one fine morning our cotton knights and iron heroes found themselves changed into patriots. So people are beginning in Germany to recognize the interior sovereignty of monopoly by according it an exterior sovereignty. Thus we are now starting to begin in Germany when France and England are beginning to end. The old and rotten state of affairs against which these countries are in theoretical rebellion and which they only tolerate as one tolerates chains, is in Germany greeted like the rising dawn of a beautiful future that scarcely dares to pass from artful[1] theory to implacable practice. While in France and England the problem is: political economy or domination of wealth by society, in Germany it is: national economy or domination of nationality by private property. Thus in France and England the problem is to abolish monopoly that has progressed to its final consequences; in Germany the problem is to progress as far as the final consequences of monopoly. There the problem is to find a solution, here it is to provoke a collision. This is a sufficient example of the German form of modern problems, an example of how our history, like a raw recruit, has so far only had a job of performing trivial historical drill after everyone else.

So if developments in Germany as a whole did not go beyond German political development, a German could no more take part in contemporary problems than can a Russian. But if the single individual is not bound by the limits of his nation, the whole nation is even less liberated by the liberation of an individual. Scythians made no progress at all towards a Greek culture because Greece counted a Scythian as one of her philosophers.[2]

Happily we Germans are no Scythians.

As the ancient peoples have experienced their pre-history in imagination, in mythology, so we Germans have experienced our future history in thought, in philosophy. We are philosophical contemporaries without being historical ones. German philosophy is the ideal prolongation of German history. So if, instead of criticizing the incomplete works of

---

[1] In German: *listig*. A pun on the name of Friedrich List, (1789–1856), German protectionist economist.

[2] Anacharsis, counted as one of the Seven Wise Men of Greece.

our real history, we criticize the posthumous works of our ideal history, philosophy, then our criticism will be at the centre of the question of which the present age says: that is the question. What in developed peoples is the practical conflict with the modern state institutions, in Germany, where these institutions do not even exist, it is a critical conflict with the philosophical reflection of these institutions.

The German philosophy of law and of the state is the only theory in German history that stands *al pari* with the official modern present. The German people must therefore add this dream history to its existing circumstances and submit to criticism not only these existing circumstances but at the same time their abstract continuation. Its future can limit itself neither to the immediate negation of its real political and juridical circumstances nor to the immediate completion of its ideal political and juridical circumstances, for it has the immediate negation of its real situation in its ideal circumstances and has already almost left behind the immediate completion of its philosophy by looking at neighbouring peoples. Thus the practical political party in Germany is justified in demanding the negation of philosophy. Their error consists not in their demand, but in being content with the demand that they do not and cannot really meet. They believe that they can complete that negation by turning their back on philosophy and murmuring at her with averted head some vexatious and banal phrases. Their limited vision does not count philosophy as part of German reality or even fancies that it is beneath the level of German practice and the theories that serve it. You demand that we start from the real seeds of life, but forget that until now the real seed of the German people has only flourished inside its skull. In a word: you cannot transcend philosophy without realizing it.

The same error but with inverted factors is committed by the theoretical party that originates in philosophy.

It saw in the present struggle nothing but the critical struggle of philosophy with the German world and did not reflect that previous philosophy itself has belonged to this world and is its completion, albeit in ideas. It was critical with regard to its opposite but not to itself for it started from the presuppositions of philosophy and remained content with the results thus obtained. Or else it presented demands and conclusions got from elsewhere as the demands and conclusions of philosophy although these, supposing them to be well founded, can only be obtained by the negation of previous philosophy, of philosophy as philosophy. We reserve for later a more detailed description of this party. Its principal fault can be summed up thus: it thought it could realize philosophy without transcending it.

The criticism of the German philosophy of the state and of law which was given its most consistent, richest and final version by Hegel, is both the critical analysis of the modern state and of the reality that depends upon it and also the decisive denial of the whole previous method of the German political and legal mind, whose principal and most general expression, raised to the level of a science, is precisely the speculative philosophy of law itself. Only Germany could give rise to a speculative philosophy of law, this abstract and exuberant thought of the modern state whose reality remains in the beyond, even though this is only beyond the Rhine. And inversely the German ideology of the modern state that abstracts from actual men was only possible because, and in so far as, the modern state itself abstracts from actual men or satisfies the whole man in a purely imaginary way. In politics the Germans have thought what other people have done. Germany was their theoretical conscience. The abstraction and conceit of its thought has always been in step with the reality of its narrow and trivial situation. So if the *status quo* of the German political system expresses the consummation of the *ancien régime*, the completion of the thorn in the flesh of the modern state, then the *status quo* of the German political consciousness expresses the incompletion of the modern state, the defectiveness of its very flesh.

Even were it only a decided opponent of the previous methods of the German political mind, the criticism of the speculative philosophy of law cannot end with itself, but in tasks for which there is only one solution: *praxis*.

This is the question: can Germany attain to a *praxis* that will be equal to her principles, i.e. can she attain to revolution that will not only raise her to the official level of modern peoples but to the human level that is the immediate future of these peoples?

The weapon of criticism cannot, of course, supplant the criticism of weapons, material force must be overthrown by material force. But theory, too, will become material force as soon as it seizes the masses. Theory is capable of seizing the masses as soon as its proofs are *ad hominem* and its proofs are *ad hominem* as soon as it is radical. To be radical is to grasp the matter by the root. But for man the root is man himself. The manifest proof of the radicalism of German theory and its practical energy is that it starts from the decisive and positive abolition of religion. The criticism of religion ends with the doctrine that man is the highest being for man, that is, with the categorical imperative to overthrow all circumstances in which man is humiliated, enslaved, abandoned and despised, circumstances best described by the exclamation of a Frenchman on hearing of an intended tax on dogs: Poor dogs! They want to treat you like men!

Even historically speaking, theoretical emancipation has a specifically practical significance for Germany. For Germany's revolutionary past is theoretical, it is the Reformation. Once it was the monk's brain in which the revolution began, now it is in the philosopher's.

Certainly, Luther removed the servitude of devotion by replacing it by the servitude of conviction. He destroyed faith in authority by restoring the authority of faith. He turned priests into laymen by turning laymen into priests. He liberated man from exterior religiosity by making man's inner conscience religious. He emancipated the body from chains by enchaining the heart.

But even though Protestantism was not the true solution, it formulated the problem rightly. The question was now no longer the battle of the layman with the exterior priest, it was the battle with his own interior priest, his priestly nature. Protestantism by turning laymen into priests emancipated the lay popes, the princes, together with their clergy, the privileged and the philistines. Similarly philosophy, by turning the priestly Germans into men, will emancipate the people. But just as emancipation did not stop with the princes, so it will not stop with the secularization of goods involved in the spoilation of the church that was above all practised by hypocritical Prussia. The peasants' war, the most radical event in German history, failed then because of theology. Today, when theology itself has failed, the most unfree event in German history, our *status quo*, will be wrecked on philosophy. On the day before the Reformation Germany was the most unconditional servant of Rome, on the day before its revolution it is the unconditional servant of less than Rome, of Prussia and Austria, cabbage squires and philistines.

However, there appears to be a major obstacle to a radical German revolution. For revolutions need a passive element, a material basis. A theory will only be realized in a people in so far as it is the realization of what it needs. Will the enormous gulf between the demands of German thought and the replies of German actuality match the same gulf that exists between civil society and the state, and within civil society itself? Will theoretical needs immediately become practical ones? It is not enough that thought should tend towards reality, reality must also tend towards thought.

But Germany has not scaled the intermediary stages of political emancipation at the same time as modern peoples. Even the stages that she has passed beyond theoretically have not yet been reached in practice. How can she with one perilous leap not only go beyond her own barriers but also beyond the barriers of modern peoples, barriers which must in reality appear to her as a desirable liberation from her real barriers. A radical revolution can only be a revolution of radical needs, whose presuppositions and breeding ground seem precisely to be lacking.

Germany, it is true, has only accompanied the development of modern peoples by the abstract activity of thought, without taking an active part in the real struggles of this development. But, on the other hand, it has shared the sufferings of this development without sharing its joys and its partial satisfactions. Abstract activity on the one hand is matched by abstract suffering on the other. Germany will therefore one fine morning find herself on a level with European decadence before it has ever stood on the level of European emancipation. She could be compared with a fetish worshipper who suffers from the maladies of Christianity.

If we consider first the German governments, we find that the conditions of the age, the situation of Germany, the outlook of German culture and finally their own happy instincts drive them to combine the civilized deficiencies of the modern political world, whose advantages we do not possess, with the barbaric deficiencies of the *ancien régime*, which we enjoy to the full. Thus Germany must participate more and more in the unreason, if not in the reason, even of forms of state that go beyond her present *status quo*. Is there, for example, a country in the world that shares so naïvely as so-called constitutional Germany all the illusions of the constitutional state without sharing its realities? Or did it not have to be the brain wave of a German regime to link the terrors of censorship with those of the French September laws[1] which presuppose freedom of the press? In the Roman Pantheon the gods of all nations were to be found and in the Holy Roman German Empire are to be found the sins of all forms of state. This eclecticism will reach a height as yet unsuspected: this is guaranteed by the politico-aesthetic gourmandize of a German king[2] who thinks to play all the roles of monarchy, the feudal as well as the bureaucratic, the absolute as well as the constitutional, the autocratic as well as the democratic, in his own person if not through the person of the people, and for himself if not for the people. Germany is the political deficiencies of the present constituted into a world of their own and as such will not be able to overthrow specifically German barriers without overthrowing the general barriers of the political present.

It is not the radical revolution that is a Utopian dream for Germany, not universal human emancipation; it is the partial, purely political revolution, the revolution which leaves the pillars of the house still standing. What is the basis of a partial, purely political revolution? It is that a part of civil society emancipates itself and attains to universal domination, that a particular class undertakes the general emancipation of society from its particular situation. This class frees the whole of society, but only under the presupposition that the whole of society is in the same situation as this class, that it possesses, or can easily acquire for example, money and education.

No class in civil society can play this role without arousing a moment of enthusiasm in itself and among the masses. It is a moment when the class fraternizes with society in general and dissolves itself into society; it is identified with society and is felt and recognized as society's general representative. Its claims and rights are truly the claims and rights of society itself of which it is the real social head and heart. A particular

---

[1] Laws introduced in September 1835 under which publishers had to provide larger financial guarantees for newspapers and were liable to larger fines for 'subversion'.

[2] i.e. Frederick William IV.

class can only vindicate for itself general supremacy in the name of the general rights of society. Revolutionary energy and intellectual self-confidence alone are not enough to gain this position of emancipator and thus to exploit politically all spheres of society in the interest of one's own sphere. So that the revolution of a people and the emancipation of a particular class of civil society may coincide, so that one class can stand for the whole of society, the deficiency of all society must inversely be concentrated in another class, a particular class must be a class that rouses universal scandal and incorporates all limitations; a particular social sphere must be regarded as the notorious crime of the whole society, so that the liberation of this sphere appears as universal self-liberation. So that one class *par excellence* may appear as the class of liberation, another class must inversely be the manifest class of oppression. The universally negative significance of the French nobility and clergy determined the universally positive significance of the class nearest to them and opposed to them: the bourgeoisie.

But not only is every particular class in Germany lacking in the consistency, insight, courage and boldness that could mark it as the negative representative of society; they are also lacking in that breadth of mind that can identify, even if only for a moment, with the mind of the people, that genius that can infuse material force with political power, that revolutionary zeal that can throw at its adversary the defiant words: I am nothing and I should be all. The principal element in the honest morality of not only individual Germans but also of classes is that modest egoism that parades its narrowness and lets it be used against itself. Thus the relationship of the different spheres of German society to each other is not dramatic but epic. For each begins to be conscious of itself and to take up a position near the others with its particular claims, not as soon as it is oppressed but as soon as the conditions of the time without any co-operation create a lower social stratum which they in their turn can oppress. Even the moral self-awareness of the German middle class rests simply on the consciousness of being the representative of philistine mediocrity of all other classes. It is thus not only the German kings that ascend the throne *mal à propos*; it is also every sphere of civil society that is defeated before it has celebrated its victory, that has developed its own limitations before it has overcome the limitations that confront it, that shows its narrow-mindedness before it can show its generosity. The result is that even the opportunity for an important role is past before it was to hand and that, as soon as that class begins to struggle with the class above it, it is engaged in a struggle with the class below. Thus the princes are fighting against the king, the bureaucracy against the nobility, the bourgeoisie against all of them, while the proletariat is already beginning its fight against the bourgeoisie. The middle class scarcely dares to conceive of emancipation from its own point of view and already the development of social circumstances and the progress of political theory declares this point of view itself to be antiquated or at least problematical.

In France it is enough that one should be something in order to wish to be all. In Germany one must be nothing, if one is to avoid giving up everything. In France partial emancipation is the basis of universal emancipation, in Germany universal emancipation is a *conditio sine qua non* of every partial emancipation. In France it is the reality, in Germany the impossibility of a gradual liberation that must give birth to total freedom. In France every class of the people is politically idealistic and is not primarily conscious of itself as a particular class but as a representative of general social needs. The role of emancipator thus passes in a dramatic movement to different classes of the French people until it comes to the class which no longer realizes social freedom by presupposing certain conditions that lie outside mankind and are yet created by human society, but which organizes the conditions of human existence by presupposing social freedom. In Germany, on the contrary, where practical life is as unintellectual as intellectual life is unpractical, no class of civil society has the need for, or capability of achieving, universal emancipation until it is compelled to by its immediate situation, by material necessity and its own chains.

So where is the real possibility of a German emancipation?

We answer: in the formation of a class with radical chains, a class in civil society that is not a class of civil society, of a social group that is the dissolution of all social groups, of a sphere that has a universal character because of its universal sufferings and lays claim to no particular right, because it is the object of no particular injustice but of injustice in general. This class can no longer lay claim to a historical status, but only to a human one. It is not in a one-sided opposition to the consequences of the German political regime, it is in total opposition to its presuppositions. It is, finally, a sphere that cannot emancipate itself without emancipating itself from all other spheres of society and thereby emancipating these other spheres themselves. In a word, it is the complete loss of humanity and thus can only recover itself by a complete redemption of humanity. This dissolution of society, as a particular class, is the proletariat.

The proletariat is only beginning to exist in Germany through the invasion of the industrial movement. For it is not formed by the poverty produced by natural laws but by artificially induced poverty. It is not made up of the human masses mechanically oppressed by the weight of society, but of those who have their origin in society's brutal dissolution and principally the dissolution of the middle class, although, quite naturally its ranks are gradually swelled by natural poverty and Germano-Christian serfdom.

When the proletariat proclaims the dissolution of the hitherto existing world order, it merely declares the secret of its own existence, since it is in fact the dissolution of this order. When it demands the negation of private property it is only laying down as a principle for society what society has laid down as a principle for the proletariat, what has already been incorporated in itself without its consent as the negative result of society. The proletarian thus finds that he has in relation to the world of the future the same right as the German king in relation to the world of the past, when he calls the people *his* people as he might call a horse *his* horse. When the king declares the people to be his private property he is only confirming that the private property owner is king.

As philosophy finds in the proletariat its material weapons so the proletariat finds in philosophy its intellectual weapons and as soon as the lightning of thought has struck deep into the virgin soil of the people, the emancipation of the Germans into men will be completed.

Let us summarize our results:

The only liberation of Germany that is practically possible is the liberation from the theoretical standpoint that declares man to be the highest being for man. In Germany emancipation from the Middle Ages is only possible as an emancipation from the partial overcoming of the Middle Ages. In Germany no form of slavery can be broken without every form of slavery being broken. Germany is thorough and cannot make a revolution without its being a thorough one. The emancipation of Germany is the emancipation of man. The head of this emancipation is philosophy, its heart is the proletariat. Philosophy cannot realize itself without transcending the proletariat, the proletariat cannot transcend itself without realizing philosophy.

When all interior conditions are fulfilled, the day of German resurrection will be heralded by the crowing of the Gallic cock.

Economic and Philosophical Manuscripts[1]

Written: April–August 1844

First published: MEGA, I (3), pp. 29–172, 589–96
Reprinted: Frühe Schriften, pp. 506–665

Translated: Karl Marx, *Economic and Philosophical Manuscripts of 1844,* trans. M. Milligan, Moscow, 1959; Karl Marx, *Manuscrits de 1844,* ed. E. Bottigelli, Paris, 1962; Karl Marx, *Early Writings,* ed. T. B. Bottomore, London, 1963, pp. 66–219; Easton and Guddatt, *Writings of the Young Marx,* pp. 284–337

There are four of these manuscripts. The first, of thirty-six pages, is divided at the beginning into three columns, headed respectively 'Wages of Labour', 'Profit of Capital' and 'Rent of Land'. These consist mostly of excerpts from classical economists and are omitted here. For the last part of the manuscript, Marx disregarded the column division and wrote the section here entitled 'Alienated Labour'. The second manuscript, usually entitled 'The Relationship of Private Property', consists of only four pages, the previous ones having been lost. The third manuscripts contains sixty-eight pages, the last twenty-three being blank. It contains the section entitled 'Private Property and Communism', preceded by a section entitled 'Private property and labour' and followed by one entitled 'Needs, Production and the Division of Labour', both here omitted. There follows (though parts of it are interspersed with the last-named section) the 'Critique of Hegel's Dialectic', which I have retained in its original place since it follows straight on from the end of the section on 'Private Property and Communism', though other editors, following the indications given in the *Preface,* have placed it at the end. This is followed by the *Preface* itself and finally by the section given the title 'Money'. The fourth manuscript consists of four pages and is merely a precis of the last chapter of the *Phenomenology.*

Of the manuscripts translated below, only the 'Preface' and 'Alienated Labour' had their titles given them by Marx: the others come from the editors of the MEGA.

Passages enclosed in pointed brackets (⟨ . . . ⟩) were later crossed out by Marx.

[1] See further: Introduction, pp. 25 ff.; the relevant passages of the books mentioned in the bibliography; D. Braybrooke, 'Diagnosis and Remedy in Marx's Doctrine of Alienation', *Social Research,* 1958; L. Easton, 'Alienation and History in the Early Marx', *Philosophy and Phenomenological Research,* 1961.

Preface

I have announced in the *Deutsch-französische Jahrbucher*[1] a forthcoming critique of legal and political science in the form of a critique of Hegel's philosophy of right. While I was working on the manuscript for publication it became clear that it was quite inopportune to mix criticism directed purely against speculation with that of other and different matters and that this mixture was an obstacle to the development of my line of thought and to its intelligibility. Moreover, the condensation of such rich and varied subjects into a single work would have permitted only a very aphoristic treatment and on the other hand such an aphoristic presentation would have created the appearance of an arbitrary systematization. I will therefore present one after another a critique of law, morality, politics, etc. in different independent brochures and then finally in a separate work try to show the connection of the whole and the relationship of the parts to each other and end with a criticism of the elaboration of the material by speculative philosophy. Therefore in the present work the connection of political economy with the state, law, morality, civil life etc. is only dealt with in so far as political economy itself professes to deal with these subjects.

I do not need to reassure the reader who is familiar with political economy that my results have been obtained through a completely empirical analysis founded on a conscientious and critical study of political economy.

It is self evident that apart from the French and English socialists I have also used the works of German socialists. However, the substantial and original German works in this field can be reduced—apart from Weitling's work—to the articles published by Hess in the '*Twenty-One Sheets*'[2] and to Engels' '*Sketch of a Critique of Political Economy*' in the *Deutsch-französische Jahrbücher*, where I also outlined the first elements of the present work in a completely general way.[3]

---

[1] Marx refers to his essay, 'Towards a Critique of Hegel's Philosophy of Right', see pp. 115 ff.

[2] Marx refers to the three essays: 'Socialism and Communism', 'Philosophy of Action' and 'Freedom One and Undivided', first published in *Twenty-One Sheets* and reprinted in M. Hess, *Philosophische und Sozialistische Aufsätzel 1837–1850*, ed. Cornu and Mönke, Berlin, 1961.

[3] In 'Towards a Critique of Hegel's Philosophy of Right'; see pp. 115 ff.

⟨Apart from these writers who have treated political economy in a critical manner, positive criticism in general, including thus the positive German criticism of political economy, owes its true foundation to the discoveries of Feuerbach. The petty jealousy of some and the real anger of others seems to have instigated a veritable conspiracy of silence against his *Philosophy of the Future*[1] and *Theses for the Reform of Philosophy* in *Anekdota*,[2] although they are used tacitly.⟩

The first positive humanist and naturalist criticism dates from Feuerbach. The less bombastic they are, the more sure, deep, comprehensive and lasting is the effect of Feuerbach's works, the only ones since Hegel's *Phenomenology* and *Logic* to contain a real theoretical revolution.

I considered the final chapter of the present work, 'The Critical Analysis of the Hegelian Dialectic and Philosophy in General', to be absolutely necessary. This is in contradistinction to the critical theologians of our time who have not completed any such task. This deficiency of theirs is inevitable for even the critical theologian remains a theologian, and thus must either begin with definite presuppositions of philosophy regarded as an authority or, if the process of criticism and the discoveries of someone else have made him doubt his philosophical presuppositions, he abandons them in a cowardly and unjustified manner, abstracts from them, and only proclaims his slavery to them and vexation at this slavery in a negative, unconscious and sophistical way.

⟨The reason for his purely negative and unconscious expression is partly that he constantly repeats an assurance of the purity of his own criticism and partly that he wishes to avert the eye of the observer and his own eye from the fact that criticism must necessarily come to terms with its birth place, the Hegelian dialectic and German philosophy in general.⟩

However much theological criticism was at the beginning of the movement the really progressive stage, on close examination it is in the last analysis nothing but the apogee and the result of the old transcendant philosophy, particularly the Hegelian, pushed to theological

---

[1] L. Feuerbach, *Grundsätze der Philosophie der Zukunft*, Zurich and Winterthur, 1843.

[2] L. Feuerbach, *Vorläufige Thesen zur Reform der Philosophie*, in *Anekdota*, ed. A. Ruge, Zurich and Winterthur, 1843.

caricature. The justice meted out by history is interesting in that theology which was always the fly in the philosophical ointment is now called to represent in itself the negative dissolution of philosophy, its process of decomposition. I shall demonstrate this historical nemesis in detail on another occasion.

⟨On the other hand, the extent to which Feuerbach's discoveries about the essence of philosophy still necessitate a critical treatment of the philosophical dialectic, at least to serve as proof, will become apparent from my development of the subject.⟩

Alienated Labour

We started from the presuppositions of political economy. We accepted its vocabulary and its laws. We presupposed private property, the separation of labour, capital and land, and likewise of wages, profit and ground rent; also division of labour; competition; the concept of exchange value etc. Using the very words of political economy we have demonstrated that the worker is degraded to the most miserable sort of commodity; that the misery of the worker is in inverse proportion to the power and size of his production; that the necessary result of competition is the accumulation of capital in a few hands, and thus a more terrible restoration of monopoly; and that finally the distinction between capitalist and landlord, and that between peasant and industrial worker disappears and the whole of society must fall apart into the two classes of the property owners and the propertyless workers.

Political economy starts with the fact of private property, it does not explain it to us. It conceives of the material process that private property goes through in reality in general abstract formulae which then have for it a value of laws. It does not understand these laws, i.e. it does not demonstrate how they arise from the nature of private property. Political economy does not afford us any explanation of the reason for the separation of labour and capital, of capital and land. When, for example, political economy defines the relationship of wages to profit from capital, the interest of the capitalist is the ultimate court of appeal, that is, it presupposes what should be its result. In the same way competition enters the argument everywhere. It is explained by

M

exterior circumstances. But political economy tells us nothing about how far these exterior, apparently fortuitous circumstances are merely the expression of a necessary development. We have seen how it regards exchange itself as something fortuitous. The only wheels that political economy sets in motion are greed and war among the greedy, competition.

It is just because political economy has not grasped the connections in the movement that new contradictions have arisen in its doctrines, for example, between that of monopoly and that of competition, freedom of craft and corporations, division of landed property and large estates. For competition, free trade and the division of landed property were only seen as fortuitous circumstances created by will and force, not developed and comprehended as necessary, inevitable and natural results of monopoly, corporations and feudal property.

So what we have to understand now is the essential connection of private property, selfishness, the separation of labour, capital and landed property, of exchange and competition, of the value and degradation of man, of monopoly and competition, etc.—the connection of all this alienation with the money system.

Let us not be like the political economist who when he wishes to explain something puts himself in an imaginary original state of affairs. Such an original state of affairs explains nothing. He simply pushes the question back into a grey and nebulous distance. He presupposes as a fact and an event what he ought to be deducing, namely the necessary connection between the two things, for example, between the division of labour and exchange. Similarly, the theologian explains the origin of evil through the fall, i.e. he presupposes as an historical fact what he should be explaining.

We start with a contemporary fact of political economy:

The worker becomes poorer the richer is his production, the more it increases in power and scope. The worker becomes a commodity that is all the cheaper the more commodities he creates. The depreciation of the human world progresses in direct proportion to the increase in value of the world of things. Labour does not only produce commodities; it produces itself and the labourer as a commodity and that to the extent to which it produces commodities in general.

What this fact expresses is merely this: the object that labour produces, its product, confronts it as an alien being, as a power independent of the producer. The product of labour is labour that has solidified itself into an object, made itself into a thing, the objectification of labour. The realization of labour is its objectification. In political economy this realization of labour appears as a loss of reality for the worker, objectification as a loss of the object or slavery to it, and appropriation as alienation, as externalization.

The realization of labour appears as a loss of reality to an extent that the worker loses his reality by dying of starvation. Objectification appears as a loss of the object to such an extent that the worker is robbed not only of the objects necessary for his life but also of the objects of his work. Indeed labour itself becomes an object that he can only have in his power with the greatest of efforts and with irregular intervals. The appropriation of the object appears as alienation to such an extent that the more objects the worker produces, the less he can possess and the more he falls under the domination of his product, capital.

All these consequences follow from the fact that the worker relates to the product of his labour as to an alien object. For it is evident from this presupposition that the more the worker externalizes himself in his work, the more powerful becomes the alien, objective world that he creates opposite himself, the poorer he becomes himself in his inner life and the less he can call his own. It is just the same in religion. The more man puts into God, the less he retains in himself. The worker puts his life into the object and this means that it no longer belongs to him but to the object. So the greater this activity, the more the worker is without an object. What the product of his labour is, that he is not. So the greater this product the less he is himself. The externalization of the worker in his product implies not only that his labour becomes an object, an exterior existence but also that it exists outside him, independent and alien, and becomes a self-sufficient power opposite him, that the life that he has lent to the object affronts him, hostile and alien.

Let us now deal in more detail with objectification, the production of the worker and the alienation, the loss of the object, his product, which is involved in it.

The worker can create nothing without nature, the sensuous exterior world. It is the matter in which his labour realizes itself, in which it is active, out of which and through which it produces.

But as nature affords the means of life for labour in the sense that labour cannot live without objects on which it exercises itself, so it affords a means of life in the narrower sense, namely the means for the physical subsistence of the worker himself.

Thus the more the worker appropriates the exterior world of sensuous nature by his labour, the more he doubly deprives himself of the means of subsistence, firstly since the exterior sensuous world increasingly ceases to be an object belonging to his work, a means of subsistence for his labour; secondly, since it increasingly ceases to be a means of subsistence in the direct sense, a means for the physical subsistence of the worker.

Thus in this double way the worker becomes a slave of his object: firstly he receives an object of labour, that is he receives labour, and secondly, he receives the means of subsistence. Thus it is his object that permits him to exist first as a worker and secondly as a physical subject. The climax of this slavery is that only as a worker can he maintain himself as a physical subject and it is only as a physical subject that he is a worker.

(According to the laws of political economy the alienation of the worker in his object is expressed as follows: the more the worker produces the less he has to consume, the more values he creates, the more valueless and worthless he becomes, the more formed the product the more deformed the worker, the more civilized the product, the more barbaric the worker, the more powerful the work, the more powerless becomes the worker, the more cultured the work, the more philistine the worker becomes and more of a slave to nature.)

Political economy hides the alienation in the essence of labour by not considering the immediate relationship between the worker (labour) and production. Labour produces works of wonder for the rich, but nakedness for the worker. It produces palaces, but only hovels for the worker; it produces beauty, but cripples the worker; it replaces labour by machines but throws a part of the workers back to a barbaric labour and turns the other part into machines. It produces culture, but also imbecility and cretinism for the worker.

The immediate relationship of labour to its products is the relationship of the worker to the objects of his production. The relationship of the man of means to the objects of production and to production itself is only a consequence of this first relationship. And it confirms it. We shall examine this other aspect later.

So when we ask the question: what relationship is essential to labour, we are asking about the relationship of the worker to production.

Up till now we have only considered one aspect of the alienation or externalization, of the worker, his relationship to the products of his labour. But alienation shows itself not only in the result, but also in the act of production, inside productive activity itself. How would the worker be able to affront the product of his work as an alien being if he did not alienate himself in the act of production itself? For the product is merely the summary of the activity of production. So if the product of labour is externalization, production itself must be active externalization, the externalization of activity, the activity of externalization. The alienation of the object of labour is only the résumé of the alienation, the externalization in the activity of labour itself.

What does the externalization of labour consist of then?

Firstly, that labour is exterior to the worker, that is, it does not belong to his essence. Therefore he does not confirm himself in his work, he denies himself, feels miserable instead of happy, deploys no free physical and intellectual energy, but mortifies his body and ruins his mind. Thus the worker only feels at home outside his work and in his work he feels a stranger. He is at home when he is not working and when he works he is not at home. His labour is therefore not voluntary but compulsory, forced labour. It is therefore not the satisfaction of a need but only a means to satisfy needs outside itself. How alien it really is is very evident from the fact that when there is no physical or other compulsion, labour is avoided like the plague. External labour, labour in which man externalizes himself, is a labour of self-sacrifice and mortification. Finally, the external character of labour for the worker shows itself in the fact that it is not his own but someone else's, that it does not belong to him, that he does not belong to himself in his labour but to someone else. As in religion the human imagination's own activity, the activity of man's head and his heart, reacts independently on the individual as an alien activity of gods or devils, so the activity of the worker is not his own spontaneous activity. It belongs to another and is the loss of himself.

The result we arrive at then is that man (the worker) only feels him-

self freely active in his animal functions of eating, drinking and procreating, at most also in his dwelling and dress, and feels himself an
animal in his human functions.

Eating, drinking, procreating, etc. are indeed truly human functions.
But in the abstraction that separates them from the other round of
human activity and makes them into final and exclusive ends they
become animal.

We have treated the act of alienation of practical human activity,
labour, from two aspects. (1) The relationship of the worker to the
product of his labour as an alien object that has power over him. This
relationship is at the same time the relationship to the sensuous exterior
world and to natural objects as to an alien and hostile world opposed to
him. (2) The relationship of labour to the act of production inside
labour. This relationship is the relationship of the worker to his own
activity as something that is alien and does not belong to him, it is
activity that is passivity, power that is weakness, procreation that is
castration, the worker's own physical and intellectual energy, his
personal life (for what is life except activity?) as an activity directed
against himself, independent of him and not belonging to him. It is
self-alienation, as above it was the alienation of the object.

We now have to draw a third characteristic of alienated labour from
the two previous ones.

Man is a species-being not only in that practically and theoretically
he makes both his own and other species into his objects, but also, and
this is only another way of putting the same thing, he relates to himself
as to the present, living species, in that he relates to himself as to a
universal and therefore free being.

Both with man and with animals the species-life consists physically
in the fact that man (like animals) lives from inorganic nature, and the
more universal man is than animals the more universal is the area of
inorganic nature from which he lives. From the theoretical point of
view, plants, animals, stones, air, light, etc. form part of human consciousness, partly as objects of natural science, partly as objects of art;
they are his intellectual inorganic nature, his intellectual means of
subsistence, which he must first prepare before he can enjoy and assimilate them. From the practical point of view, too, they form a part of
human life and activity. Physically man lives solely from these products

of nature, whether they appear as food, heating, clothing, habitation, etc. The universality of man appears in practice precisely in the universality that makes the whole of nature into his inorganic body in that it is both (i) his immediate means of subsistence and also (ii) the material object and tool of his vital activity. Nature is the inorganic body of man, that is, in as far as it is not itself a human body. That man lives from nature means that nature is his body with which he must maintain a constant interchange so as not to die. That man's physical and intellectual life depends on nature merely means that nature depends on itself, for man is a part of nature.

While alienated labour alienates (1) nature from man, and (2) man from himself, his own active function, his vital activity, it also alienates the species from man; it turns his species-life into a means towards his individual life. Firstly it alienates species-life and individual life, and secondly in its abstraction it makes the latter into the aim of the former which is also conceived of in its abstract and alien form. For firstly, work, vital activity and productive life itself appear to man only as a means to the satisfaction of a need, the need to preserve his physical existence. But productive life is species-life. It is life producing life. The whole character of a species, its generic character, is contained in its manner of vital activity and free conscious activity is the species-characteristic of man. Life itself appears merely as a means to life.

The animal is immediately one with its vital activity. It is not distinct from it. They are identical. Man makes his vital activity itself into an object of his will and consciousness. He has a conscious vital activity. He is not immediately identical to any of his characterizations. Conscious vital activity differentiates man immediately from animal vital activity. It is this and this alone that makes man a species-being. He is only a conscious being, that is his own life is an object to him, precisely because he is a species-being. This is the only reason for his activity being free activity. Alienated labour reverses the relationship so that, just because he is a conscious being, man makes his vital activity and essence a mere means to his existence.

The practical creation of an objective world, the working-over of inorganic nature is the confirmation of man as a conscious species-being, that is as a being that relates to the species as to himself and to himself as to the species. It is true that the animal, too, produces. It builds itself a nest, a dwelling, like the bee, the beaver, the ant, etc. But it only produces what it needs immediately for itself or its offspring; it produces one-sidedly whereas man produces universally; it produces only under the pressure of immediate physical need, whereas man produces free from physical need and only truly produces when he is thus free; it produces only itself whereas man reproduces the whole of nature. Its product belongs immediately to its physical body whereas man can freely separate himself from his product. The animal only fashions things according to the standards and needs of the species it belongs to, whereas man knows how to produce according to the measure of every species and knows everywhere how to apply its inherent standard to the object; thus man also fashions things according to the laws of beauty.

Thus it is in the working over of the objective world that man first really affirms himself as species-being. This production is his active species-life. Through it nature appears as his work and his reality. The object of work is therefore the objectification of the species-life of man; for he duplicates himself not only intellectually, in his mind, but also actively in reality and thus can look at his image in a world he has created. Therefore when alienated labour tears from man the object of his production, it also tears from him his species-life, the real objectivity of his species and turns the advantage he has over animals into a disadvantage in that his inorganic body, nature, is torn from him.

Similarly, in that alienated labour degrades man's own free activity to a means, it turns the species-life of man into a means for his physical existence.

Thus consciousness, which man derives from his species, changes itself through alienation so that species-life becomes a means for him.

Therefore alienated labour:

(3) makes the species-being of man, both nature and the intellectual faculties of his species, into a being that is alien to him, into a means for his individual existence. It alienates from man his own body, nature exterior to him, and his intellectual being, his human essence.

(4) An immediate consequence of man's alienation from the product of his work, his vital activity and his species-being, is the alienation of man from man. When man is opposed to himself, it is another man that is opposed to him. What is valid for the relationship of man to his work,

the product of his work and himself, is also valid for the relationship of man to other men and their labour and the objects of their labour.

In general, the statement that man is alienated from his species-being, means that one man is alienated from another as each of them is alienated from the human essence.

The alienation of man and in general of every relationship in which man stands to himself is first realized and expressed in the relationship with which man stands to other men.

Thus in the situation of alienated labour each man measures his relationship to other men by the relationship in which he finds himself placed as a worker.

We began with a fact of political economy, the alienation of the worker and his production. We have expressed this fact in conceptual terms: alienated, externalized labour. We have analysed this concept and thus analysed a purely economic fact.

Let us now see further how the concept of alienated, externalized labour must express and represent itself in reality.

If the product of work is alien to me, opposes me as an alien power, whom does it belong to then?

If my own activity does not belong to me and is an alien, forced activity to whom does it belong then?

To another being than myself.

Who is this being?

The gods? Of course in the beginning of history the chief production, as for example, the building of temples etc. in Egypt, India and Mexico was both in the service of the gods and also belonged to them. But the gods alone were never the masters of the work. And nature just as little. And what a paradox it would be if, the more man mastered nature through his work and the more the miracles of the gods were rendered superfluous by the miracles of industry, the more man had to give up his pleasure in producing and the enjoyment in his product for the sake of these powers.

The alien being to whom the labour and the product of the labour belongs, whom the labour serves and who enjoys its product, can only be man himself. If the product of labour does not belong to the worker but stands over against him as an alien power this is only possible in that it belongs to another man apart from the worker.

If his activity torments him it must be a joy and a pleasure to some-one else. This alien power above man can be neither the gods nor nature, only man himself.

Consider further the above sentence that the relationship of man to himself first becomes objective and real to him through his relationship to other men. So if he relates to the product of his labour, his objectified labour, as to an object that is alien, hostile, powerful and independent of him, this relationship implies that another man is the alien, hostile, powerful and independent master of this object. If he relates to his own activity as to something unfree, it is a relationship to an activity that is under the domination, oppression and yoke of another man.

Every self-alienation of man from himself and nature appears in the relationship in which he places himself and nature to other men distinct from himself. Therefore religious self-alienation necessarily appears in the relationship of layman to priest, or, because here we are dealing with a spiritual world, to a mediator, etc. In the practical, real world, the self-alienation can only appear through the practical, real relation-ship to other men. The means through which alienation makes progress are themselves practical. Through alienated labour then man creates not only his relationship to the object and act of production as to alien and hostile men; he creates too the relationship in which other men stand to his production and his product and the relationship in which he stands to these other men. Just as he turns his production into his own loss of reality and punishment and his own product into a loss, a product that does not belong to him, so he creates the domination of the man who does not produce over the production and the product. As he alienates his activity from himself, so he hands over to an alien person an activity that does not belong to him.

Up till now we have considered the relationship only from the side of the worker and we will later consider it from the side of the non-worker.

Thus through alienated, externalized labour the worker creates the relationship to this labour of a man who is alien to it and remains ex-terior to it. The relationship of the worker to his labour creates the relationship to it of the capitalist, or whatever else one wishes to call the master of the labour. Private property is thus the product, result and necessary consequence of externalized labour, of the exterior relationship of the worker to nature and to himself.

Thus private property is the result of the analysis of the concept of externalized labour, i.e. externalized man, alienated work, alienated life, alienated man.

We have, of course, obtained the concept of externalized labour (externalized life) from political economy as the result of the movement of private property. But it is evident from the analysis of this concept, that although private property appears to be the ground and reason for externalized labour, it is rather a consequence of it, just as the gods are originally not the cause but the effect of the aberration of the human mind, although later this relationship reverses itself.

It is only in the final culmination of the development of private property that these hidden characteristics come once more to the fore in that firstly it is the product of externalized labour and secondly it is the means through which labour externalizes itself, the realization of this externalization.

This development sheds light at the same time on several previously unresolved contradictions.

1. Political economy starts from labour as the veritable soul of production, and yet it attributes nothing to labour and everything to private property. Proudhon has drawn a conclusion from this contradiction that is favourable to labour and against private property. But we can see that this apparent contradiction is the contradiction of alienated labour with itself and that political economy has only expressed the laws of alienated labour.

We can therefore also see that wages and private property are identical: for wages, in which the product, the object of the labour, remunerates the labour itself, are just a necessary consequence of the alienation of labour. In the wage system the labour does not appear as the final aim but only as the servant of the wages. We will develop this later and for the moment only draw a few consequences.

An enforced raising of wages (quite apart from other difficulties, apart from the fact that, being an anomaly, it could only be maintained by force) would only mean a better payment of slaves and would not give this human meaning and worth either to the worker or to his labour.

Indeed, even the equality of wages that Proudhon demands only changes the relationship of the contemporary worker to his labour into that of all men to labour. Society is then conceived of as an abstract capitalist.

Wages are an immediate consequence of alienated labour and alienated labour is the immediate cause of private property. Thus the disappearance of one entails also the disappearance of the other.

2. It is a further consequence of the relationship of alienated labour to private property that the emancipation of society from private property, etc, from slavery, is expressed in its political form by the emancipation of the workers. This is not because only their emancipation is at stake but because general human emancipation is contained in their emancipation. It is contained within it because the whole of human slavery is involved in the relationship of the worker to his product and all slave relationships are only modifications and consequences of this relationship.

Just as we have discovered the concept of private property through an analysis of the concept of alienated, externalized labour, so all categories of political economy can be deduced with the help of these two factors. We shall recognize in each category of market, competition, capital, money, only a particular and developed expression of these first two fundamental elements.

However, before we consider this structure let us try to solve two problems:

1. To determine the general essence of private property as it appears as a result of alienated labour in its relationship to truly human and social property.

2. We have taken the alienation and externalization of labour as a fact and analysed this fact. We now ask, how does man come to externalize, to alienate his labour? How is this alienation grounded in human development? We have already obtained much material for the solution of this problem in that we have turned the question of the origin of private property into the question of the relationship of externalized labour to the development of human history. For when we speak of private property we think we are dealing with something that is exterior to man. When we speak of labour, then we are dealing directly with man. This new formulation of the problem already implies its solution.

As to point 1, the general nature of private property and its relationship to truly human property.

Externalized labour has been broken down into two component parts that determine each other or are only different expressions of one and the same relationship. Appropriation appears as alienation, as externalization, and externalization as appropriation and alienation as true enfranchisement. We have dealt with one aspect, alienated labour as regards the worker himself, that is, the relationship of externalized labour to itself. As a product and necessary result of this relationship we have discovered the property relationship of the non-worker to the worker and his labour.

As the material and summary expression of alienated labour, private property embraces both relationships, both that of the worker to his labour, the product of his labour and the non-worker, and that of the non-worker to the worker and the product of his labour.

We have already seen that for the worker who appropriates nature through his work, this appropriation appears as alienation, his own activity as activity for and of someone else, his vitality as sacrifice of his life, production of objects as their loss to an alien power, an alien man: let us now consider the relationship that this man, who is alien to labour and the worker, has to the worker, to labour and its object.

The first remark to make is that everything that appears in the case of the worker to be an activity of externalization, of alienation appears in the case of the non-worker to be a state of externalization, of alienation.

Secondly, the real, practical behaviour of the worker in production and towards his product (as a state of mind) appears in the case of the non-worker opposed to him as theoretical behaviour. Thirdly, the non-worker does everything against the worker that the worker does against himself but he does not do against himself what he does against the worker.

Let us consider these three relationships in more detail.[1]

Private Property and Communism

The overcoming of self-alienation follows the same course as self-alienation itself. At first, private property is considered only from its

[1] The manuscript breaks off unfinished here.

objective aspect, but still with labour as its essence. The form of its existence is therefore capital, that is to be abolished 'as such' (Proudhon). Or else the source of the nocivity of private property, its alienation from human existence, is thought of as consisting in the particular type of labour, labour which is levelled down, fragmented and therefore un-free. This is the view of Fourier who like the physiocrats also considered agriculture as labour *par excellence*. Saint-Simon on the other hand declares industrial labour to be the essential type and demands as well exclusive rule by industrialists and the improvement of the condition of the workers. Finally, communism is the positive expression of the overcoming of private property, appearing first of all as generalized private property. In making this relationship universal communism is:

1. In its original form only a generalization and completion of private property. As such it appears in a dual form: firstly, it is faced with such a great domination of material property that it wishes to destroy everything that cannot be possessed by everybody as private property; it wishes to abstract forcibly from talent, etc. It considers immediate physical ownership as the sole aim of life and being. The category of worker is not abolished but extended to all men. The relationship of the community to the world of things remains that of private property. Finally, this process of opposing general private property to private property is expressed in the animal form of opposing to marriage (which is of course a form of exclusive private property) the community of women where the woman becomes the common property of the community. One might say that the idea of the community of women reveals the open secret of this completely crude and unthinking type of communism. Just as women pass from marriage to universal prostitution, so the whole world of wealth, that is the objective essence of man, passes from the relationship of exclusive marriage to the private property owner to the relationship of universal prostitution with the community. By systematically denying the per-sonality of man this communism is merely the consistent expression of private property which is just this negation. Universal envy setting itself up as a power is the concealed form of greed which merely asserts itself and satisfies itself in another way. The thoughts of every private property owner as such are at least turned against those richer than they as an envious desire to level down. This envious desire is precisely

the essence of competition. Crude communism is only the completion of this envy and levelling down to a preconceived minimum. It has a particular and limited standard. How little this abolition of private property constitutes a real appropriation is proved by the abstract negation of the whole world of culture and civilization, a regression to the unnatural simplicity of the poor man without any needs who has not even arrived at the stage of private property, let alone got beyond it.

In this theory the community merely means a community of work and equality of the wages that the communal capital, the community as general capitalist, pays out. Both sides of the relationship are raised to a sham universality, labour being the defining characteristic applied to each man, while capital is the universality and power of society.

The infinite degradation in which man exists for himself is expressed in his relationship to woman as prey and servant of communal lust; for the secret of this relationship finds an unambiguous, decisive, open and unveiled expression in the relationship of man to woman and the conception of the immediate and natural relationship of the sexes. The immediate, natural and necessary relationship of human being to human being is the relationship of man to woman. In this natural relationship of the sexes man's relationship to nature is immediately his relationship to man, and his relationship to man is immediately his relationship to nature, his own natural function. Thus, in this relationship is sensuously revealed and reduced to an observable fact how far for man his essence has become nature or nature has become man's human essence. Thus, from this relationship the whole cultural level of man can be judged. From the character of this relationship we can conclude how far man has become a species-being, a human being, and conceives of himself as such; the relationship of man to woman is the most natural relationship of human being to human being. Thus it shows how far the natural behaviour of man has become human or how far the human essence has become his natural essence, how far his human nature has become nature for him. This relationship also shows how far the need of man has become a human need, how far his fellow men as men have become a need, how far in his most individual existence he is at the same time a communal being.

The first positive abolition of private property, crude communism, is thus only the form in which appears the ignominy of private property that wishes to establish itself as the positive essence of the community.

2. The second form of communism is: (a) still political in nature, whether democratic or despotic; (b) with the abolition of the state, but still incomplete and still under the influence of private property, i.e. the alienation of man. In both forms communism knows itself already to be the reintegration or return of man into himself, the abolition of man's self-alienation. But since it has not yet grasped the positive essence of private property or the human nature of needs, it is still imprisoned and contaminated by private property. It has understood its concept, but not yet its essence.

3. Thirdly, there is communism as the positive abolition of private property and thus of human self-alienation and therefore the real reappropriation of the human essence by and for man. This is communism as the complete and conscious return of man conserving all the riches of previous development for man himself as a social, i.e. human being. Communism as completed naturalism is humanism and as completed humanism is naturalism. It is the genuine solution of the antagonism between man and nature and between man and man. It is the true solution of the struggle between existence and essence, between objectification and self-affirmation, between freedom and necessity, between individual and species. It is the solution to the riddle of history and knows itself to be this solution.

The whole movement of history, therefore, both as regards the real engendering of this communism, the birth of its empirical existence, and also as regards its consciousness and thought, is the consciously comprehended process of its becoming. On the other hand, the communism that is still incomplete seeks an historical proof for itself in what already exists by selecting isolated historical formations opposed to private property. It tears isolated phases out of the movement (Cabet, Villegardelle, etc. in particular ride this hobby horse) and asserts them as proofs of its historical pedigree. But all it succeeds in showing is that the disproportionately larger part of this movement contradicts its assertions and that if it has ever existed, it is precisely its past being that refutes its pretension to essential being.

We can easily see how necessary it is that the whole revolutionary movement should find not so much its empirical as its theoretical basis in the development of private property and particularly the economic system.

This material, immediately sensuous, private property, is the material, sensuous expression of man's alienated life. Its movement of production and consumption is the sensuous revelation of the movement of all previous production, i.e. the realization or reality of man. Religion, family, state, law, morality, science and art are only particular forms of production and fall under its general law. The positive abolition of private property and the appropriation of human life is therefore the positive abolition of all alienation, thus the return of man out of religion, family, state, etc. into his human, i.e. social being. Religious alienation as such occurs only in man's interior consciousness, but economic alienation is that of real life and its abolition therefore covers both aspects. It is obvious that the movement begins differently with different peoples according to whether the actual conscious life of the people is lived in their minds or in the outer world, is an ideal or a real life. Communism begins immediately with atheism (Owen) and atheism is at first still very far from being communism, for this atheism is still rather an abstraction.[1] The philanthropy of atheism is therefore at first only an abstract philosophical philanthropy whereas that of communism is immediately real and directly orientated towards action.

We have seen how presupposing the positive supercession of private property man produces man, himself and other men; how also the object, which is the direct result of his personal activity, is at the same time his own existence for other men and their existence for him. In the same way, both the materials of his labour and man its author are the result and at the same time the origin of the movement. (And private property is historically necessary precisely because there must be this origin.) So the general character of the whole movement is a social one; as society produces man as man, so it is produced by man. Activity and

---

[1] Prostitution is only a particular expression of the general prostitution of the worker, and because prostitution is a relationship which includes both the person prostituted and the person prostituting—whose baseness is even greater —thus the capitalist, too, etc. is included within this category. (Footnote by Marx.)

N

enjoyment are social both in their content and in their mode of existence; they are social activity and social enjoyment. The human significance of nature is only available to social man; for only to social man is nature available as a bond with other men, as the basis of his own existence for others and theirs for him, and as the vital element in human reality; only to social man is nature the foundation of his own human existence. Only as such has his natural existence become a human existence and nature itself become human. Thus society completes the essential unity of man and nature, it is the genuine resurrection of nature, the accomplished naturalism of man and the accomplished humanism of nature.

Social activity and social enjoyment by no means exist only in the form of a directly communal activity and directly communal enjoyment. But communal activity and enjoyment, i.e. activity and enjoyment that is expressed and confirmed in the real society of other men, will occur everywhere where this direct expression of sociability arises from the content of the activity or enjoyment and corresponds to its nature.

But even if my activity is a scientific one etc., an activity that I can seldom perform directly in company with other men, I am still acting socially since I am acting as a man. Not only the material of my activity —like language itself for the thinker—is given to me as a social product, my own existence is social activity; therefore what I individually produce, I produce individually for society, conscious of myself as a social being.

My universal consciousness is only the theoretical form whose living form is the real community, society, whereas at the present time universal consciousness is an abstraction from real life and as such turns into its enemy. Thus the activity of my universal consciousness is as such my theoretical existence as a social being.

It is above all necessary to avoid restoring society as a fixed abstraction opposed to the individual. The individual is the social being. Therefore, even when the manifestation of his life does not take the form of a communal manifestation performed in the company of other men, it is still a manifestation and confirmation of social life. The individual and the species-life of man are not different, although, necessarily, the mode of existence of individual life is a more particular or a more general mode of species-life or the species-life is a more particular or more general individual life.

Man confirms his real social life in his species-consciousness and in his thought he merely repeats his real existence just as conversely his species-being is confirmed in his species-consciousness and exists for itself in its universality as a thinking being.

However much he is a particular individual (and it is precisely his particularity that makes him an individual and a truly individual communal being) man is just as much the totality, the ideal totality, the subjective existence of society as something thought and felt. Man exists also in reality both as the contemplation and true enjoyment of social existence and as the totality of human manifestations of life.

Thus thought and being are indeed distinct, but at the same time they together form a unity.

Death appears as the harsh victory of the species over the particular individual and seems to contradict their unity; but the particular individual is only a determinate species-being and thus mortal.

⟨4. Private property is only the sensuous expression of the fact that man is both objective to himself and even more becomes a hostile and inhuman object to himself, that the expression of his life entails its externalization, its realization becomes the loss of its reality, an alien reality. Similarly the positive supersession of private property, that is, the sensuous appropriation by and for man of human essence and human life, of objective man and his works, should not be conceived of only as direct and exclusive enjoyment, as possession and having. Man appropriates his universal being in a universal manner, as a whole man. Each of his human relationships to the world—seeing, hearing, smell, tasting, feeling, thinking, contemplating, feeling, willing, acting, loving—in short all the organs of his individuality, just as the organs whose form is a directly communal one, are in their objective action, or their relation to the object, the appropriation of this object. The appropriation of human reality, their relationship to the object, is the confirmation of human reality. It is therefore as manifold as the determinations and activities of human nature. It is human effectiveness and suffering, for suffering, understood in the human sense, is an enjoyment of the self for man.⟩

Private property has made us so stupid and narrow-minded that an object is only ours when we have it, when it exists as capital for us or when we directly possess, eat, drink, wear, inhabit it, etc. in short, when we use it. Yet private property itself in its turn conceives of all these direct realizations of property merely as means of life, and the life which they serve is that of private property, labour and capitalization.

Thus all physical and intellectual senses have been replaced by the simple alienation of all these senses, the sense of having. Man's essence had to be reduced to this absolute poverty, so it might bring forth out of itself its own inner riches. (On the category of having see Hess in *Twenty-One Sheets*.)[1]

The supersession of private property is therefore the complete emancipation of all human senses and qualities, but it is this emancipation precisely in that these senses and qualities have become human, both subjectively and objectively. The eye has become a human eye when its object has become a social, human object produced by man and destined for him. Thus in practice the senses have become direct theoreticians. They relate to the thing for its own sake but the thing itself is an objective human relationship to itself and to man and vice versa. (I can in practice only relate myself humanly to an object if the object relates itself humanly to man.) Need and enjoyment have thus lost their egoistic nature and nature has lost its mere utility in that its utility has become human utility.

In the same way I can appropriate the senses and enjoyment of other men. Apart, then, from these immediate organs, social organs are constituted in the form of society: thus, for example, direct social activity with others is an organ of the manifestation of life and a manner in which to appropriate human life.

It is evident that the human eye enjoys things differently from the crude, inhuman eye, the human ear differently from the crude ear, etc.

We have seen that man does not lose himself in his object provided that it is a human object or objective humanity. This is only possible if it becomes a social object for him and he himself becomes a social being, while society becomes a being for him in this object.

Therefore in so far as generally in society reality becomes the

---

[1] See M. Hess, *Philosophische und Sozialistische Aufsätze*, ed. Cornu and Mönke, Berlin, 1961, p. 225.

reality of man's faculties, human reality, and thus the reality of his own faculties, all objects become for him the objectification of himself. They are objects that confirm and realize his individuality, his own objects, i.e. he becomes an object himself. How they become his own depends on the nature of the object and the faculty that corresponds to it. For it is just the distinctness of this relationship that constitutes the specific real mode of affirmation. The eye perceives an object differently from the ear and the object of the eye is different from that of the ear. What makes each faculty distinct is just its particular essence and thus also the particular mode of its objectification, of its objectively real, living being. Thus man is affirmed in the objective world not only in thought but through all his senses.

⟨Just as society that is being born finds all of the material for its cultural formation through the development of private property with its material and intellectual wealth and poverty, so society when formed produces man in the whole wealth of its being, man rich in profound and manifold sensitivity as its constant reality.⟩

It can be seen how subjectivism and objectivism, spiritualism and materialism, activity and passivity lose their opposition and thus their existence as opposites only in a social situation; ⟨ it can be seen how the solution of theoretical opposition is only possible in a practical way, only through the practical energy of man and their solution is thus by no means an exercise in epistemology but a real problem of life that philosophy could not solve just because it conceived of it as a purely theoretical task.⟩

⟨It can be seen how the history of industry and its previous objective existence is an open book of man's faculties and his psychology available to view. It was previously not conceived of in its connection with man's essence but only under the exterior aspect of utility, because man, moving inside the sphere of alienation, could only apprehend religion as the generalized existence of man, or history in its abstract and universal form of politics, art, literature, etc., as the reality of human faculties and the human species-act. In every day, material industry (which one can just as well consider as a part of that general development, or the general development can be considered as a particular part of industry, because all human activity has hitherto been labour, i.e. industry, self-alienated activity) we have the objectified faculties of man before us in the form of sensuous, alien, utilitarian objects, in the form of alienation. A psychology for which this book, and therewith the most tangible and accessible part of history, remains closed cannot become a genuine science with a real content.⟩ What should one think of a science whose preconceptions disregarded this large field of man's labour and which is not conscious of its incompleteness even though so broad a wealth of man's labour means nothing to it apart, perhaps, from what can be expressed in a single word 'need', and 'common need'?

The natural sciences have developed an enormous activity and appropriated an ever-increasing amount of material. However, philosophy has remained as alien to them as they to philosophy. The momentary union was only an imaginary illusion. The wish was there, but the ability lacking. Historians themselves only afford natural science a passing glance, as making for enlightenment, utility and isolated great discoveries. But natural science by means of industry has penetrated human life all the more effectively, changed its form and prepared for human emancipation, even though in the first place it had to complete dehumanization. Industry is the real historical relationship of nature, and therefore of natural science, to man. If then it is conceived of as the open revelation of human faculties, then the human essence of nature or the natural essence of man will also be understood. Natural science will then lose its one-sidedly materialist, or rather idealistic, orientation and become the basis of human science as it has already, though in an alienated form, become the basis of actual human life. And to have one basis for life and another for science would be in itself a falsehood. ⟨Nature as it is formed in human history—the birth process of human society—is the real nature of man and thus nature as fashioned by industry is true anthropological nature, though in an alienated form.⟩

Sense-experience (see Feuerbach) must be the basis of all science. Science is only real science when it starts from sense-experience in the dual form of sense perception and sensuous need, so when it starts from nature. The whole of history is a preparation for 'man' to become the object of sense perception and for needs to be the needs of 'man as man'. History itself is the real part of natural history, of nature's becoming man. Natural science will later comprise the science of man just as much as the science of man will embrace natural science; they will be one single science.

Man is the direct object of natural science; for directly sensuous nature for man is man's sense-experience (the expressions are identical) in the shape of other men presented to him in a sensuous way. For it is only through his fellow man that his sense-experience becomes human for him. But nature is the direct object of the science of man. Man's first object—man himself—is nature, sense-experience; and particular human sensuous faculties are only objectively realized in natural objects and can only attain to self-knowledge in the science of nature in general. The elements of thought itself, the element of the vital manifestation of thought, language, is sensuous in character. The social reality of nature and human natural science or the natural science of man are identical expressions.

⟨It can be seen how the wealthy man and the plenitude of human need take place of economic wealth and poverty. The wealthy man is the man who needs a complete manifestation of human life and a man in whom his own realization exists as an inner necessity, as a need. Not only the wealth of man but also his poverty contain equally, under socialism, a human and therefore social meaning. Poverty is the passive bond that lets man feel his greatest wealth, his fellow man, as a need. The domination of the objective essence within me, the sensuous eruption of my essential activity is the passion that here becomes the activity of my essence.⟩

5. A being only counts itself as independent when it stands on its own feet and it stands on its own feet as long as it owes its existence to itself. A man who lives by grace of another considers himself a dependent being. But I live completely by the grace of another when I owe him not only the maintenance of my life but when he has also created my life, when he is the source of my life. And my life necessarily has such a ground outside itself if it is not my own creation. The idea of creation is thus one that it is very difficult to drive out of the minds of people. They find it impossible to conceive of nature and man existing through themselves since it contradicts all the evidences of practical life.

The idea of the creation of the world received a severe blow from the science of geogeny, the science which describes the formation and coming into being of the earth as a process of self-generation. Spontaneous generation is the only practical refutation of the theory of creation.

Now it is easy to say to the single individual what Aristotle already said: you are engendered by your father and your mother and so in your case it is the mating of two human beings, a human species-act, that has produced the human being. You see, too, that physically also man owes his existence to man. So you must not only bear in mind the aspect of the infinite regression and ask further: who engendered my father and his grandfather, etc., you must also grasp the circular movement observable in that progression whereby man renews himself by procreation and thus always remains the subject. But you will answer: I grant you this circular movement but then grant me the progression that pushes me ever further backwards until I ask, who created the first man and the world as a whole? I can only answer you: your question itself is a product of abstraction. Ask yourself how you come to ask such a question; ask yourself whether your question is not put from a standpoint that I cannot accept because it is an inverted one. Ask yourself whether that progress exists as such for rational thought. When you enquire about the creation of the world and man, then you abstract from man and the world. You suppose them non-existent and yet require me to prove to you that they exist. I say to you: give up your abstraction and you will give up your question or if you wish to stick to your abstraction, then be consistent and if you think of man and the world as non-existent, then think of yourself as non-existent, also, for you too are a part of the world and man. Do not think, do not ask me questions, for immediately you think and ask, your abstraction from the being of nature and man has no meaning. Or are you such an egoist that you suppose everything to be nothing and yet wish to exist yourself?

You can reply to me: I do not wish to suppose the nothingness of the world and so on; I am only asking you about their origins, as I ask an anatomist about the formation of bones, etc.

But since for socialist man what is called world history is nothing but the creation of man by human labour and the development of nature for man, he has the observable and irrefutable proof of his self-creation and the process of his origin. Once the essential reality of man in nature, man as the existence of nature for man, and nature for man as the existence of man, has become evident in practical life and sense experience, then the question of an alien being, of a being above nature and man—a question that implies an admission of the unreality of nature and man—has become impossible in practice. Atheism, as a denial of this unreality, has no longer any meaning, for atheism is a denial of God and tries to assert through this negation the existence of man; but socialism as such no longer needs this mediation; it starts from the theoretical and practical sense-perception of man and nature as the true reality. It is the positive self-consciousness of man no longer mediated through the negation of religion, just as real life is the positive reality of man no longer mediated through communism as the negation of private property. Communism represents the positive in the form of the negation of the negation and thus a phase in human emancipation and rehabilitation, both real and necessary at this juncture of human development. Communism is the necessary form and dynamic principle of the immediate future, but communism is not as such the goal of human development, the form of human society.

Critique of Hegel's Dialectic and General Philosophy

6. Perhaps this is the place to make some remarks towards an understanding and justification of my attitude to Hegel's dialectic in general and in particular its elaboration in the *Phenomenology* and *Logic* and finally about its relationship to the modern critical movement.

Modern German criticism was so busy with the content of what it had inherited, and its progress, though imprisoned within its material, was so forceful that there developed a completely uncritical attitude to the method of criticism and a total unawareness of the apparently merely formal but in fact essential question: where do we stand now concerning Hegel's dialectic? The unawareness of the relationship of modern criticism to Hegel's philosophy in general and his dialectic in particular was so great that critics like Strauss[1] and Bruno Bauer are completely imprisoned within Hegel's logic, the former completely and the latter at least implicitly in his *Synoptics*[2] (where, in opposition to Strauss, he replaces the substance of 'abstract nature' with the 'self-

---

[1] D. F. Strauss, *Das Leben Jesu*, Tübingen, 1835/6.
[2] Bruno Bauer, *Kritik der evangelischen Geschichte der Synoptiker*, Leipzig and Braunschweig, 1841/2.

consciousness' of abstract man) and even in his *Christianity Revealed*.[1] Thus we read for example in *Christianity Revealed:* 'as though self-consciousness, in positing the world, that which is different, and in producing itself in what it produces, since it then suppresses the difference between its product and itself and is only itself in the productive movement, did not have its purpose in this movement'[2] etc. Or: 'they (the French materialists) have not yet appreciated that the movement of the universe only becomes really explicit and achieves unity with itself in the movement of self consciousness'.[3] Not only do these expressions not differ in their vocabulary from the Hegelian conception, they even repeat it literally.

How little during the process of criticism (Bauer in his *Synoptics*) an awareness was shown of its relationship to Hegel's dialectic and how little this awareness arose even after the process of material criticism, is shown by Bauer when in his *Good Cause of Freedom*[4] he brushes aside the indiscrete question of Herr Gruppe 'what will now happen to logic?' by referring him to future critics.

But now Feuerbach, both in his *Theses*[5] in the *Anekdota* and in more detail in his *Philosophy of the Future*,[6] has radically reversed the old dialectic and philosophy and the criticism that was unable to accomplish this itself, has seen it done by someone else, and proclaimed itself pure, decisive and absolute criticism that has a clear vision of itself.[7] This criticism has now in its spiritual pride reduced the whole movement of history to the relationship between itself and the rest of the world that by contrast falls into the category of 'the mass', and dissolved all dogmatic oppositions into the single dogmatic opposition between its own cleverness and the stupidity of the world, between the critical Christ and the 'rabble' of humanity. It has daily and hourly demonstrated its own excellence in comparison with the stupidity of the mass

[1] Bruno Bauer, *Das entdeckte Christentum*, Zurich and Winterthur, 1843.

[2] Bruno Bauer, op. cit., p. 113.

[3] Bruno Bauer, op. cit., pp. 114 f.

[4] Bruno Bauer, *Die gute Sache der Freiheit und meine eigene Angelegenheit*, Zurich and Winterthur, 1842, pp. 193 ff.

[5] See p. xxi.

[6] See p. xxi.

[7] Marx refers to Bruno Bauer's *Allgemeine Literatur Zeitung*, Charlottenburg, 1844.

and has finally announced the critical last judgment in that the day is approaching when the whole of fallen humanity will be assembled before it, be divided into groups and each particular rabble receive its certificate of poverty.[1] The critical school has published its superiority to human sentiments and to the world over which, enthroned in superior solitude, it lets echo from time to time from its sarcastic lips the laughter of the Olympian gods. After all these entertaining antics of idealism (Young Hegelianism) whose death agony takes the form of criticism, it has not once breathed a word of the necessity of a critical debate with its own source, Hegel's dialectic; indeed it has not even been capable of giving any criticism of Feuerbach's dialectic. It is thoroughly devoid of self-criticism.

Feuerbach is the only person to have a serious and critical relationship to the Hegelian dialectic and to have made real discoveries in this field; in short, he has overcome the old philosophy. The greatness of his achievement and the unpretentious simplicity with which Feuerbach presents it to the world are in a strikingly opposite inverse ratio.

Feuerbach's great achievement is:

1. To have proved that philosophy is nothing but religion conceptualized and rationally developed; and thus that it is equally to be condemned as another form and mode of existence of human alienation.

2. To have founded true materialism and real science by making the social relationship of 'man to man' the basic principle of his theory.

3. To have opposed to the negation of the negation that claims to be the absolute positive, the positive that has its own self for foundation and basis.

This is how Feuerbach explains Hegel's dialectic and thus justifies his taking the positive knowledge afforded by the senses as his starting point:

Hegel starts from the alienation of substance (in logical terms: infinity, abstract universality), from the absolute and unmoved abstraction, i.e. in popular language, he starts, from religion and theology.

Secondly, he supersedes the infinite and posits the actual, the perceptible, the real, the finite and the particular. (Philosophy as supersession of religion and theology.)

[1] Marx refers to an article by Hirzel in *Allgemeine Literatur Zeitung*, no. 5, p. 15.

Thirdly, he supersedes the positive in its turn and reinstates the abstraction, the infinite. Reinstatement of religion and theology.

Thus Feuerbach conceives of the negation of the negation only as an internal contradiction of philosophy, as philosophy that affirms theology (transcendance, etc.) after it has just denied it and thus affirms it in opposition to itself.

The positing of self-affirmation and self-confirmation present in the negation of the negation is not considered to be an independent affirmation since it is not yet sure of itself, still burdened with its opposite, doubtful of itself and thus needing proof and not demonstrated by the fact of its own existence. It is therefore contrasted directly with affirmation that is verified by the senses and based on itself.

But Hegel has nevertheless discovered an expression of the historical movement that is merely abstract, logical and speculative in that he conceived of the positive aspect of the negation of the negation as the sole, unique positive and the negative aspect in it as the only true self-affirming act of all being. This history is not yet the real history of man as a presupposed subject but only the history of the act of creation and the origin of man. We shall explain both the abstract form of this movement in Hegel and also what differentiates it from modern criticism and the same process in Feuerbachs' *Essence of Christianity*; or rather, we explain the critical form of the process that is still uncritical in Hegel.

Let us look at Hegel's system. We must begin with Hegel's *Phenomenology*, the true birth place and secret of Hegel's philosophy.

PHENOMENOLOGY

(A) SELF–CONSCIOUSNESS

I. *Consciousness*

(a) Sense certainty or the 'this' and meaning.

(b) Perception or the thing with its properties and illusion.

(c) Power and understanding, phenomena and the super-sensible world.

II. *Self-consciousness*. The truth of the certainty of oneself.

    (*a*) Dependence and independence of self-consciousness. Mastery and servitude.

    (*b*) Freedom of self-consciousness. Stoicism and scepticism. The unhappy consciousness.

III. *Reason*. Certainty and truth of reason.

    (*a*) Observational reason: observation of nature and self-conciousness.

    (*b*) Realization of rational self-consciousness through itself. Pleasure and necessity. The law of the heart and the madness of self-conceit. Virtue and the way of the world.

    (*c*) Individuality which is real in and for itself. Legislative reason. Reason as testing laws.

(B) SPIRIT

  I. True spirit: customary morality.

  II. Self-alienated spirit, culture.

III. Spirit sure of itself, morality.

(C) RELIGION

Natural religion, the religion of art, revealed religion.

(D) ABSOLUTE KNOWLEDGE

Hegel's *Encyclopaedia* begins with logic, with pure speculative thought and ends with absolute knowledge, with the philosophical or absolute, i.e. super-human, abstract mind that is self-conscious and self-conceiving. Similarly the whole of the *Encyclopaedia* is nothing but the extended being of philosophical mind, its self-objectification; and philosophical mind is nothing but the alienated mind of the world conceiving of itself and thinking inside its self-alienation, i.e. abstractly. Logic is the money of the mind, the speculative thought-value of man and nature, their essence which has become indifferent to any real determination and thus unreal. It is externalized thought that abstracts from nature and real man, abstract thought. The exterior character of this abstract thought . . . nature as it exists for this abstract thought. Nature is exterior to it and represents its loss of itself. And mind understands nature as exterior, as an abstract thought, but as alien abstract thought. Finally spirit, which is thought returning to its birthplace and which, as anthropological, phenomenological, psychological, moral and artistic–religious spirit, only considers itself valid when it finally discovers and affirms itself as absolute knowledge in absolute, i.e. abstract, spirit, receives its conscious and appropriate existence. For its real mode of existence is abstraction.

Hegel has committed a double error.

The first is most evident in the *Phenomenology*, the birthplace of the Hegelian philosophy. When he considers, for example, wealth and the power of the state as beings alienated from man's being, this happens only in their conceptual form. . . . They are conceptual beings and thus simply an alienation of pure, i.e. abstract, philosophical thought. The whole process therefore ends with absolute knowledge. What these objects are alienated from and what they affront with their pretention to reality, is just abstract thought. The philosopher, who is himself an abstract form of alienated man, sets himself up as the measure of the alienated world. The whole history of externalization and the whole recovery of this externalization is therefore nothing but the history of the production of abstract, i.e. absolute thought, logical, speculative thought. Alienation, which thus forms the real interest of this externalization and its supersession is the opposition inside thought itself of the implicit and the explicit, of consciousness and self-consciousness of object and subject, that is, it is the opposition inside thought itself, of abstract thought and sensuous reality or real sensuous experience.

All other oppositions and their movements are only the appearance, the cloak, the exoteric form of these two opposites that alone are interesting and which give meaning to other, profane contradictions. What is supposed to be the essence of alienation that needs to be transcended is not that man's being objectifies itself in an inhuman manner in opposition to itself, but that it objectifies itself in distinction from, and in opposition to, abstract thought.

The appropriation of man's objectified and alienated faculties is thus firstly only an appropriation that occurs in the mind, in pure thought, i.e. in abstraction. It is the appropriation of these objects as thoughts and thought processes. Therefore in the *Phenomenology* in spite of its thoroughly negative and critical appearance and in spite of the genuine criticism, often well in advance of later developments, that is contained within it, one can already see concealed as a germ, as a secret potentiality, the uncritical positivism and equally uncritical idealism of Hegel's later works, this philosophical dissolution and restoration of existing empirical reality. Secondly, the vindication of the objective world for man (for example, the knowledge that sense perception is not abstract sense perception but human sense perception; that religion, wealth, etc., are only the alienated reality of human objectification, of human faculties put out to work and therefore only the way to true human reality), this appropriation or the insight into this process appears in Hegel in such a way that sense perception, religion, state power, etc., are spiritual beings; for spirit alone is the true essence of man and the true form of spirit is thinking spirit, logical, speculative spirit. The human character of nature and of historically produced nature, the product of man, appears as such in that they are products of abstract mind, and thus phases of mind, conceptual beings. The *Phenomenology* is thus concealed criticism that is still obscure to itself and mystifying; but in so far as it grasps the alienation of man, even though man appears only in the form of mind, it contains all the elements of criticism concealed, often already prepared and elaborated in a way that far surpasses Hegel's own point of view. The 'unhappy consciousness', the 'honest consciousness', the struggle of the 'noble and base consciousness' etc. etc., these single sections contain the elements, though still in an alienated form, of a criticism of whole spheres like religion, the state, civil life, etc. Just as the essence, the object appears as a conceptual being, so the subject is always consciousness or self-consciousness, or rather the object only appears as abstract consciousness, man only as self-consciousness. Thus the different forms of alienation that occur are only different forms of consciousness and self-consciousness. Since the abstract consciousness that the object is regarded as being, is only in itself a phase in the differentiation of self-consciousness, the result of the process is the identity of consciousness and self-consciousness, absolute knowledge, the process of abstract thought that is no longer outward looking but only takes place inside itself. In other words, the result is the dialectic of pure thought.

Therefore the greatness of Hegel's *Phenomenology* and its final product, the dialectic of negativity as the moving and creating principle, is on the one hand that Hegel conceives of the self-creation of man as a process, objectification as loss of the object, as externalization and the transcendence of this externalization. This means, therefore, that he grasps the nature of labour and understands objective man, true, because real, man as the result of his own labour. The real, active relationship of man to himself as a species-being or the manifestation of himself as a real species-being, i.e. as a human being, is only possible if he uses all his species powers to create (which is again only possible through the co-operation of man and as a result of history), if he relates himself to them as objects, which can only be done at first in the form of alienation.

We shall now describe in detail the one-sidedness and limitations of Hegel using as a text the final chapter of the *Phenomenology* on absolute knowledge, the chapter which contains both the quintessence of the *Phenomenology*, its relationship to speculative dialectic, and also Hegel's attitude to both and to their interrelations.

For the moment we will only say this in anticipation: Hegel adopts the point of view of modern economics. He conceives of labour as the self-confirming essence of man. He sees only the positive side of labour, not its negative side. Labour is the means by which man becomes himself inside externalization or as externalized man. The only labour that Hegel knows and recognizes is abstract, mental labour. Thus Hegel conceives of what forms the general essence of philosophy, the externalization of man who knows himself or externalized science that thinks itself, as the essence of labour and can therefore, in contrast to previous philosophy, synthesize its individual phases and present his philosophy as the philosophy. What other philosophers have done—to conceive of single phases of nature and man's life as phases of self-consciousness, indeed of abstract self-consciousness—this Hegel knows by doing philosophy. Therefore his science is absolute.

Let us now proceed to our subject.

Absolute knowledge. Last chapter of the *Phenomenology*.

The main point is that the object of consciousness is nothing but self-consciousness or that the object is only objectified self-consciousness, self-consciousness as object. (Positing that man = consciousness.)

It is necessary therefore to overcome the objects of consciousness. Objectivity as such is considered to be an alien condition not fitting man's nature and self-consciousness. Thus the reappropriation of the objective essence of man, which was produced as something alien and determined by alienation, not only implies the transcendance of alienation, but also of objectivity. This means that man is regarded as a non-objective, spiritual being.

Hegel describes the process of the overcoming of the object of consciousness as follows:

The object does not only show itself as returning into the Self: that is according to Hegel the one-sided conception of this process. Man is equated with Self. But the Self is only man abstractly conceived and produced by abstraction. It is the Self that constitutes man. His eye, his ear, etc., take their nature from his Self; each of his faculties belongs to his Self. But in that case it is quite false to say: self-consciousness has eyes, ears and faculties. Self-consciousness is rather a quality of human nature, of the human eye, etc., human nature is not a quality of self-consciousness.

The Self, abstracted and fixed for itself, is man as abstract egoist, egoism raised to its pure abstraction in thought (we will return to this point later).

For Hegel, the human essence, man, is the same as self-consciousness. All alienation of man's essence is therefore nothing but the alienation of self-consciousness. The alienation of self-consciousness is not regarded as the expression of the real alienation of man's essence reflected in knowledge and thought. The real alienation (or the one that appears to be real) in its inner concealed essence that has first been brought to the light by philosophy, is nothing but the appearance of the alienation of the real human essence, self-consciousness. The science that comprehends this is therefore called 'phenomenology'. Thus all reappropriation of the alienated objective essence appears as an incorporation into self-consciousness. Man making himself master of his own essence is only self-consciousness making itself master of objective essence. The return of the object into the Self is therefore the reappropriation of the object.

o

Universally expressed the overcoming of the object of consciousness implies:

1. That the object presents itself to consciousness as about to disappear.

2. That it is the externalization of self-consciousness that creates 'thingness'.

3. That this externalization has not only a negative but also a positive significance.

4. That this significance is not only implicit and for us but also for self-consciousness itself.

5. For self-consciousness, the negative aspect of the object or its self-supersession has a positive significance, or, in other words, it knows the nullity of the object because it externalizes itself, for in this externalization it posits itself as object or establishes the object as itself, in virtue of the indivisible unity of being for itself.

6. At the same time, this other phase is also present that self-consciousness has just as much superseded and re-absorbed this alienation and objectivity and thus is at home in its other being as such.

7. This is the movement of consciousness and consciousness is therefore the totality of its phases.

8. Similarly, consciousness must have related itself to the object in all its determinations, and have conceived it in terms of each of these determinations. This totality of determinations makes the object intrinsically a spiritual being, and it becomes truly so for consciousness by the perception of every one of these determinations as the Self, or by what was earlier called the spiritual attitude towards them.

Concerning 1. That the object as such presents itself to the consciousness as about to disappear is the above mentioned return of the object into the Self.

Concerning 2. The externalization of self-consciousness posits 'thingness'. Because man is equated with self-consciousness, his externalized objective essence or 'thingness' is equated with externalized self-consciousness and 'thingness' is posited through this externalization. ('Thingness' is what is an object for man and the only true object for him is the object of his essence or his objectified essence. Now since it is not real man as such—and therefore not nature, for man is only human nature—that is made the subject, but only self-consciousness, the abstraction of man, 'thingness' can only be externalized self-consciousness.) It is quite understandable that a natural, living being equipped and provided with objective, i.e. material faculties should have real, natural objects for the object of its essence and that its self-alienation should consist in the positing of the real, objective world, but as something exterior to it, not belonging to its essence and overpowering it. There is nothing incomprehensible and paradoxical in that. Rather the opposite would be paradoxical. It is equally clear that a self-consciousness, i.e. its externalization can only posit 'thingness', i.e. only an abstract thing, a thing of abstraction and no real thing. It is further clear that 'thingness' is not something self-sufficient and essential in contrast to self-consciousness, but a mere creation established by it. And what is established is not self-confirming, but only confirms the act of establishment which has for a moment, but only a moment, crystallized its energy into a product and in appearance given it the role of an independant and real being.

When real man of flesh and blood, standing on the solid, round earth and breathing in and out all the powers of nature posits his real objective faculties, as a result of his externalization, as alien objects, it is not the positing that is the subject; it is the subjectivity of objective faculties whose action must therefore be an objective one. An objective being has an objective effect and it would not have an objective effect if its being did not include an objective element. It only creates and posits objects because it is posited by objects, because it is by origin natural. Thus in the act of positing it does not degenerate from its 'pure activity' into creating an object; its objective product only confirms its objective activity, its activity as an activity of an objective, natural being.

We see here how consistent naturalism or humanism is distinguished from both idealism and materialism and constitutes at the same time their unifying truth. We see also how only naturalism is capable of understanding the process of world history.

⟨Man is a directly natural being. As a living natural being he is on the one hand equipped with natural vital powers and is an active natural being. These powers of his are dispositions, capacities, instincts. On the other hand, man as a natural, corporeal, sensuous, objective being is a passive, dependent and limited being, like animals and plants, that is, the objects of his instincts are exterior to him and independent of him and yet they are objects of his need, essential objects that are indispensable for the exercise and confirmation of his faculties. The fact that man is an embodied, living, real, sentient objective being means that he has real, sensuous objects as the objects of his life-expression. In other words, he can only express his being in real, sensuous objects. To be objective, natural and sentient and to have one's object, nature and sense outside oneself or oneself to be object, nature and sense for a third person are identical.⟩ Hunger is a natural need; so it needs a natural object outside itself to satisfy and appease it. Hunger is the objective need of a body for an exterior object in order to be complete and express its being. The sun is the object of the plant, an indispensable object that confirms its life, just as the plant is the object of the sun in that it is the expression of the sun's life-giving power and objective faculties.

A being that does not have its nature outside itself is not a natural being and has no part in the natural world. A being that has no object outside itself is not an objective being. A being that is not itself an object for a third being has no being for its object, i.e. has no objective relationships and no objective existence.

A non-objective being is a non-being.

Imagine a being which is neither itself an object nor has an object. Firstly, such a being would be the only being, there would be no being outside it, it would exist solitary and alone. For as soon as there are objects outside myself, as soon as I am not alone, I am something distinct, a different reality from the object outside me. Thus for this third object, I am a reality different from it, i.e. its object. Thus an object that is not the object of another being supposes that no objective being exists. As soon as I have an object, this object then has me as an object. But a non-objective being is an unreal, non-sensuous being that is only thought of, i.e. an imaginary being, a being of abstraction. To be sensuous, i.e. to be real, is to be an object of sense, a sensuous object, thus to have sensuous objects outside oneself, to have objects of sense perception. To be sentient is to suffer.

Man as an objective, sentient being is therefore a suffering being, and, since he is a being who feels his sufferings, a passionate being. Passion is man's faculties energetically striving after their object.

⟨But man is not only a natural being, he is a human natural being. This means that he is a being that exists for himself, thus a species-being that must confirm and exercise himself as such in his being and knowledge. Thus human objects are not natural objects as they immediately present themselves nor is human sense, in its purely objective existence, human sensitivity and human objectivity. Neither nature in its objective aspect nor in its subjective aspect is immediately adequate to the human being.⟩ And as everything natural must have an origin, so man too has his process of origin, history, which can, however, be known by him and thus is a conscious process of origin that transcends itself. History is the true natural history of man. (We shall return to this point later.)

Thirdly, since the positing of 'thingness' is itself only an appearance, an act that contradicts the essence of pure activity, it must again be transcended and 'thingness' be denied.

Concerning 3, 4, 5, 6. (3). This externalization of consciousness has not only negative but also positive significance and (4) this significance is not only implicit and for us, but also for self-consciousness itself. (5) For self-consciousness the negative aspect of the object or its self-transcendance has a positive significance or in other words it knows the nullity of the object because it externalizes itself, for in this externalization it knows itself as object, or in virtue of the indivisible unity of being for itself, establishes the object for itself. (6) At the same time, this other phase is also present that self-consciousness has just as much superseded and reabsorbed this alienation and objectivity and thus is at home in its other being as such.

We have already seen that the appropriation of the alienated objective essence or the supersession of objectivity regarded as alienation, which must progress from indifferent strangeness to a really inimical alienation, means for Hegel at the same time, or even principally, the supersession of objectivity, since what offends self-consciousness in alienation is not the determinate character of the object but its objective character. The object is thus a negative, self-annulling being, a nullity. This nullity has for consciousness not only a negative but also a positive meaning, for this nullity of the object is precisely the self-confirmation of its non-objectivity and abstraction. For consciousness itself the nullity of the object has a positive significance because it knows this nullity, objective being as its own self-externalization; because it knows that this nullity only exists through its self-externalization . . .

The way that consciousness is and that something is for it, is knowledge. Knowledge is its only act. Thus something exists for it in so far as it knows this something. Knowing is its only objective relationship. It knows the nullity of the object, i.e. that the object is not distinct from itself, the non-being of the object for itself, because it recognizes the object as its own self-externalization. In other words, it knows itself, knows knowledge as object, because the object is only the appearance of an object, a mirage, that essentially is nothing but knowledge itself that opposes itself to itself and is thus faced with a nullity, something that has no objectivity outside knowledge. Knowing knows that in so far as it relates itself to an object it is only exterior to itself, alienates itself. It knows that it only appears to itself as an object or that what appears to it as an object is only itself.

On the other hand, says Hegel, there is implied this other aspect: that consciousness has equally superseded this externalization and objectivity and taken it back into itself and thus is at home in its other being as such.

In this discussion we have assembled all the illusions of speculation.

Firstly, self-consciousness at home in its other being as such. It is, therefore, if we here abstract from the Hegelian abstraction and substitute man's self-consciousness for self-consciousness, at home in its other being as such. This implies, for one thing, that consciousness, knowing as knowing, thinking as thinking, pretends to be directly the opposite of itself, sensuous reality, life; it is thought over-reaching itself in thought (Feuerbach). This aspect is entailed in so far as consciousness as mere consciousness is not offended by alienated objectivity but by objectivity as such.

The second implication is that in so far as self-conscious man has recognized the spiritual world (or the general spiritual mode of existence of his world) as self-externalization and superseded it, he nevertheless confirms it again in this externalized form and declares it to be his true being, restores it, pretends to be at home in his other being as such. Thus, for example, after the supersession of religion and the recognition of it as the product of self-alienation, man nevertheless finds himself confirmed in religion as such. Here is the root of Hegel's false positivism or his merely apparent criticism. This is what Feuerbach has characterized as the positing, negation and restoration of religion or theology, although it should be understood to have a wider application. Thus reason finds itself at home in unreason as such. Man who has recognized that he has been leading an externalized life in law, politics, etc., leads his true human life in this externalized life as such. Thus the true knowledge and the true life is the self-affirmation and self-contradiction in contradiction with itself and with the knowledge and the nature of the object.

So there can be no more question of a compromise on Hegel's part with religion, the state, etc., for this falsehood is the falsehood of his very principle.

If I know religion as externalized human self-consciousness, then what I know in it as religion is not my self-consciousness, but the confirmation in it of my externalized self-consciousness. Thus I know that the self-consciousness that is part of my own self is not confirmed in religion, but rather in the abolition and supersession of religion.

Therefore, in Hegel the negation of the negation is not the confirmation of true being through the negation of apparent being. It is the confirmation of apparent being or self-alienated being in its denial or the denial of this apparent being as a being dwelling outside man and independent of him, its transformation into a subject.

Therefore supersession plays a very particular role in which negation and conservation are united.

Thus for example, in Hegel's *Philosophy of Right*, private right superseded equals morality, morality superseded equals the family, the family superseded equals civil society, civil society superseded equals the state, and state superseded equals world history. In reality private right, morality, family, civil society, state, etc., remain, only they become 'phases', modes of men's existence, which have no validity in isolation but which dissolve and create themselves. They are mere phases in the process. In their real existence, this moving being of theirs is concealed. It only comes to the fore and is revealed in thought, in philosophy, and therefore my true religious existence is my existence in the philosophy of religion, my true political existence is my existence in the philosophy of law, my true natural existence is in the philosophy of nature, my true artistic existence is in the philosophy of art, my true human existence is my existence in philosophy. Similarly, the true existence of religion, the state, nature and art is the philosophy of religion, the state, nature and art. But if the philosophy of religion, etc., is the only true existence of religion, then it is only as a philosopher of religion that I am really religious and so I deny real religiousness and really religious men. But at the same time I confirm them, too, partly inside my own existence or inside the alienated existence that I oppose to them (for this is merely their philosophical expression), partly in their peculiar and original form, for I count them as only apparently other being, as allegories, forms of their own true existence (i.e. my philosophical existence), concealed by sensuous veils.

Similarly, quality superseded equals quantity, quantity superseded equals measure, measure superseded equals essence, essence superseded equals appearance, appearance superseded equals reality, reality superseded equals concept, concept superseded equals objectivity, objectivity superseded equals the absolute idea, absolute idea superseded equals nature, nature superseded equals subjective spirit, subjective spirit superseded equals ethical objective spirit, ethical objective spirit superseded equals art, art superseded equals religion, religion superseded equals absolute knowledge.

On the one hand, this supersession is a supersession of something thought and thus private property as thought is superseded in the thought of morality. And because this thought imagines that it is directly the opposite of itself, sensuous reality, and thus also that its action is sensuous, real action, this supersession in thought that lets its object remain in reality believes it has really overcome it. On the other hand, since the object has now become for it a phase in its thought process, it is therefore regarded in its real existence as being a self-confirmation of thought, of self-consciousness and abstraction.

From one angle, therefore, the being that Hegel transcends in philosophy is not actual religion, state, nature, but religion as itself already an object of knowledge, dogmatics; and similarly with jurisprudence, political science, natural science. From this angle, therefore, he stands in opposition both to actual being and to direct, non-philosophical science or to the non-philosophical conception of this being. Thus he contradicts current conceptions.

From another angle the man who is religious, etc., can find his final confirmation in Hegel.

Let us consider, within the framework of alienation, positive phases of the Hegelian dialectic.

(a) Supersession as an objective movement absorbing externalization. ⟨This is the insight expressed within alienation of the reappropriation of objective being through the supersession of its alienation. It is the alienated insight into the real objectification of man, into the real appropriation of his objective essence through the destruction of the alienated character of the objective world, through its supersession in its alienated character of the objective world, through its supersession in its alienated existence. In the same way, atheism as the supersession of God is the emergence of theoretical humanism, and communism as the supersession of private property is the indication of real human life as man's property, which is also the emergence of practical humanism. In other words, atheism is humanism mediated with itself through the supersession of religion, and communism is humanism mediated with itself through the supersession of private property. Only through the supersession of this mediation, which is, however, a necessary precondition, does positive humanism that begins with itself come into being.⟩

But atheism and communism are no flight, no abstraction, no loss of the objective world engendered by man, or of his faculties that have created his objectivity, no poverty-stricken regression to unnatural and underdeveloped simplicity. They are rather the first real emergence and genuine realization of man's essence as something actual.

Thus in considering the positive side of self-referring negation (although still in an alienated form) Hegel conceives of the alienation of man's self and his being, the loss of his object and his reality as self-discovery, manifestation of being, objectification, realization. ⟨In short, Hegel conceives, inside his abstraction, labour to be the self-engendering act of man, his relation to himself as an alien being and the manifestation of his own being as something alien, as the emergence of the species-consciousness and species-life.⟩

In Hegel, apart from or rather as a consequence of, the inversion we have already described, this act appears as merely formal because it is abstract, and the human essence itself is only regarded as an abstract, thinking being, as self-consciousness.

Secondly, because the conception is formal and abstract, the supersession of externalization becomes a confirmation of externalization. In other words for Hegel the process of self-creation and self-objectification as self-externalization and self-alienation is the absolute and therefore final manifestation of human life which has itself for aim, is at peace with itself and has attained its true nature.

Therefore, this movement in its abstract form as dialectic is regarded as true human life and because it is still an abstraction, an alienation of human life, it is viewed as a divine process, but the divine process of man, a process gone through by his absolute, pure, abstract being separated from himself.

Thirdly, this process must have an agent, a subject; but the subject only comes into being as the result; this result, the subject knowing itself as absolute self-consciousness, is therefore God, absolute spirit, the idea that knows and manifests itself. Real man and real nature become mere predicates or symbols of this hidden, unreal man and unreal nature. The relationship of subject and predicate to each other is thus completely inverted: a mystical subject–object or subjectivity reaching beyond the object, absolute subject as a process (it externalizes itself returns to itself from its externalization and at the same time reabsorbs its externalization); a pure and unceasing circular movement within itself.

First, the formal and abstract conception of man's act of self-creation or self-objectification.

Because Hegel equates man with self-consciousness, the alienated object, the alienated reality of man's being is nothing but consciousness, only the thought of alienation, its abstract and therefore empty and unreal expression, negation. The supersession of externalization is, therefore, equally nothing but an abstract, empty supersession of this empty abstraction, the negation of the negation. The full, living, sensuous, concrete activity of self-objectification, therefore, becomes its mere abstraction, absolute negativity, an abstraction that is in its turn crystallized as such and conceived as independent activity, activity itself. Because this so-called negativity is nothing but the abstract and empty form of that real, living act, its content, too, can only be a formal one produced by abstracting from all content. They are, therefore, general, abstract forms of abstraction that fit any content and thus are also indifferent to every content and equally valid for all. They are forms of thought, logical categories, detached from real mind and real nature. (We shall develop the logical content of absolute negativity below.)

The positive side of what Hegel has elaborated here in his speculative logic is that he presents determinate concepts, general static forms of thought in their independence of nature and mind as a necessary result of the universal alienation of man's being and thus also of man's thought, and therefore collects them together as phases of the process of abstraction. For example, being superseded is essence, essence superseded is concept, concept superseded is . . . absolute idea. But what is the absolute idea? It supersedes itself again, if it is not willing to go through again the whole process of abstraction from the beginning and content itself with being a totality of abstractions or abstraction that comprehends itself. But abstraction that comprehends itself as such, knows itself to be nothing. It must abandon itself, abstraction, and thus it arrives at a being that is its exact opposite, nature. The whole logic is thus the proof that abstract thought is nothing for itself, that the absolute idea is nothing for itself and that only nature is something.

The absolute idea, the abstract idea which 'considered from the aspect of unity with itself is intuition' (Hegel's *Encyclopaedia*, 3rd edition, p. 222) and which (loc. cit.) 'in its own absolute truth decides to let a phase of its particularity or its first determination or other-being, the immediate idea as its reflection, emerge freely from itself as nature'; this whole idea which conducts itself in such a peculiar and baroque manner and which has caused Hegelians frightful headaches is just nothing but abstraction, i.e. the abstract thinker. Instructed by experience and enlightened about its own truth, abstraction resolves, subject to manifold conditions, themselves false and still abstract, to abandon itself and to substitute its other being, the particular and determinate, for its self-sufficient nullity, its universality and indeterminateness. It thus resolves to let nature, that it had concealed within itself as a mere abstraction and creature of thought, emerge freely from itself, i.e. it decides to leave abstraction and at last regard nature free from abstraction. The abstract idea which is directly intuition, is nothing but abstract thought that gives itself up and resolves to rely on intuition. This whole transformation of logic into philosophy of nature is nothing but the transition from abstraction to intuition that the abstract thinker finds so difficult to effect and therefore describes in such bizarre terms. The mystical feeling that drives the philosopher from abstract thought to intuition is boredom, the longing for a content.

(Man alienated from himself is also the thinker alienated from his natural human essence. His thoughts are therefore spirits that have a static abode outside nature and man. Hegel has shut up all these static spirits together in his logic and then conceived each of them firstly as negation, i.e. as externalization of human thought, then as negation of the negation, i.e. as supersession of this externalization and as the true manifestation of human thought. But, being itself still imprisoned within alienation, this negation of the negation is partly the restoration of the static spirits in their alienation and partly immobilization in their final act, the self-reference in externalization as their true being. That is, Hegel substitutes the circular act of abstraction for the other static abstractions. He has thereby the merit of having pointed out the source of all these inadequate concepts which originally belonged to different philosophies, grouped them together and made the exhaustive range of abstraction instead of a particular abstraction into the object of criticism.) (We shall see later why Hegel separates thought from the subject; but it is already clear that if man is not human, then the manifestation of his nature cannot be human and, therefore, that thought cannot be conceived as a manifestation of man's nature, of a human, natural subject, with eyes, ears, etc., living in society, the world and nature.) (Also, in so far as this abstraction conceives itself and feels an infinite boredom with itself, in Hegel the abandonment of abstract thought that only moves within itself and has no eyes, teeth, ears or anything, appears as a resolution to recognize nature as being and rely on intuition).

But nature also, taken in the abstract, for itself, and fixed in its separation from man is nothing for man. It is self-evident that the abstract thinker who has resolved on intuition, regards nature in an abstract way. As nature lay enclosed in the thinker as absolute idea and a creature of thought in a form that was concealed from him and enigmatic, so when he let it emerge from himself, it was still only this abstract nature, nature as a creature of thought, though now in the sense that it is the opposite of thought, real, intuitive nature, distinct from abstract thought, or, to speak in human terms, in his intuition of nature the abstract thinker sees that the beings that he imagined he created out of nothing, out of pure abstraction in the divine dialectic, the beings that he thought were pure products of an intellectual labour shuttling back and forth within itself and never looking out into reality, are nothing but the abstractions of natural qualities. Thus the whole of nature only repeats to him in a sensuous, exterior form the abstractions of logic. He re-analyses nature and these abstractions. His intuition of nature is thus only the way he confirms his abstraction from the intuition of nature, the process of creating his abstraction consciously repeated. Thus, for example, Time is equated with self-referring Negativity (loc. cit., p. 238). What corresponds to superseded Becoming as Being, in its natural form is superseded Movement as Matter. Light is, in the natural form, Reflection-in-itself. Body as moon and comet is the natural form of the antithesis that according to the Logic consists in the positive grounded upon itself and the negative grounded upon itself. The earth is the natural form of the logical ground, as the negative unity of the antitheses, etc.

Nature as nature, i.e. in so far as it is still sensuously distinguished from the hidden meaning concealed within itself, nature separated and different from these abstractions is nothing, a nothing that verifies itself as such. It is meaningless or only has the meaning of something exterior that has been superseded.

'In the finite-teleological view, is to be found the correct pre-supposition that nature does not contain its absolute end within itself' (p. 225). Its end is the confirmation of abstraction. 'Nature has revealed itself as the idea in the form of other-being. Because the idea is thus the negation of itself, in other words, exterior to itself, nature is not only exterior relative to this idea but exteriority constitutes the form in which it exists as nature' (p. 227).

Exteriority here is not to be understood as sensuous reality that externalizes itself and opens up to light and men's senses. It must be understood in the sense of externalization, as a fault, a defect that ought not to be. For the truth is still always the idea. Nature is only the form of its other-being. And since abstract thinking is the essence, so anything exterior to it is something exterior by essence. The abstract thinker recognizes at the same time that sensuousness, exteriority in contrast to thought shuttling back and forth inside itself, is the essence of nature.

But he also expressses this antithesis in such a way that this exteriority of nature, its antithesis to thought, is its defect and that it is a defective being in so far as it is different from abstraction. A being that is deficient, not simply for me and in my eyes, but in itself has something outside itself that it lacks. That is, its being is other than itself. Therefore, for the abstract thinker nature must supersede itself because it is already posited by him as a potentially superseded being.

'For us, spirit has nature as a presupposition. It is its truth and absolute first. In this truth nature has disappeared and spirit has surrendered itself as the idea that has attained being-for-itself whose subject and object is the concept. This identity is absolute negativity since in nature the concept has its completely exterior objectivity, but has superseded this alienation and has become in it identical with itself. It is their identity only in so far as it is a return from nature' (p. 392).

'The manifestation as abstract idea is the immediate transition to and becoming of nature; as the manifestation of spirit that is free it is the establishment of nature as its world; this establishment, being reflection, presupposes at the same time the world as independent nature. Manifestation in the concept is the creation of nature as its being in which it acquires the affirmation and truth of its freedom.' 'The absolute is spirit: this is the highest definition of the absolute.'

Money

If the feelings, passions and so forth of men are not merely anthropological determinations in the narrow sense but also truly ontological affirmations of his essence (nature) and if they only really affirm themselves when they are objects of sense perceptions, then it is evident:

1. That the modes of their affirmation are certainly not one and the same, but rather that the different modes constitute the particularity of their being and life. The mode in which the object exists for them is the specific mode of their enjoyment.

2. Where the sensuous affirmation involves immediate destruction of the object in its independent form (eating, drinking, working on an object) this is the affirmation of the object.

3. In so far as man is human and thus in so far as his feelings and so on

are human, the affirmation of the object by another person is equally his own enjoyment.

4. It is only through the development of industry, i.e. through the mediation of private property that the ontological essence of human passion comes into being in its totality and humanity. The science of man is thus itself a product of the practical self-formation of man.

5. The meaning of private property freed from its alienation, is the existence of essential objects for man, as objects both of enjoyment and of activity.

Money, since it has the property of being able to buy anything, and to appropriate all objects to itself, is thus the object *par excellence*. It is the universal character of this property that creates the omnipotence of money; this is the reason for its being regarded as an almighty being . . . money is the pander between need and its object, between man's life and his means of subsistence. But what mediates my life also mediates the existence of other men for me, it is for me the other person.

> What, man! confound it, hands and feet
> And head and backside, all are yours!
> And what we take while life is sweet,
> Is that to be declared not ours?
> 　　Six stallions, say, I can afford,
> Is not their strength my property?
> I tear along, a sporting lord,
> As if their legs belonged to me.
>
> 　　　　　　　(Goethe, Faust–Mephistopheles)[1]

Shakespeare in Timon of Athens

> Gold? Yellow, glittering, precious gold? No, gods,
> I am no idle votarist: roots, you clear heavens!
> Thus much of this will make black, white; foul, fair;
> Wrong, right; base, noble; old, young; coward, valiant;
> . . . Why, this
> Will lug your priests and servants from your sides;
> Pluck stout men's pillows from below their heads:
> This yellow slave
> Will knit and break religions; bless th' accurst;
> Make the hoar leprosy adored; place thieves,

[1] Part I, scene 4, trans. P. Wayne, Penguin Books, 1949.

And give them title, knee, and approbation,
With senators on the bench: this is it
That makes the wappen'd widow wed again;
She whom the spittal house and ulcerous sores
Would cast the gorge at, this embalms and spices
To th' April day again. Come, damned earth,
Thou common whore of mankind, what putt'st odds
Among the rout of nations, I will make thee
Do thy right nature.[1]

And later on:

O thou sweet king-killer and dear divorce
'Twixt natural son and sire! Thou bright defiler
Of Hymen's purest bed! Thou valiant Mars!
Thou ever young, fresh, loved and delicate
Whose blush doth thaw the consecrated snow
That lies on Dian's lap! Thou visible god!
That solder'st close impossibilities,
And mak'st them kiss! That speak'st with every tongue,
To every purpose! O thou touch of hearts!
Think, thy slave man rebels; and by thy virtue
Set them into confounding odds, that beasts
May have the world in empire![2]

Shakespeare portrays the essence of money excellently. To understand him let us begin with an exegesis of the passage of Goethe.

What I have thanks to money, what I pay for, i.e. what money can
buy, that is what I, the possessor of the money, am myself. My power is
as great as the power of money. The properties of money are my—
(its owner's)—properties and faculties. Thus what I am and what I am
capable of is by no means determined by my individuality. I am ugly,
but I can buy myself the most beautiful women. Consequently I am
not ugly, for the effect of ugliness, its power of repulsion, is annulled by
money. As an individual, I am lame, but money can create twenty-four
feet for me; so I am not lame; I am a wicked, dishonest man without
conscience or intellect, but money is honoured and so also is its possessor.
Money is the highest good and so its possessor is good. Money relieves
me of the trouble of being dishonest; so I am presumed to be honest. I

[1] Act IV, scene 3.   [2] Ibid.

may have no intellect, but money is the true mind of all things and so how should its possessor have no intellect? Moreover he can buy himself intellectuals and is not the man who has power over intellectuals not more intellectual than they? I who can get with money everything that the human heart longs for, do I not possess all human capacities? Does not my money thus change all my incapacities into their opposite?

If money is the bond that binds me to human life, that binds society to me and me to nature and men, is not money the bond of all bonds? Can it not tie and untie all bonds? Is it not, therefore, also the universal means of separation? It is the true agent both of separation and of union, the galvano-chemical power of society.

Shakespeare brings out two particular properties of money:

1. It is the visible god-head, the transformation of all human and natural qualities into their opposites, the general confusion and inversion of things; it makes impossibilities fraternize.

2. It is the universal whore, the universal pander between men and peoples.

The inversion and confusion of all human and natural qualities, the fraternization of impossibilities, this divine power of money lies in its being the externalized and self-externalizing species-being of man. It is the externalized capacities of humanity.

What I cannot do as a man, thus what my individual faculties cannot do, this I can do through money. Thus money turns each of these faculties into something that it is not, i.e. into its opposite.

If I long for a meal, or wish to take the mail coach because I am not strong enough to make the journey on foot, then money procures the meal and the mail coach for me. This means that it changes my wishes from being imaginary, and translates them from their being in thought, imagination and will into a sensuous, real being, from imagination to life, from imaginary being to real being. The truly creative force in this mediation is money.

Demand also exists for the man who has no money but his demand is simply an imaginary entity that has no effective existence for me, for a third party or for other men and thus remains unreal and without an object. The difference between a demand that is based on money and effective and one that is based on my needs, passions, wishes, etc. and is ineffective is the difference between being and thought, between a

P

representation that merely exists within me and one that is outside me as a real object.

If I have no money for travelling, then I have no need, no real and self-realizing need, to travel. If I have a vocation to study, but have no money for it, then I have no vocation to study, no effective, genuine vocation. If, on the contrary, I do not really have a vocation to study, but have the will and the money, then I have an effective vocation thereto. Money is the universal means and power, exterior to man, not issuing from man as man or from human society as society, to turn imagination into reality and reality into mere imagination. Similarly it turns real human and natural faculties into mere abstract representations and thus imperfections and painful imaginings, while on the other hand it turns the real imperfections and imaginings, the really powerless faculties that exist only in the imagination of the individual into real faculties and powers. This description alone suffices to make money the universal inversion of individualities that turns them into their opposites and gives them qualities at variance with their own. As this perverting power, money then appears as the enemy of man and social bonds that pretend to self-subsistence. It changes fidelity into infidelity, love into hate, hate into love, virtue into vice, vice into virtue, slave into master, master into slave, stupidity into intelligence and intelligence into stupidity.

Since money is the existing and self-affirming concept of value and confounds and exchanges all things, it is the universal confusion and exchange of all things, the inverted world, the confusion and exchange of all natural and human qualities.

He who can buy courage is courageous though he be a coward. Because money can be exchanged not for a particular quality, for a particular thing or human faculty but for the whole human and actual objective world, from the point of view of its possessor it can exchange any quality for any other, even contradictory qualities and objects; it is the fraternization of incompatibles and forces contraries to embrace.

If you suppose man to be man and his relationship to the world to be a human one, then you can only exchange love for love, trust for trust, etc. If you wish to appreciate art, then you must be a man with some artistic education; if you wish to exercise an influence on other men, you must be a man who has a really stimulating and encouraging effect on other men. Each of your relationships to man—and to nature —must be a definite expression of your real individual life that corresponds to the object of your will. If you love without arousing a reciprocal love, that is, if your love does not as such produce love in return, if through the manifestation of yourself, as a loving person you do not succeed in making yourself a beloved person, then your love is impotent and a misfortune.

Letter to Ludwig Feuerbach

Written: 11th August 1844

First published: Probleme des Friedens und des Sozialismus, Berlin, 1960, vol. 2, pp. 8 ff.
Reprinted: Karl Marx, *Texte zu Methode und Praxis*, ed. G. Hillmann, Hamburg, 1966, vol. 2, pp. 185–8

This letter, published for the first time only recently, shows how enthusiastic Marx was about Feuerbach's ideas during the period when he was composing the *Paris Manuscripts*.

Paris, 11th August 1844

Dear Sir,

I take the opportunity presented to me of sending you an article of mine, in which are sketched some elements of my critical philosophy of law which I had already finished once but then subjected to a new rewriting so as to be generally intelligible. I lay no particular value on this article, but I am glad to find an opportunity of being able to assure you of the exceptional respect and—allow me the word—love that I have for you. Your *Philosophy of the Future* and *Essence of Faith* are, in spite of their limited scope, of more weight than the whole of contemporary German literature put together.

In these writings you have—whether intentionally I do not know—given a philosophical basis to socialism, and the communists, too, have similarly understood these works in that sense. The unity of man with man based on the real differences between men, the concept of human species transferred from the heaven of abstraction to the real earth, what is this other than the concept of society!

Two translations of your *Essence of Christianity*, an English and a French one, are being prepared and are already almost ready to be printed. The first will appear in Manchester (Engels has been in charge of it), the second in Paris (the Frenchman Dr. Guerrier and the German communist Ewerbeck have translated it with the help of a French stylist).

184

At a time like this the French will immediately fall on the book, for both parties—clerics and Voltairians and materialists—are looking round for foreign help. It is a remarkable phenomenon how, in contrast to the eighteenth century, religiousness has risen into the middle and upper classes, whereas irreligiousness—but the irreligiousness of man experiencing himself as man—has penetrated down into the French proletariat. You have to have participated in one meeting of French workers to be able to believe the virgin freshness and nobility among these work-worn men. The English proletariat also makes gigantic progress, but it lacks the culture of the French. But I should not forget to emphasize the theoretical merits of the German manual labourers in Switzerland, London and Paris; only the German manual labourer is still too much of a manual labourer.

But anyway history is preparing among these 'barbarians' of our civilized society the practical element for a human emancipation.

The contrast of the French character with our German one was never presented to me so sharply and strikingly as in a Fourierist work that begins with the following sentences: 'Man is completely defined by his passions', 'Have you ever met a man who thought in order to think, who remembered in order to remember and who imagined in order to imagine? Who wished in order to wish? Has that ever happened to you yourself?... No, of course not!'

The prime mover of nature as of society is therefore the magic, passionate, non-reflective attraction and 'every being, man, plant, animal or world has received a sum of forces linked to its mission in the universal order'.

It follows from this: 'attractions are proportionate to destinies'.

Do not all these sentences look as though the Frenchman had intentionally opposed his 'passion' to the *actus purus* of German thought? One does not think in order to think etc. Bruno Bauer, my friend of long standing (though now more estranged from me) has given a new proof in his critical Berlin *Literatur-Zeitung* of how difficult it is for Germans to emerge from their contrasted one-sidedness. I do not know whether you have read this journal. There is a lot of covert polemic against you in it.

The character of this *Literatur-Zeitung* can be reduced to this: 'Criticism' has been transformed into a transcendent being. Those

Berliners do not consider themselves to be men who criticize but as critics who incidentally have the misfortune to be men. They therefore only recognize one real need, that of theoretical criticism. So people like Proudhon are reproached with taking a 'practical' 'need' as a starting point. This criticism, therefore, loses itself in a sad and pompous spiritualism. Consciousness or self-consciousness is considered to be the sole human quality. Love, for example, is rejected, because in it the beloved is only an 'object'. Down with objects! This criticism thus considers itself the only active element in history. Opposite it stands the whole of humanity as mass, inert mass whose only value is opposition to spirit. So it is considered to be the worst sort of crime when the critic is spirited or impassioned; he should, on the contrary, be an ironical, ice-cold sophos.

Thus Bauer explains literally: 'The critic must take part in neither the sorrows nor the joys of society; he must know neither friendship and love nor hate and jealousy; he must be enthroned in an isolation whence shall echo from his lips sometimes only the laughter of the Olympian gods over the perversity of the world.'

The tones of Bauer's *Literatur-Zeitung* is therefore a tone of passionless contempt and he achieves this all the more easily in that he only uncovers contradictions and then, satisfied with this operation, retires with a contemptuous 'hm'. He explains that criticism has no results, it is so far too spiritual for that. Indeed, he goes as far as expressing the hope that 'the time is not far off when the whole of decaying humanity will mass itself over against criticism'—and criticism is himself and company —'they would then divide this mass into different groups and deliver to each of them its certificate of poverty'.

It is plain that Bauer fights out of rivalry with Christ. I intend to publish a small brochure[1] against this aberration of criticism. It would be of the greatest value to me if you were willing to give me your opinion beforehand, and indeed any quick sign of life from you would make me glad. The German workers here, that is, the communist part of them, several hundreds, have during this summer been attending twice weekly lectures by their secret leaders[2] on your *Essence of Christianity* and have shown themselves remarkably receptive. The small

[1] K. Marx and F. Engels, *The Holy Family*, Frankfurt, 1845.
[2] The League of the Just.

excerpt from the letter of a German lady in the supplement to no. 64 of *Vorwärts* was printed, without the knowledge of its author, from a letter of my wife who is visiting her mother in Trier.

With best wishes for your well-being,

Yours

Karl Marx.

On James Mill

Written: During 1844

First published: MEGA, I (3), 425–34

Reprinted: Karl Marx, *Texte zu Methode und Praxis*, ed. G. Hillmann, Hamburg, 1966, vol. 2, pp. 166–81

Translated: Easton and Guddat, *Writings of the Young Marx*, pp. 265–88

This extract is taken from a series of comments on Say, Ricardo, McCullough and Boisguilbert that Marx wrote in his notebook. It forms a parallel passage to that on '*Alienated Labour*' in the *Economic and Philosophical Manuscripts* and gives Marx's positive ideas on the future communist society.

See further: D. McLellan, 'Marx's Concept of the Unalienated Society', *Review of Politics*, 1969.

In the compensation of money and the value of metal, as in his statement that the cost of production is the only factor in determining value, Mill makes the mistake common to the whole of Ricardo's school of expressing the abstract law without taking into account the changes and continual supersession in which it has its origin. If it is a steady law that the price is determined in the last instance (or rather on the periodical and arbitrary occasions when supply and demand coincide) by the cost of production, it is just as steady a law that there is no such coincidence and thus that value and cost of production stand in no necessary relationship. Indeed, supply and demand only momentarily coincide because of previous fluctuations of supply and demand, because of the disproportion between the cost of production and exchange value, just as this fluctuation and disproportion follow on the momentary coincidence. This real process, of which that law is only an abstract, arbitrary and one-sided phase, is turned by our latest economists into something accidental and inessential. Why? Because in the acute and precise formulae to which they reduce economics, the basic formula, if they wished to express that movement abstractly would have to be: economic laws are determined by . . . their opposite, chaos.

The true law of economics is chance, from whose movement we, the professionals, fix certain phases arbitrarily in the form of laws.

The essence of the matter is brought excellently into focus when Mill characterizes money as the medium of exchange. The essence of money is not, to begin with, that it constitutes the externalization of property, but that the mediating activity or movement, the human, social act whereby man's products complete each other, is alienated and becomes the property of a material thing outside man, money. By externalizing this mediating activity itself, man has now lost himself and becomes sub-human, man's relationship to things and his activity with them becomes the activity of a being outside and above man. Through this alien mediator—for instead man himself should be the mediator for man—man views his will, activity and relationship to other men as a power that is independent of him and them. His slavery thus arrives at its culmination. It is clear that this mediator has now become a real God, for the mediator is the real power over what it mediates to me. Its cult becomes an end in itself. Objects that are separated from this mediator have lost their value. Thus they only have value in so far as they represent money whereas originally it appeared that it only had value in as far as they represented it. This reversal of the original relationship is inevitable. This mediator is thus the lost and alienated essence of private property that has become exterior to itself, externalized private property, just as private property is the externalized mediator of human production with itself, the externalized species-activity of man. Therefore, all the properties involved in the production of this activity are transferred to this mediator. Thus man becomes poorer as man, i.e. separated from this mediator, the richer the mediator becomes.

Christ represents originally (i) men before God; (ii) God for men; (iii) man to man.

Similarly the idea of money originally represents (i) private property for private property; (ii) society for private property; (iii) private property for society.

But Christ is the externalization of God and the externalization of man. Both God and man only have further value in so far as they represent Christ. So with money.

Why must private property involve the use of money? Because man as a social being is compelled to exchange, and exchange—presupposing private property—must become value. The mediating process between men's exchanges is not a human process or a human relationship, it is the abstract relationship of private property to private property and this abstract relationship is value whose real existence as value is principally money. Because men, when they exchange, do not relate to each other as men, the thing loses the significance of human, personal property. The social relationship of private property to private property is already a relationship in which private property is alienated from itself. The self-sufficient existence of this relationship, money, is therefore the externalization of private property, the abstraction from its specific, personal nature.

The opposition of modern economics to the money system cannot, therefore, gain any decisive victory in spite of its cleverness. For the crude economic superstition of the people and governments holds fast to the sensuous, tangible, visible money bag and believes in the absolute value of the precious metal and its possession as the sole reality of wealth. And when the enlightened and worldly economist then comes and proves to them that money is a commodity like any other whose value, like that of any other commodity, consequently depends on the relationship of the cost of production to demand (competition) and supply, to the quantity of supply of other commodities, then he receives the correct reply that nevertheless the real value of things is their exchange value and that this in the last instance resides in money as the value of money resides in precious metals and thus that money is the true value of all things and thus the most desirable thing. Indeed, the doctrines of the economists themselves result in this piece of wisdom; the only difference is that he possesses the capacity to view the question abstractly and recognize the existence of money under all forms of commodity and therefore not believe that its value is limited to its official metal existence. The metal existence of money is only the official manifest expression of the soul of money that is hidden in all parts of the products and processes of civil society.

The opposition of modern economists to the money system is only that they have understood the nature of money in its abstract universality and are thus enlightened about the sensuous superstition that believes in its exclusive existence in precious metal. They substitute refined superstition for crude superstition. But since both have their root in the nature of money, the enlightened form of the superstition is not able to suppress the crude, sensuous form completely, because it does not attack the essence but only its particular form. The personal existence of money as money, and not only as the inner, self-sufficient and hidden relationship of conversation or rank of commodities to each other, this existence corresponds all the more to the being of money, the more abstract it is, the less natural a relationship it has to other commodities, the more it appears as a product and yet a non-product of man, the less natural the means of its existence, the more created by man or, in economic terms, the greater the inverted relationship of its value as money to the exchange value or money value of the material in which it exists. Therefore, paper money and all the paper representations of money (such as note of hand, mandates, bonds, etc.) are a more complete existence of money as money and a necessary phase in the progressive development of the nature of money. In the world of credit, whose full expression is the world of the bank, it seems as though the powers of the alien, material force were broken, the relationship of self-alienation superseded and man reinstated in his human relations with man. The Saint-Simonians were taken in by this appearance and considered the development of money, notes of hand, paper money, paper representatives of money, credit, banks as a gradual supersession of the separation of man from things, capital from labour, poverty from money and money from man, the separation of man from man. Therefore, their ideal is an organized banking system. But this supersession of the alienation, this return of man to himself and therefore to other men is only an appearance. It is a self-alienation and dehumanization that is all the more infamous and extreme in that its element is no longer a commodity, metal, paper, but the very heart of man, his moral and social being, and that under the appearance of man's trust in man it is extreme mistrust and complete alienation. What constitutes the essence of credit? We completely disregard here the content of credit that is again money. We are thus disregarding the content of the trust exemplified when a man recognizes another man by advancing him money and in the best instance, when he does not demand payment for the credit and is not a profiteer, pays his fellow man the compliment of trusting that he is not a swindler but a 'good' man. Under 'good' man here the man with the trust understands, like

Shylock, a man 'who can repay'. Credit is conceivable as two relationships and under two distinct conditions. The two relationships are:
firstly a rich man gives credit to a poor man whom he considers indust-
rious and orderly. This sort of credit belongs to the romantic, senti-
mental type of economics, to its aberrations, excesses, exceptions not to
the rule. But even supposing this exception and admitting this romantic
possibility, the life and active talent of the poor man serves as the rich
man's guarantee of the refunding of the money he has lent. In other
words, all the social virtues of the poor man, the whole content of his
vital activity, his existence itself represents for the rich man the re-
imbursing of his capital with the customary interest. The death of the
poor man is thus the worst catastrophe for his creditor. It is the death
of his capital and its interest. Consider how base it is to value a man for
money, as happens in the credit relationship. It is self-evident that the
creditor, apart from moral guarantees, has the guarantee of judicial
force and more or less real guarantees for his man. If a man to whom
credit has been made has means of his own then credit becomes merely
a means of facilitating exchange, i.e. it is money itself raised to a completely ideal form. Credit is the economic judgement on the morality
of a man. In credit, instead of metal or paper, man himself has become
the mediator of exchange, only not as man, but as the existence of capital
and interest. Thus the medium of exchange has certainly returned and
been transferred to man, but only because man has been transferred outside himself and himself taken on a material form. Money is not
transcended in man inside the credit relationship but man himself has
been changed into money or money become incarnate in him. Human
individuality, human morality has itself become both an article of
commerce and the material in which money exists. Instead of money,
paper is my own personal being, my flesh and blood, my social value
and status, the material body of the spirit of money. Credit no longer
analyses money value into money but into human flesh and the human
heart. This is because all progress and inconsequence inside a false
system produce the worst regression and the worst and basest consequences. Inside the system of credit man's nature alienated from itself
confirms itself, under the appearance of an extreme economic recognition of man, in a double way: (1) the antithesis between capitalist and
worker and between large and small capitalist becomes even greater in

that credit is only given to him who already has and is a new opportunity for the rich man to accumulate; or in that the poor man either confirms or denies his whole existence according to the arbitrary will and judgement that the rich man passes on him, and sees his whole existence depend upon this arbitrariness. (2) The reciprocal dissimulation, hypocrisy and pretended sanctity is forced to a culmination so that the man who has no credit not only has the simple judgement passed on him that he is poor, but also the moral judgement that he possesses no trust or recognition, thus that he is a social pariah, a bad man. Also the poor man undergoes this humiliation in addition to his privation and has to make a humiliating request for credit to the rich man. (3) Because of this completely ideal existence of money, man cannot detect what is counterfeit in any other material than his own person and must himself become counterfeit, obtain credit by stealth and lies, and this credit relationship both on the side of the man who trusts and of the man who needs trust, becomes an object of commerce, an object of mutual deception and misuse. Here there is still plain in all its clarity the mistrust that is the basis of economic trust, the mistrustful consideration of whether to give credit or not, the spying into the secrets of the private life, etc., of the person seeking credit; the betrayal of temporary difficulties in order to ruin a rival through the sudden shaking of his credit. The whole system of bankruptcy, ghost companies, etc. . . . in state credit, the state occupies exactly the same place as man does above . . . his play with papers of state shows how he has become a plaything of businessmen. (4) The credit system has its final completion in the banking system. The creation of bankers, the state domination of the banks, the concentration of capital in these hands, this economic Areopagus of the nation, is the worthy completion of the world of money. In that the moral recognition of a man, trust in the state, etc., in the credit system take the form of credit, the secret that is contained in the lie of moral recognition, the immoral baseness of this morality and the hypocrisy and egoism in that trust of the state come to the fore and show themselves for what they really are.

Exchange, both of human activity within production itself and also of human products with each other, is equivalent to species-activity and species-enjoyment whose real, conscious and true being is social activity and social enjoyment. Since human nature is the true communal nature of man, men create and produce their communal nature by their natural action, they produce their social being which is no abstract, universal power over against single individuals, but the nature of each individual, his own activity, his own life, his own enjoyment, his own wealth. Therefore this true communal nature does not originate in reflection, it takes shape through the need and egoism of individuals, i.e. it is produced directly by the effect of their being. It is not dependent on man whether this communal being exists or not; but so long as man has not recognized himself as man and has not organized the world in a human way, this communal nature appears in the form of alienation, because its subject, man, is a self-alienated being. Men, not in the abstract, but as real, living, particular individuals, are this nature. It is, therefore, as they are. Therefore, to say that man alienates himself is the same as to say that the society of this alienated man is a caricature of his real communal nature, his true species-life, that therefore his activity appears to him as a suffering, his own creation appears as an alien power, his wealth as poverty, the natural tie that binds him to other men appears as an unnatural tie and the separation from other men as his true being; his life appears as sacrifice of life, the realization of his essence as a loss of the reality of his life, his production as a production of his own nothingness, his power over the object as the power of the object over him, and he himself, the master of his creation, appears as its slave.

Economics conceives of the communal nature of man, or his self-affirming human nature, the mutual completion that leads to the species-life, to the truly human life, under the form of exchange and commerce. Society, says Destutt de Tracy, is a series of mutual exchanges. It is precisely this movement of mutual integration. Society, says Adam Smith, is a commercial society and each of its members is a tradesman.

We can see how economics rigidifies the alienated form of social intercourse, as the essential, original form that corresponds to man's nature.

Economics, as does the actual process, starts from the relationship of man to man as that of private property owner to private property owner. If man as private property owner is presupposed, i.e. man as an exclusive owner who keeps his personality and distinguishes himself from other men by means of this exclusive property (private property is his personal, peculiar and thus essential being), then the loss or surrender of private property is an externalization of man and of private property itself. Here we shall only take up the last point. If I hand over my private property to another, then it ceases to be mine; it becomes a thing that is independent of me lying outside my control, exterior to me. Thus, I externalize my private property. Thus, in relation to myself I turn it into externalized private property. But I only turn it into an externalized thing, I only abolish my personal relationship to it, I give it back to the elementary powers of nature when I only externalize it with reference to myself. It only becomes externalized private property when it ceases to be my private property without thereby ceasing altogether to be private property, i.e. when it enters into the same relationship with another man apart from me that it had to me, in a word, when it becomes the private property of another man. Violence excepted, how would I come to externalize my private property in favour of another man? Economics correctly answers; out of necessity, out of need. The other man is also a private property owner, but he owns another thing that I want and cannot and will not do without, that appears to me as necessary to the completion of my being and the realization of my essence.

The tie that binds the two private property owners to each other is the specific nature of the object that is the stuff of their private property. The desire and need for both these objects shows each of the private property owners and makes him realize that he has another essential relationship to objects apart from that of private property, that he is not the particular being that he imagined but a total being whose needs in relation also to the products of another's work are an inner property. For the need of a thing is the most evident and irrefutable proof that the thing belongs to my essence, that its being is for me, its property is the property and peculiarity of my essence. Thus, owners of private property are driven both to give up their private property but to do so in such a way that it confirms private property at the same time, or to give up the private property inside the relationship of private property. Thus each externalizes a part of his private property to the other. The social connection or relationship between the two owners of private property is therefore a reciprocal externalization, the relationship of externalization supposed on both sides or externalization as the relationship between both owners, whereas in private property by itself the externalization is only in relation to oneself, i.e. one-sided.

Thus exchange or trade is the social species-act, the communal nature, the social commerce and integration of man inside private property and thus the exterior, externalized species-act. This is the reason that it appears as trade. This is also the reason that it is the opposite of the social relationship.

Through this reciprocal externalization or alienation of private property, private property itself gets into the position of externalized private property. For firstly it has ceased to be the product of labour, the exclusive, peculiar personality of its owner. This latter has externalized it, it has left the owner whose product it was and has acquired a personal meaning for the man whose product it is not. It has lost its personal meaning for its owner. Secondly, it has been related to another piece of private property and made equivalent to it. It has been replaced by the private property of a different nature, as it itself replaces private property of a different nature. Thus, on both sides private property appears as representing private property of a different nature. It appears as the equivalent of another natural product and both sides are inter-related in such a way that each represents the being of the other and both relate to each other as substitutes for themselves and the other. The being of private property has therefore as such become a substitute, and an equivalence. Instead of possessing a direct self-identity it is only a relation with something else. As an equivalence, its being is no longer its own. It has therefore become a value and most directly an exchange value. Its existence as value is different from its immediate existence; it is exterior to its specific being, an externalized aspect of itself; it is only a relative existence of the same.

We must leave to another place a more precise definition of the nature of this value and also of the process by which it turns into a price.

If the relationship of exchange is presupposed, labour immediately becomes labour of wages. The condition of alienated labour reaches its culmination in that: (1) on one side wage labour and the product of the worker stands in no direct relationship to his need or the nature of his work, but is determined on both sides by social combinations hostile to the worker; and (2) the person who buys the product is not a producer himself but exchanges for it what another has produced. In the crude form of externalized private property, barter, each of the private property owners has produced under the impulse of direct need, of his situation and of the material available to him. Therefore, each exchanges with the other only the superfluity of his own production. Labour was, of course, the direct source of his existence, but at the same time it was also the affirmation of his individual existence. Through exchange his labour has become partly a source of gain. Its aim and its nature have become different. The product is produced for value, exchange-value, equivalency and no longer because of its direct, personal connection with the producer. The more varied the production becomes, so the producer's needs are more varied while his activity becomes more one-sided and his labour can more and more be characterized as wage-labour, until finally it is purely this and it becomes quite accidental and inessential both whether the producer has the immediate enjoyment of a product that he personally needs and also whether the very activity of his labour enables him to enjoy his personality, realize his natural capacities and spiritual aims.

In wage-labour is contained: (1) the alienation and disconnection between labour and the man who labours; (2) the alienation and disconnection between labour and its object; (3) that the worker is governed by social needs that are alien and do violence to him: he subjects himself to them out of egoistic need and necessity and they only have significance for him as a means of satisfying his want just as to them he appears as a slave of his needs; (4) that to the worker the purpose of his activity seems to be the maintenance of his individual life and what he actually does is regarded as a means; his life's activity is in order to gain the means to live.

Thus, the greater and more elaborate appears the power of society inside the private property relationship, the more egoistic, antisocial and alienated from his own essence becomes man.

Thus, the mutual exchange of the products of human activity appears as commerce and barter: similarly mutual completion and exchange of activity itself appears as division of labour which makes of man an extremely abstract being, a machine etc., and leads to an abortion of his intellectual and physical faculties.

It is precisely the unity of human labour that is viewed only as its division because man's social being only comes into existence as its opposite and in its alienated form. Division of labour grows with civilization.

Q

Within the presuppositions of the division of labour the product, the material of private property, is considered by the individual more and more as an equivalent. Moreover, just as he no longer exchanges what is superfluous and the object of his production can simply be immaterial to him, so he does not exchange his product for what is immediately necessary to him. The equivalent exists as a money equivalent which is the immediate result of wage labour and the medium of exchange (see above).

The complete domination of the alienated thing over man is fully manifested in money, the complete indifference both with regard to the nature of the material and the specific nature of the private property, and to the personality of the private property owner.

What was domination of person over person, is now the general domination of the thing over the person, of the product over the producer. Just as the characteristic externalization of private property lay in the equivalent and value, so money is the existence of this externalization that is sensuous and objective to itself.

It is self evident that political economy can only grasp this whole development as a fact, a result of the fortuitous force of circumstances.

The separation of work from itself = the separation of the worker from the capitalist = the separation of work from capital whose original form separates into landed property and moveable property . . . the original characteristic of private property is monopoly; and so as soon as it provides itself with a political constitution, it is that of monopoly. The completion of monopoly is competition. For the political economist production, consumption and their mediator, exchange or distribution, are separate. The separation of production and consumption of activity and enjoyment in different individuals and in the same individual is the separation of work from its object and from itself as enjoyment. Distribution is the self-confirming power of private property. The separation of work, capital and private property from each other and similarly the separation of work from work, of capital from capital and landed property from landed property, and finally the separation of labour from wages, of capital from profit and profit from rent, and lastly of landed property from ground rent permits self-alienation to appear both in its own form and in that of mutual alienation.

Man—and this is the basic presupposition of private property—only produces in order to have. The aim of production is possession. Not only does production have this utilitarian aim; it also has a selfish aim; man produces only his own exclusive possession. The object of his production is the objectification of his immediate, selfish need. Thus, in this savage and barbaric condition man's production is measured, is limited by the extent of his immediate need whose immediate content is the object produced.

Thus, in these circumstances man no longer produces according to his immediate needs. His need is limited by his production. Demand and supply are thus exactly coterminous. His production is measured by his need. In this case there is no exchange or it is reduced to the exchange of his labour against the product of his labour and this exchange is the hidden form or kernel of real exchange.

As soon as exchange exists, production goes beyond the immediate limits of possession. But over-production does not leave selfish need behind. It is rather an indirect way of satisfying a need that can only be objectified in the production of another and not in this production. Production has become the source of wages, wage-labour. Thus, while in the first situation need is the measure of production, in the second situation production or rather the ownership of the product is the measure of how far needs can be satisfied.

I have produced for myself and not for you, as you have produced for yourself and not for me. You are as little concerned by the result of my production in itself as I am directly concerned by the result of your production. That is, our production is not a production of men for men as such, that is, social production. Thus, as a man none of us is in a position to be able to enjoy the product of another. We are not present to our mutual products as men. Thus, neither can our exchange be the mediating movement which confirms that my product is for you, because it is an objectification of your own essence, your need. For what links our productions together is not the human essence. Exchange can only set in motion and activate the attitude that each of us has to his own product and thus to the product of another. Each of us sees in his own product only his own selfish needs objectified, and thus in the product of another he only sees the objectification of another selfish need independent and alien to him.

Of course as man you have a human relationship to my product; you have a need for my product. Therefore, it is present to you as an object of your desires and will. But your need, your desires, your will are powerless with regard to my product. This means, therefore, that your human essence, which as such necessarily has an intrinsic relationship to my production, does not acquire power and property over my production, for the peculiarity and power of the human essence is not recognized in my production. They are more a fetter that makes you depend on me because they manoeuvre you into a position of dependence on my product. Far from being the means of affording you power over my production, they are rather the means of giving me power over you.

When I produce more of an object than I myself directly require, my over-production is calculated and refined according to your need. It is only in appearance that I produce more of this object. In reality I produce another object, the object of your production that I count on exchanging for my surplus, an exchange that I have already completed in my thought. The social relationship in which I stand to you, my work for your need, is also a mere appearance and similarly our mutual completion is a mere appearance for which mutual plundering serves as a basis. An intention to plunder and deceive is necessarily in the background, for since our exchange is a selfish one both on your side and on mine and since each selfishness tries to overcome the other person's, of necessity we try to deceive each other. Of course, the measure of the power that I gain for my object over yours needs your recognition in order to become a real power. But our mutual recognition of the mutual power of our objects is a battle in which he conquers who has more energy, strength, insight and dexterity. If I have enough physical strength, I plunder you directly. If the kingdom of physical strength no longer holds sway, then we seek to deceive each other and the more dextrous beats the less. Who defeats whom is an accident as far as the totality of the relationship is concerned. The ideal intended victory is with both sides, i.e. each has, in his own judgement, defeated the other.

Thus, exchange is brought about necessarily on both sides by the object of each man's production and possession. The ideal relationship to the mutual objects of our reproduction is of course our mutual need. But the actual and true relationship, the one that has a real effect is simply the mutual exclusive possession of mutual production. What gives your need of my things a value, a worth and an effect for me is only your object, the equivalent of my object. Thus, our mutual product is therefore the means, the mediation, the instrument, the recognized power of our mutual need of each other. Your demand, therefore, and the equivalent of your possession are expressions that have the same meaning and value for me and your demand is only effective and therefore becomes meaningful when it has effect and meaning in relation to me. Simply as a man without this instrument your demand is for you an unsatisfied desire, and for me a non-existent imagining. Thus, as a man you stand in no relationship to my object, because I myself have no human relationship to it. But the true power over an object is the means and thus we mutually regard our products as the power of each over another and over himself. This means that our own product has reared up against us. It seemed to be our property, but in reality we are its property. We ourselves are excluded from true property because our property excludes other men.

The only intelligible language that we speak to one another consists in our objects in their relationships to one another. We would not understand a human speech and it would remain ineffective; on the one hand it would be seen and felt as an entreaty or a prayer and thus as a humiliation and therefore used with shame and a feeling of abasement, while on the other side it would be judged brazen and insane and as such rejected. Our mutual alienation from the human essence is so great that the direct language of this essence seems to us to be an affront to human dignity and in contrast the alienated language of the values of things seems to be the language that justifies a self-reliant and self-conscious human dignity.

Of course in your eyes your product is an instrument, a means to be able to control my product and thus to satisfy your needs. But in my eyes it is the aim of our exchange. For me you are only an instrumental means for the production of this object, that is an end for me while you yourself conversely have the same relationship to my object. But: (1) each of us really acts as the other sees him. You have really made yourself into the means, the instrument, the producer of your own object in order to gain power over mine; (2) your object is to you only the perceivable cloak, the hidden form of my object; for what its production means and expresses is: power to purchase my object. So actually you have for yourself become a means and instrument of your object of which your desire is a slave, and you have performed the service of a slave so that the object of your desires shall no more afford you its charity. If this mutual enslavement to an object at the beginning of the process appears now as in a relationship of lordship and slavery, that is only the crude and open expression of our true relationship.

Our mutual value is for us the value of our mutual products. Thus, man himself is for us mutually worthless.

Supposing that we had produced in a human manner; each of us would in his production have doubly affirmed himself and his fellow men. I would have: (1) objectified in my production my individuality and its peculiarity and thus both in my activity enjoyed an individual expression of my life and also in looking at the object have had the individual pleasure of realizing that my personality was objective, visible to the senses and thus a power raised beyond all doubt. (2) In your enjoyment or use of my product I would have had the direct enjoyment of realizing that I had both satisfied a human need by my work and also objectified the human essence and therefore fashioned for another human being the object that met his need. (3) I would have been for you the mediator between you and the species and thus been acknowledged and felt by you as a completion of your own essence and a necessary part of yourself and have thus realized that I am confirmed both in your thought and in your love. (4) In my expression of my life I would have fashioned your expression of your life, and thus in my own activity have realized my own essence, my human, my communal essence.

In that case our products would be like so many mirrors, out of which our essence shone.

Thus, in this relationship what occurred on my side would also occur on yours.

If we consider the different stages as they occur in our supposition:

My work would be a free expression of my life, and therefore a free enjoyment of my life. Presupposing private property, my work is an alienation of my life, because I work in order to live, to furnish myself with the means of living. My work is not my life.

Secondly: In work the peculiarity of my individuality would have been affirmed since it is my individual life. Work would thus be genuine, active property. Presupposing private property, my individuality is so far externalized that I hate my activity: it is a torment to me and only the appearance of an activity and thus also merely a forced activity that is laid upon me through an exterior, arbitrary need, not an inner and necessary one.

My labour can only appear in my object as what it is. It cannot appear as what it essentially is not. Therefore, it appears still as merely the expression of my loss of self and my powerlessness that is objective, observable, visible and therefore beyond all doubt.

Critical Remarks on the Article:
The King of Prussia and Social Reform.
By a Prussian[1]

Written: Beginning of August 1844

First Published: Vorwärts, Paris, 7th and 10th August 1844

Reprinted: MEGA, I (3), pp. 5–23; MEW, I pp. 392–409

Translated: Easton and Guddatt, *Writings of the Young Marx*, pp. 338–58

This article takes up the theme already outlined in the *Introduction to a Critique of Hegel's Philosophy of Right* of the difference between a political and a social revolution. The article rejects any conception of democracy that does not go beyond the political state and thus embodies Marx's final break with Ruge.

Number 60 of *Vorwärts* contains an article entitled 'The King of Prussia and Social Reform' and signed 'A Prussian'.

The so-called Prussian quotes first of all from the Cabinet Order of the Prussian king concerning the Silesian worker's revolt[2] and adds the opinion on the Cabinet Order of the French paper *La Réforme*. '*La Réforme*', he says, considers that the order has its source in the 'terror and religious feelings of the King'; it even finds in this document a premonition of the great reforms that await civil society. The Prussian then gives *La Réforme* the following lesson:

The King and German society has not yet arrived at a 'premonition of their reform'[3] and even the Silesian and Bohemian revolts have not given rise to this feeling. It is impossible to make an unpolitical country like Germany view the particular distress of the industrial districts as an affair of general concern let alone as an injury to the whole civilized world. The event has the same character for the Germans as any local drought or famine. So the King views it as a result of faulty administration or lack of charity. For this reason and also because only

[1] See Introduction, pp. xxix ff.

[2] 4th–6th June 1844.

[3] Note the stylistic and grammatical nonsense. 'The King of Prussia and society *has* not yet arrived at a premonition of *their* (who does the "*their*" refer to?) [Marx's note].

a few troops were required to deal with the feeble weavers, the destruction of factories and machines does not inspire the King and the authorities with 'terror'. Moreover it was not even religious feeling that dictated the Cabinet Order. It is a very insipid expression of Christian statecraft and of a doctrine whose only remedy, 'the good disposition of Christian hearts', sweeps away all difficulties. Poverty and crime are two great evils. Who can cure them? The state and the authorities? No, but the union of all Christian hearts.

The so-called Prussian denies the 'terror' of the King on the grounds, among others, that only a few troops were required to deal with the feeble weavers.

Thus in a country where a banquet with liberal toasts and liberal champagne froth—the Düsseldorf feast springs to mind[1]—provoke a royal Cabinet Order, where not a single soldier was necessary to destroy the desires of the whole liberal bourgeoisie for freedom of the press and a constitution in a land where passive obedience is the order of the day; in such a land is not the fact that armed force had to be used against feeble weavers an event and a terrible one? And the feeble weavers had the upper hand in the first encounter, though they were suppressed later by a reinforcement of troops. Is the revolt of a crowd of weavers not less dangerous because it needs no army to stifle it? Let our clever Prussian compare the revolt of the Silesian weavers with those of English workers and the Silesians will appear to him to be strong weavers.

We will explain from the general relationship of politics to social evils why the revolt of the weavers could not inspire the King with any particular 'terror'. The following remarks will suffice as a preliminary: the revolt was not aimed directly against the King of Prussia, but against the bourgeoisie. Being an aristocrat and an absolute monarch, the King of Prussia cannot love the bourgeoisie; he is even less upset when their subjection and powerlessness is increased by a tense and difficult relationship with the proletariat. Further: an orthodox Catholic is more hostile to an orthodox Protestant than to an atheist, as a legitimist is more hostile to a liberal than to a communist. This is not

[1] Marx refers to a banquet given in Düsseldorf by some liberals in honour of the Seventh Rhenish Parliament, and the subsequent decree of Frederick William IV that no government employees were to take part in such manifestations.

because the atheist and the communist are nearer to the Catholic and the legitimist, but because they are further removed from him than the protestant and the liberal, because they are outside his sphere of reference. As a politician the King of Prussia has his direct opposite inside politics in liberalism. An opposition to the proletariat exists as little for the King, as the King for the proletariat. The proletariat would already have had to attain a marked power in order to stifle antipathies and political oppositions and concentrate on itself all political enmity. Finally, it must have afforded the well-known character of the King, so eager for what is interesting and important, an extremely pleasant surprise to discover the 'interesting' pauperism with its 'great future' on his own home ground and with it a fresh opportunity to get himself talked about. How contented he must have felt at the news that he now had his 'own' royal Prussian pauperism!

Our 'Prussian' is still unhappier when he denies that 'religious feeling' was the source of the Cabinet Order.

Why is religious feeling not the source of this Cabinet Order? Because it is a 'very insipid expression of Christian statecraft', an 'insipid' expression of the doctrine whose 'only remedy, the good disposition of Christian hearts, sweeps away all difficulties'.

Is religious feeling not the source of Christian statecraft? Is a doctrine that has its universal remedy in the good disposition of Christian hearts not based on religious feeling? Does an insipid expression of religious feeling cease to be an expression of religious feeling? I further affirm that it is a very conceited and very intoxicated religious feeling that seeks in the 'union of Christian hearts' the 'salvation of great evils' that it denies to 'the state and the authorities'. It is a very intoxicated religious feeling which, according to the admission of the Prussian, sees the cause of the whole evil as the lack of the religious sense and thus directs the authorities to the only means of strengthening this sense, i.e. an exhortation. According to the Prussian, a Christian disposition is the aim of Cabinet Order. Religious feeling, of course, when it is inebriated and not insipid, considers itself the only good. Whenever it sees evil, it ascribes the existence of the evil to its own absence. For if it is the only good, it also has the exclusive ability to create what is good. Thus the Cabinet Order, dictated by religious feeling, logically dictates religious feeling. A politician of insipid religious feeling would never in his 'perplexity' seek 'salvation' in the 'exhortation to the Christian disposition of a pious preacher'.

How then does the so-called Prussian prove to *La Réforme* that the Cabinet Order was not inspired by religious feeling? By describing it throughout as a result of religious feeling. Should we expect from such an illogical mind an insight into social movements? Let us listen to his verbiage about the relationship of German society to the workers' movement and social reform in general.

Let us distinguish, as the Prussian has failed to do, the different categories that are included in the expression 'German society': Government, bourgeoisie, press and lastly the workers themselves. These are the different groups that are here in question. The Prussian lumps these groups together and then condemns them *en bloc* from his elevated standpoint. According to him, German society 'has not yet arrived at the presentiment of its reform'.

Why has it not got this instinct?

'In an unpolitical land like Germany', answers the Prussian, 'it is impossible to view the particular distress of the industrial districts as an affair of general concern let alone as an injury to the whole civilized world. The event has the same character for the Germans as any local drought or famine. So the King views it as a result of faulty administration or lack of charity.'

Thus the Prussian explains this inverted conception of the workers' misery by the particular characteristics of an unpolitical country.

It will be conceded that England is a political country and further that England is the country of pauperism and that even the word is of English origin. So the surest way of considering the relationship of a political country to pauperism is to consider England's situation. In England the misery of the workers is not partial but universal; it is not limited to industrial districts but extends to the agricultural regions. The movements are not in their infancy there: they have arisen periodically for nearly a century.

Now what is the significance of pauperism for the English bourgeoisie and for the government and press that go with them?

In so far as the English bourgeoisie admits that politics is to blame for pauperism the Whig holds the Tory responsible and the Tory the Whig. According to the Whig the main source of pauperism is the monopoly of large landed properties and the law forbidding the importation of corn. According to the Tory, the whole evil lies in liberalism, in competition and an over-grown factory system. Neither party finds politics in general to be the cause, rather each finds it exclusively in the political policy of the opposite party; neither party permits itself so much as to dream of social reform.

The most striking expression of the English insight into pauperism—I am still speaking of the English bourgeoisie and government—is English economics, which is the scientific reflection of the economic situation in England.

MacCullough, a pupil of the cynical Ricardo and one of the best and most famous of English economists, who knows the present situation and must possess an overall picture of the movements of bourgeois society, even dares in a public lecture and amid applause to apply to economics what Bacon says of philosophy:

'Man who, with genuine and tireless wisdom, suspends his judgement, progresses step by step, overcomes one after another the obstacles that stand like mountains in the path of research, will in time reach the peak of knowledge where one enjoys peace and a clear air, where Nature offers herself to the eye in all her beauty, and from where, by means of a comfortably sunken path, one can descend to the last practical details.'

Good pure air in the pestilential basement dwellings of England! Great natural beauty in the fantastic ragged clothes of the English poor and the wrinkled, shrivelled skin of the women eaten out by work and suffering; the children lying in dung heaps; the monstrosities produced by overwork among the monotonous factory machinery! And the last, charming, practical details: prostitution, murder and the gallows.

Even the part of the English bourgeoisie who are fully convinced of the dangers of pauperism conceive this danger, and the manner of meeting it, in a way that is not only peculiar but also, to put it bluntly, infantile and absurd.

Dr. Kay, for example, in his pamphlet *Recent Measures for the Promotion of Education in England* reduces everything to a deficiency of education. Guess for what reason! It is through a deficiency in education that the worker does not appreciate the 'natural laws of commerce', laws which necessarily lead him to pauperism. Therefore he resists. This could 'harm the prosperity of English manufacturing and trade, destroy business men's mutual trust, and diminish the stability of social and political institutions'.

This shows how little thought the English bourgeoisie and its press has given to pauperism, this national epidemic of England. Supposing then that the reproaches that our Prussian directs against German society are well-founded. Does the reason lie in the unpolitical situation of Germany? The bourgeoisie in unpolitical Germany may not know how to appreciate the general significance of a partial misery, but the bourgeoisie of political England knows how to misconceive the general meaning of universal misery, a misery whose general importance can be appreciated partly because it recurs periodically in time, partly because it increases in space, and partly because all attempts to remedy it have failed.

The Prussian also blames it on the unpolitical situation of Germany when the King of Prussia finds the cause of pauperism in a deficient administration and lack of charity and thus seeks the remedy to pauperism in administrative and charitable measures.

Is this way of looking at things peculiar to the King of Prussia? Take a quick look at England, the only country where you can talk of a large-scale political campaign against pauperism.

The present English Poor Law dates from the law in the forty-third act of Elizabeth's reign (it is not necessary for our purpose to go back to the workers' statute under Edward III). What are the remedies used by this legislation? Obliging Parishes to accept their poor workers, the poor rate, legal charity. This legislation—charity via administration— has lasted for two centuries. After long and painful experiences what do we find to be Parliament's standpoint in its amendment bill of 1834?

Parliament begins by declaring that the enormous increase in pauperism is due to a 'deficiency in administration'.

So the administration of the poor rate, which consisted in officials from the various parishes, was reformed. Unions of about twenty parishes were formed and united under a single administration. The Board of Guardians, a committee of officials elected by the rate payers, met on a particular day in the Union Building and decided upon the distribution of the assistants. These committees are guided and supervised by government delegates, the central commission of Somerset House, and Ministry of Pauperism as a Frenchman has trenchantly called it. The capital that this organization controls is almost equal to France's war budget. The number of local organizations that follow its directives runs to five hundred and each of these local organizations employs at least twelve men.

The English Parliament did not stop at a formal revision of administration.

It found the chief source of the crisis in English pauperism in the Poor Law itself, legal remedies for social evils, i.e. charity really favours social evils. As far as pauperism in general is concerned, it was seen as an eternal law of nature, according to the theory of Malthus:

'Since the population continually tends to increase faster than the means of subsistence, charity is stupid and a public encouragement to misery. The state can therefore do nothing but leave misery to its fate and at most ease the deaths of the sufferers.'

The English Parliament combines with this humanitarian theory the view that pauperism is a misery that the workers have brought upon themselves and thus not a misfortune to be prevented but rather a crime to be stamped out and punished.

This was the origin of the system of workhouses, houses for the poor whose interior organization frightened off those in misery and prevented them from finding in them a refuge from starvation. In the workhouses the charity of the bourgeoisie is cleverly interwoven with their vengeance on the miserable wretch who appealed to their charity. Thus England first tried to root out pauperism through charity and administrative measures. Then it saw in the continuing process of pauperism not the necessary consequence of modern industry, but rather the consequence of the English poor rate. It viewed the universal misery as merely a particular characteristic of English legislation. What was induced before by a lack of charity, was now induced by a superfluity of it. Finally poverty was treated as the fault of the poor and was punished as such.

The general impression that political England has gleaned from pauperism is that in the course of its development in spite of administrative measures pauperism has grown into a national institution and therefore inevitably has become the object of a ramified and extensive organization, an organization that no longer has the task of doing away with it, but of disciplining it and making it eternal. This organization has ceased to stop up the source of pauperism with positive remedies. It contents itself, whenever pauperism springs up on the surface of official soil, with using the mildness of the police to dig it a deathbed. So far from going beyond administrative and charitable measures, the English state is still far behind them. It only administers the fraction of pauperism that is desperate enough to let itself be caught and shut up.

So far the Prussian has not shown us anything peculiar in the conduct of the King of Prussia. 'But why?' cries the great man with a rare naïvety, 'why does not the King immediately order the education of all destitute children?' Why does he turn first to the authorities and await their plans and projects?

The overclever Prussian will be comforted to hear that the King of Prussia has as little originality here as in his other actions, and even that he has taken the only way open to a head of state.

Napoleon wanted to destroy beggary at one blow. He gave his authorities orders to prepare plans to extinguish beggary in the whole of France. The project got delayed. Napoleon lost patience, wrote to Crétet, his Minister of the Interior, ordering him to destroy beggary within a month, and saying:

'We ought not to pass over this earth without leaving traces to recommend our memory to posterity. Do not ask me for three or four more months to collect information. You have young auditors, clever prefects, well-informed civil engineers: set all these in motion and do not go to sleep in your normal office work.'

In a few months all was done. On 5th July 1808, the law was promulgated that suppressed beggary. How? By means of dépôts that transformed themselves so quickly into prisons that the poor man could soon only get inside these institutions after going before a police tribunal. This did not prevent Monsieur Noaille du Gard, a member of the legislative body, from crying:

'Eternal recognition to the hero who assures a refuge for indigence and means of subsistence for poverty. Children will no longer be abandoned, poor families will no longer be deprived of resources nor workers of encouragement and occupation. Our steps will no longer be halted by the disgusting picture of illness and shameful misery.'

The last cynical sentence is the only true one in this panegyric.

If Napoleon addresses himself to the insight of his auditors, prefects and engineers, why should not the King of Prussia address himself to his authorities?

Why did Napoleon not order immediate suppression of beggary? Of the same value is the question of the Prussian: 'Why does the King of Prussia not immediately order the education of destitute children?' Does the Prussian know what the King would have to order? Nothing less than the destruction of the proletariat. To educate children you must feed them and free them from earning their living. The feeding and education of destitute children implies the feeding and education of all proletarian youth and thus the abolition of the proletariat and of pauperism. The Convention had for a moment the boldness to order the suppression of pauperism, not indeed 'immediately' as the Prussian requires of his King, but only when it had ordered the Committee of Public Safety to prepare the necessary plans and projects, and this Committee had used the detailed studies of the Constituent Assembly on the state of poverty in France and proposed through Barère the establishment of a 'Book of National Charity'. What was the result of the order of the Convention? That there was one more order in the world and one year later famished women besieged the Convention.

Yet the Convention realized the maximum of political energy, political power and political intelligence.

No government in the world has ever given orders concerning pauperism immediately and without consulting the authorities. The English Parliament even sent envoys to every country in Europe to learn of the different administrative remedies that they employed against pauperism. But as far as states have dealt with pauperism they have gone no further than administrative and charitable measures or even not got as far as them.

Can the state act otherwise?

The state will never find the cause of social evils in the state and the organization of society as the Prussian requires of his King. Where there are political parties, each one finds the cause of every evil in the fact that their opponents are at the helm instead of themselves. Even the radical and revolutionary politicians do not look for the cause of evil in the essence of the state, but in its particular form which they wish to replace by a different form.

From the political point of view the state and any organization of society are not two distinct things. The state is the organization of society. In so far as the state admits the existence of social abuses, it seeks their origin either in natural laws that no human power can control or in the private sector which is independent of it or in the inadequacy of the administration that depends on the state. Thus, England sees misery as founded in the natural law according to which population must always outstrip the means of subsistence. On the other hand, it explains pauperism by the cussedness of the poor, as the King of Prussia explains it by the unchristian spirit of the rich and the Convention by the counter-revolutionary and suspicious attitude of the property owners. Therefore, England punishes the poor, the King of Prussia exhorts the rich and the Convention beheads the property owners.

In short, all states look for the causes in accidental or intended faults of administration, and therefore seek the remedy for its evils in administrative measures. Why? Simply because the administration is the organizing activity of the state.

The state cannot abolish the contradiction which exists between the role and good intentions of the administration on the one hand and the means at its disposal on the other, without abolishing itself, for it rests on this contradiction. It rests on the contrast between public and private life, on the contrast between general and particular interests. The administration must therefore limit itself to a formal and negative activity, for its power ceases just where civil life and work begin. Indeed, in the face of the consequences that spring from the unsocial nature of this civil life, this private property, this commerce, this industry, this reciprocal plundering of different civil groups, in face of these consequences, impotence is the natural law of the administration. For this tearing apart, this baseness, this slavery of civil society is the natural basis on which the modern state rests, as the civil society of slavery was the natural basis on which the classical state rested. The existence of the state and the existence of slavery are inseparable. The classical state and classical slavery—frank and open class oppositions— were not more closely forged together than the modern state and modern world of haggling, hypocritical, Christian oppositions. If the modern state wished to do away with the impotence of its administration, it would have to do away with the contemporary private sphere

R

for it only exists in contrast to the private sphere. But no living being believes that the defects of its specific existence are grounded in what is essential to its own life, but in circumstances exterior to its life. Suicide is unnatural. So the state cannot believe in the intrinsic impotence of its administration, i.e. of itself. It can appreciate only its formal, accidental defects, and try to remedy them. And if these modifications are fruit- less then it thinks that social evils are a natural imperfection independent of man, a law of God, or else that the will of individuals is too perverted to be able to match the good intentions of the administration. And what perverse individuals! They complain about the government whenever it limits freedom and yet require the government to prevent the necessary consequences of this freedom!

The more powerful the state, and thus the more political a country is, the less is it inclined to look in the state itself, that is in the present organization of society whose active, self-conscious and official expres- sion is the state, for the cause of social evils, and thus understand their general nature. Political intelligence is political just because it thinks inside the limits of politics. The sharper and livelier it is the less capable it is of comprehending social evils. The classical period of political intelligence is the French Revolution. Far from seeing the source of social defects in the state, the heroes of the French Revolution see in social defects the source of political misfortunes. Thus Robespierre sees in extremes of poverty and riches only an impediment to pure demo- cracy. So he wishes to establish a general Spartan frugality. The prin- ciple of politics is the will. The more one-sided, and thus the more perfect political intelligence is, the more it believes in the omnipotence of the will, the blinder it is to the natural and intellectual limits of the will, and thus the more incapable it is of discovering the sources of social evils. No further explanation is necessary to refute the stupid hope of the Prussian that it is the vocation of 'the political intelligence to discover the root of social misery in Germany'.

It would not only be stupid to attribute the King of Prussia a power superior to that of the Convention and Napoleon together; it would also be stupid to attribute to him an attitude that goes beyond the limits of all politics, an attitude that the clever Prussian himself is not nearer to possessing than the King. This whole declaration is all the more stupid in that the Prussian admits:

Fine words and good intentions are cheap, insight and successful action is dear; in this case they are more than dear, they are not to be had.

If they are not to be had, then the effects of the man who tries to do what is possible in his own situation should be realized. For the rest I leave it to the tact of the reader to judge whether commercial gypsy-speech of 'cheap', 'dear', 'more than dear', 'not yet to be had', falls into the category of 'fine words and intentions'.

So, granted that the remarks of the Prussian on the German government and the German bourgeoisie—the latter being surely included in 'German society'—are fully justified: is this part of the society more clueless in Germany than in England and France? Can one be more clueless than in England for example, where cluelessness has been made into a system? If workers' revolts break out today all over England, the bourgeoisie and government there are not better advised than in the last third of the eighteenth century. Their one resort is material force. And because material force diminishes in proportion to the spread of pauperism and the increase in understanding of the proletariat, the English cluelessness necessarily grows in geometrical proportion.

Finally it is untrue, factually untrue, that the general significance of the Silesian revolt completely escaped the German bourgeoisie. In many cities the masters are trying to associate themselves with the apprentices. All liberal German newspapers, the organs of the liberal bourgeoisie, gush articles on the organization of labour, reform of society, criticisms of monopolies and competition. All this as a consequence of workers' movements. The newspapers of Trier, Aachen, Cologne, Wesel, Mannheim, Breslau and even Berlin offer very many intelligent articles on social questions from which the Prussian can always complete his education. Indeed, letters from Germany express continued amazement at how little opposition the bourgeoisie affords to social tendencies and ideas.

The Prussian, were he better acquainted with the history of the social movement, would have put his question in the reverse form. Why does even the German bourgeoisie give to this partial misery an importance that is relatively universal? Whence comes the animosity and cynicism of the political bourgeoisie, whence the lack of resistance and sympathy of the unpolitical bourgeoisie in relation to the proletariat?

Let us turn now to the oracular utterances of the Prussian concerning the German workers:

The German poor [he jokes] are no cleverer than the poor Germans, that is, nowhere do they see further than their own home, their own factory, their own district. Up to the present time the whole question has been left on one side by the all-penetrating political soul.

In order to be able to compare the conditions of the German workers with that of the English and French workers, the Prussian should have compared the first form, the beginning of the English and French workers' movements with the present beginning of the German move- ment. This he fails to do. Thus his reasoning ends in a sort of trivial statement that industry in Germany is not yet so developed as in England, or that the origins of the movement appear different from its later progress. He wanted to speak of the particular characteristics of the German workers' movement. All he says is irrelevant to this subject.

If, on the other hand, the Prussian were to look at it from the right standpoint, he would find that not a single one of the French and English workers' revolts had so theoretical and conscious a character as the revolt of the Silesian weavers.

Think first of the Weavers' Song, of these bold, fighting words where home, factory and district are not once mentioned, and the proletariat immediately shouts out its opposition to a society of private property in a manner that is brutal, sharp, reckless and violent. The Silesian revolt begins precisely where the English and French workers' revolts end, with a realization of what the proletariat is. Even their actions have this superior character. Not only the machines, the workers' rivals, are destroyed but also the commercial books and titles to property, and, while all other movements turned first against the visible enemy, the captains of industry, this movement turned at the same time against the hidden enemy, the banker. Finally not a single English workers' revolt was managed with such superior courage and endurance.

As far as in general concerns the level of education or capacity for it of the German worker, I may draw attention to the brilliant works of Weitling which from the theoretical point of view often surpass even Proudhon, however inferior they may be in execution. Where could the bourgeoisie, its philosophers and scholars included, produce work similar to Weitling's *Guarantees of Harmony and Freedom* concerning the emancipation of the bourgeoisie, that is political emancipation? Compare the insipid, timid mediocrity of German political literature with this boundless and brilliant literary debut of the German workers. Compare the gigantic size of the proletariat's infant shoes with the dwarf-like size of the German bourgeoisie's worn out political ones, and you will forecast an athlete's body for the German Cinderella. It must be admitted that the German proletariat is the theoretician of the European proletariat, as the English proletariat is its economist and the French its politician. It must be admitted that Germany has a vocation to social revolution that is all the more classic in that it is incapable of political revolution. For as the impotence of the German bourgeoisie is the political impotence of Germany, so the situation of the German proletariat, even without speaking of German theory, is the social situation of Germany. The disproportion between philosophical and political development in Germany is no abnormality. It is a necessary disproportion. It is only in socialism that a philosophical people can find a corresponding activity, thus only in the proletariat that it finds the active element of its freedom.

But I have at this moment neither the time nor the inclination to explain to the Prussian the relationship of 'German society' to social transformation and to explain by means of this relationship both the weakly feeble reaction of the German bourgeoisie against socialism and the excellent situation of the German proletariat for socialism. He can find the first elements towards an understanding of this phenomenon in my *Introduction to a Critique of Hegel's Philosophy of Right* (*Deutsch-Französische Jahrbücher*).

Thus the cleverness of the German poor stands in inverse proportion to the cleverness of the poor Germans. But people who have to make public exercises of style out of every object, get to disfigure the content by this formality, while the disfigured content for its part reacts by stamping the form with vulgarity. So the attempt of the Prussian to use the occasion of the unrest of the Silesian workers to move in antitheses has misled him into the greatest antitheses to the truth. The sole task of a thinking and truth-loving mind *vis-à-vis* the first explosion of the Silesian workers in revolt was not to play the school-master of the event but rather to study its particular character. But of course this latter needs some knowledgeable insight in humanity, whereas for the former operation a ready turn of phrase dipped in a hollow egoism is more than sufficient.

Why does the Prussian condemn the German workers with so much contempt? Because he finds that the whole question, namely that of the workers' misery, is 'as yet still' neglected by the 'all-penetrating political soul'. And this is how he expands on his platonic love for the political soul:

All revolts that break out in this wretched isolation of man from his common essence and the separation of his thoughts from social principles will be stifled in blood and ignorance; but if first misery gives rise to understanding and the political understanding of the Germans discovers the root of social misery, then even in Germany these events will be felt as symptoms of a great transformation.

Let the Prussian first allow us a remark on the style. His antithesis is imperfect. The first half reads: If misery gives rise to understanding, and in the second half: If political understanding discovers the root of social misery. The simple understanding in the first half of the antithesis becomes political understanding in the second half, just as the simple misery of the first half of the antithesis becomes social misery in the second half. Why has our stylist furnished both halves of the antithesis so unequally? I do not think that he saw clearly here. I will interpret to him his real instinct. Had the Prussian written: If social need creates political understanding and political understanding discovers the root of social need, then the nonsense of this antithesis would not have escaped any unprejudiced reader. Everyone would have immediately asked why the anonymous author does not link social understanding with social misery and political understanding with political misery as the simplest logic requires. But, to the subject matter.

So far from the social need creating political understanding, it is rather the reverse: social well-being creates political understanding. Political understanding is spiritualist and is given to him who has already, who is already established in clover. Let our Prussian listen to a French economist on that subject, Herr Michel Chevalier:

In the year 1789, when the bourgeoisie rose, the only thing that they required in order to be free was participation in governing the land. Liberation for them consisted in taking the direction of public affairs, the high civil, military and religious functions, out of the hands of the privileged who owned the monopoly of these functions. Being rich and enlightened and capable of being self-sufficient and self-governing, they wished to get rid of an arbitrary form of government.

We have already demonstrated to the Prussian how incapable political understanding is of discovering the source of social need. One more word about this belief of his. The more developed and universal the political understanding of the people is, the more the proletariat squanders its strength at least in the beginning of its movement, in uncomprehending, useless revolts that are stifled in blood. Because it thinks politically it sees the cause of all evils in the will and the only means of remedying them in violence and overthrow of a particular form of the state. The proof is in the first explosions of the French proletariat.[1] The workers in Lyons thought they were only pursuing political ends and were only soldiers of the republic, whereas in reality they were soldiers of socialism. Their political understanding obscured for them the roots of social misery, falsified their insight into their true aims, and belied their social instinct.

But if the Prussian expects misery to create understanding, why does he throw 'stifled in blood' and 'stifled in misunderstanding' together? If misery is a means, their bloody misery must be a very acute means of creating understanding. The Prussian should therefore say: stifling in blood will stifle misunderstanding and procure the necessary draught of air for understanding. The Prussian predicts the suppression of revolts that break out in 'the wretched isolation of men from their common essence and the separation of their thoughts from social principles'. We have shown that the Silesian revolt did not take place in a separation of thought from social principles. So we have only to deal with the 'wretched isolation of man from his common essence'. By 'common essence' here, a political essence, the essence of the state is to be understood. It is the old refrain about Germany being unpolitical.

But do not all revolts without exception break out in the wretched isolation of man from his common essence? Is not isolation a necessary presupposition of any revolt? Would the revolution of 1789 have taken

[1] Marx refers to revolts of the Lyons workers in November 1831 and April 1834.

place without the wretched isolation of the French bourgeois from their common essence? Their very aim was to do away with their isolation.

But the common essence from which the worker is isolated is a common essence of quite a different reality and compass from the political collectivity. This collectivity from which his own work separates him is life itself, physical and intellectual life, human morality, human activity, human enjoyment, human essence. The human essence is the true collectivity of man. And so isolation from this essence is out of all proportion more universal, insupportable, terrifying and full of contradictions than isolation from the political collectivity, the abolition of this isolation or even a partial reaction and revolt against it is all the more immeasurable as man is more immeasurable than the citizen and human life than political life. An industrial revolt can therefore be as partial as it likes, it contains within it a universal soul: a political revolt can be as universal as it likes, even under the most colossal form it conceals a narrow spirit.

The Prussian ends his essay with the following fitting sentence:

A social revolution without a political soul (i.e. with an organizing intelligence operating from the standpoint of the whole) is impossible.

We have seen. A social revolution, even though it be limited to a single industrial district, involves from the standpoint of the whole, because it is a human protest against a dehumanized life, because it starts from the standpoint of the single, real individual, because the collectivity against whose separation from himself the individual reacts is the true collectivity of man, the human essence. The political soul of revolution consists on the contrary in a tendency of the classes without political influence to end their isolation from the top positions in the state. Their standpoint is that of the state, an abstract whole, that only exists through a separation from real life, that is inconceivable without the organized opposition, the general concept of humanity and its individual existence. Thus a revolution with a political soul also organizes, in conformity with its limited and double nature, a ruling group in society to society's detriment.

We wish to confide in the Prussian what a 'social revolution with a political soul' is; we entrust him at the same time with the secret that he is never able even in his stylish phrases to raise himself above the narrow political standpoint.

A 'social revolution with a political soul' is either a contradiction in terms, if the Prussian understands by social revolution a social revolution in opposition to a political one and nevertheless gives the social revolution a political soul instead of a social one. Or a 'social revolution with a political soul' is just a paraphrase for what used to be called a political revolution, is simply a revolution. Every revolution is social in as far as it destroys the old society. Every revolution is political in so far as it destroys the old power.

Let the Prussian choose between paraphrase and nonsense! A political revolution with a social soul is as rational as a social revolution with a political soul is paraphrastic or nonsensical. Revolution in general—the overthrow of the existing power and dissolution of previous relationships—is a political act. Socialism cannot be realized without a revolution. But when its organizing activity begins, when its peculiar aims, its soul comes forward, then socialism casts aside its political cloak.

This long development was necessary to tear apart the web of errors that lie hidden in a single newspaper column. Not all readers have the education and time necessary to give an account of such literary charlatanism. Thus does not the anonymous Prussian have a duty *vis-à-vis* the reading public to forego for the time being all writing on political and social matters and declamations on the situation in Germany, and rather begin with a conscientious attempt to clarify his own situation?

Bibliography

German Texts

Marx–Engels, *Gesamtausgabe*, Frankfurt, from 1927 (= MEGA).

K. Marx–F. Engels, *Werke*, Berlin, from 1957.

K. Marx, *Frühe Schriften*, Stuttgart, 1962.

K. Marx, *Texte zu Methode und Praxis*, Hamburg, 1966.

Translations

K. Marx, *Economic and Philosophical Manuscripts*, trans. M. Milligan, Moscow, 1957.

K. Marx, *Early Writings*, trans. T. B. Bottomore, London, 1963.

K. Marx, *Œuvres Philosophiques*, trans. Molitor, Paris, 1935 (= Molitor).

K. Marx–F. Engels, *Études philosophiques*, Paris, 1951.

K. Marx–F. Engels, *Sur la Religion*, trans. G. Badia et al., Paris, 1960.

K. Marx, *Manuscrits de 1844*, trans. E. Bottigelli, Paris, 1962.

K. Marx, *Writings of the Young Marx on Philosophy and Society*, trans. and ed. Lloyd D. Easton and Kurt H. Guddat, New York, 1967.

Commentaries

S. Avineri, *The Social and Political Thought of Karl Marx*, Cambridge, 1968.

I. Berlin, *Karl Marx*, 3rd ed., London, 1963.

B. Delfgaauw, *The Young Marx*, London, 1967.

L. Dupré, *The Philosophical Foundations of Marxism*, New York, 1966.

E. Fromm, *Marx's Concept of Man*, New York, 1961.

S. Hook, *From Hegel to Marx*, 2nd ed., Michigan, 1962.

E. Kamenka, *The Ethical Foundations of Marxism*, London, 1962.

D. McLellan, *The Young Hegelians and Karl Marx*, London, 1969.

D. McLellan, *Marx before Marxism*, London, 1970.

R. Tucker, *Philosophy and Myth in Karl Marx*, Cambridge, 1961.